DON'T MENTION THE WAR

DON'T MENTION THE WAR

THE AUSTRALIAN DEFENCE FORCE, THE MEDIA AND THE AFGHAN CONFLICT

KEVIN FOSTER

Monash University Publishing
Building 4, Monash University
Clayton, Victoria 3800, Australia
www.publishing.monash.edu

Monash University Publishing brings to the world publications which advance the best traditions of humane and enlightened thought.

Monash University Publishing titles pass through a rigorous process of independent peer review.

http://www.publishing.monash.edu/books/dmw-9781922235183.html

Series: Investigating Power

Design: Les Thomas

Cover image reproduced courtesy of the Department of Defence.

National Library of Australia Cataloguing-in-Publication entry:

Author:	Foster, Kevin D. (Kevin Dennis), 1961- author.
Title:	Don't mention the war : the Australian Defence Force, the media and the Afghan conflict / Kevin Foster.
ISBN:	9781922235183 (paperback)
Series:	Investigating power series.
Notes:	Includes index.
Subjects:	Australian Defence Force--Public relations. Armed Forces and mass media--Australia. Afghan War, 2001---Press coverage. Afghan War, 2001---Mass media and the war. War--Press coverage. Mass media--Objectivity--Australia.
Dewey Number:	070.4499581046

Printed in Australia by Griffin Press an Accredited ISO AS/NZS 14001:2004 Environmental Management System printer.

The paper this book is printed on is certified against the Forest Stewardship Council ® Standards. Griffin Press holds FSC chain of custody certification SGS-COC-005088. FSC promotes environmentally responsible, socially beneficial and economically viable management of the world's forests.

CONTENTS

For Thérèse – still fighting the good fight

'In a situation of officially-defined crisis and bipartisan support, with little opportunity for independent gathering of evidence, the news media were reduced to passive conveyors of official views. To the limited extent that they departed from this official stance, it was to add "colour"'.[1]

1 Rodney Tiffen, 'News Coverage of Vietnam', *Australia's Vietnam: Australia in the second Indo-China war*, ed. Peter King, Sydney: George Allen and Unwin, 1983, p.172.

ACKNOWLEDGMENTS

In the course of researching and writing this book I have been assisted by many people in many places. As always I thank the teachers who have taken an interest in and helped me over the years, Vincent Burke, David Langston, Angela Dale, Ron Weston, Chris Dobbyn, Peter Millard and Len Findlay. At Monash I would like to thank the Dean of the Faculty of Arts, Professor Rae Frances, and the Executive of the Research Unit in Media Studies for approving a publication grant to assist with the costs of producing this book. I also thank my colleagues, Brett Hutchins, Shane Homan, Sue Kossew, Chris Worth, Stewart King, Brian McFarlane, Brian Nelson and Louella D'Costa. Robin Gerster read an early draft of the manuscript and provided valuable feedback, for which I thank him. At the University of New South Wales I thank Tony Burke, Marilyn Anderson-Smith, Shirley Ramsay, and David Lovell with whom I organised a conference and who subsequently offered valuable feedback on the manuscript. In Canberra I am indebted to General Peter Leahy, Major Chris Linden, Lieutenant Colonel Jason Logue, Brigadier Alison Creagh, Lieutenant Colonel Peter Power, Commodore Richard Menhinick, Rear Admiral James Goldrick, Nick Butterly, Shane Wright and Karen Middleton. I would also like to thank Marilyn Lake, Amin Saikal, Donald Matheson, Tom Hyland, Chris Masters, Thom Cookes, John Martinkus, Ian McPhedran, Sean Hobbs, General Peter Cosgrove, Adrian D'Hagé, the late Prakash Mirchandani, Chris Clark, Gregory P. Gilbert, Brian Humphreys, Mark Doggett, Ian Jackson, Zoë Hibbert, Jacqui Ewart, Michael Gillies Smith, Fay Anderson, Richard Trembath, Jim Molan, Chelsea Mannix, Peter Young, Ross Tapsell, Sharon Mascall-Dare, Frank Cain, Damian Dwyer, Patrick Fuery, Kelli Fuery, David Sheehy, Belinda Glynn and Jason Pallant. In the Netherlands I thank Peter ter Velde, Hans de Vreij, Jaus Müller, Robin Middel, Manon van Kester, Jos van der Leij, Gerben van Es, Dave de Vaal and Dr Joop Veen. In the UK, Thomas Harding, Kim Sengupta, Richard Norton-Taylor, Nick Gurr and Mark Wenham were each very helpful. In Ottawa, Murray Brewster, Gloria Galloway, Stephen Thorne and Christian Lemay helped to fill in the Canadian context for me. I am grateful to Professor Chris Waddell of the School of Journalism and Communication at Carleton University and to Dominique Price for granting me access to her unpublished thesis. At the University of Saskatchewan, I thank my old Professor, Len Findlay.

Don Anderson was an ideal host during my visit to the United States Air Force Academy in Colorado. Friends put up with repeated visits and the obsessive rambling that went with them. In Canberra, Andrew Probyn, Felicity Hamilton, Jonty, Clancy and Maggie, have welcomed, fed and entertained me time and again. In Brisbane, despite their recent collision with the great traditions of British workmanship, Wayne Murphy and Suzanne Oberhardt have not held it against me and remain cherished friends. In Melbourne I thank Bern Murphy, Deb McLatchie, James Ley and Kate McFadyen. George Wright, Susana de Pedro and Maria Wright de Pedro have fed and accommodated us more times than I can count: convivial and generous, they are true and valued friends. In London, Mark Odell gave me the run of his house, while Jo Younger, Pia and Billy fed, smoked and drenched me in tea, and nobody could stop laughing. Up north, my old school friend Colin Chapman has been a sure guide and great company on the ascent of a few of Scotland's Munro Hills, in Edinburgh I thank Mac and the troops for keeping a watchful eye on the border, while Tony Burke has provided incomparable dispatches from Manchester. My greatest debt is to my family. I thank my brothers, Martin, Robert, David and Damien, and their families, Yoko, Jane, Alex, Sam, Mandy, Tom, Polly, Will, Ellis, Henry, Emma, Isaac and Finley for their love and support. My parents, Kevin and Jean, have backed me in all that I have done. My dad died while I was writing this book: I love and miss him and this book honours his memory. My mum remains an example and an inspiration to me – cheerful, practical, generous in all that she does, she is always ready to see the good in others and the funny side of every story. My sons, James and William, are my greatest pride and joy: lovely, funny boys, they give me purpose and keep me smiling. My wife (she hates being called that), Thérèse, has had to wait a bit longer for her book than either of us had anticipated. She has borne the greater burden of the domestic chores while I've been on my travels or locked away writing and hasn't complained about it … too much. Though she's under no obligation to read it all the way through, here it is, at last, with love, as always.

I first tried out a few of the ideas developed at greater length here in *Overland*. My thanks to Jeff Sparrow for publishing and promoting the earlier work.

The author and publisher gratefully acknowledge the Department of Defence for its permission to reproduce the cover photograph and other images used in this book.

ABBREVIATIONS

3PPCLI	3rd Princess Patricia's Canadian Light Infantry
AAP	Australian Associated Press
ABC	Australian Broadcasting Corporation
ADF	Australian Defence Force
ADFPP	Australian Defence Force Parliamentary Program
AFP	Australian Federal Police
ANA	Afghan National Army
ANP	Afghan National Police
ANSF	Afghan National Security Forces
ASPI	Australian Strategic Policy Institute
CBC	Canadian Broadcasting Corporation
CDF	Chief of the Defence Force (Australia)
CDS	Chief of the Defence Staff (Canada)
CEFCOM	Canadian Expeditionary Force Command
CF	Canadian Forces
CFB	Canadian Forces Base
CFMEP	Canadian Forces Media Embedding Program
CP	Canadian Press
CTV	Canadian Television
DFT	Deployable Field Team (Australia, see also MCT)
DGPA	Director General Public Affairs (Australia, see also DGSC)
DGSC	Director General Strategic Communication (see also DGPA)
DIA	Defence Intelligence Agency (USA)
DND	Department of National Defence (Canada)
DoD	Department of Defence (Australia)
DOD	Department of Defense (USA)
DPA	Defence Public Affairs
EMC	Essential Media Communications (Australia)
FOB	Forward Operating Base
IED	Improvised Explosive Device

ISAF	International Security Assistance Force
JIB	Joint Information Bureau (USA)
JPAU	Joint Public Affairs Unit (Australia)
JTF 633	Joint Task Force 633 (Australia)
KMNB	Kabul Multi-National Brigade
MCT	Military Camera Team (Australia, see also DFT)
MECC	Ministerial and Executive Coordination and Communication
MIA	Missing in Action
MoD	Ministry of Defence (UK)
MOLA	Media Opinion Leaders – Afghanistan
MRT	Media Reporting Teams (USA/UK)
MT	Mentoring Team
MTF	Mentoring Task Force (Australia)
MvD	*Ministerie van Defensie* (Netherlands)
NATO	North Atlantic Treaty Organisation
NIOD	Netherlands Institute for War Documentation
OMLT	Operational and Mentoring Liaison Team (Australia)
PA	Public Affairs
PAG	Public Affairs Guidance (USA)
PAO	Public Affairs Officer (USA/Canada)
PIO	Public Information Officer (Netherlands)
PMO	Prime Minister's Office (Canada)
PRT	Provincial Reconstruction Team
RAAF	Royal Australian Air Force
RAN	Royal Australian Navy
RMTF	Reconstruction and Mentoring Task Force (Australia)
RPG	Rocket Propelled Grenade
RTF	Reconstruction Task Force (Australia)
SBS	Special Broadcasting Service (Australia)
SIEV	Suspected Illegal Entry Vessel
SIGAR	Special Inspector General for Afghanistan Reconstruction
SOTG	Special Operations Task Group (Australia)
TOLA	Trans-Atlantic Opinion Leaders – Afghanistan
USAF	United States Air Force

INTRODUCTION

'EYE-WITNESS' RETURNS

In the days and weeks after Britain declared war on Germany on 4 August 1914, a newly literate population, served by a mass-market popular press, clamoured for details of the British Expeditionary Force's exploits in France and Belgium.[1] The military, however, were not forthcoming. The Secretary of State for War, Lord Kitchener, 'had hated war correspondents since the Sudan' and refused point blank to accredit a single reporter to accompany British forces and report on their progress.[2] Instead, he appointed a uniformed officer with a 'tincture of letters' to furnish reports from the front.[3] Lieutenant Colonel Ernest Swinton of the Royal Engineers had few illusions about where his allegiances lay. His primary role, he believed, was not 'the purveyance of news to our own people' but to 'avoid helping the enemy.'[4] As a consequence he determined to tell only 'as much of the truth as was compatible with safety.'[5] That, as it turned out, wasn't much. Having gathered his information, shaped his account and purged it of any tell tale detail, Swinton passed his material to his senior officers for vetting. They handed it on to Kitchener himself who, having put his own blue pencil to work, approved it for release to the press where it appeared under the ironic by-line 'Eye-witness'. 'As many historians point out, little truth escaped this thicket of restrictions.'[6] Swinton's reports, intended 'to offer civilians an aestheticized vision of martial endeavour', were notable not only for the rigour they demonstrated in excluding any concrete detail regarding ground

---

1 For more on the rise of the mass market popular press and the newly literate classes who consumed it see John McEwen, 'The National Press During the First World War: Ownership and Circulation', *Journal of Contemporary History*, Vol. 17, No. 3, 1982, pp.459–86; and Deian Hopkin, 'Domestic Censorship in the First World War', *Journal of Contemporary History*, Vol. 5, No. 4, pp.151–69, 1970.

2 Philip Knightley, *The First Casualty: The War Correspondent as Hero and Myth-Maker from the Crimea to Iraq*, Third Edition, Baltimore: Johns Hopkins University Press, 2004, p.89.

3 Susan Carruthers, *The Media at War*, Second Edition, New York: Palgrave, 2011, p.53. Before the war, Swinton wrote two novels under the nom de plume 'Ole Luk-Oie'.

4 Quoted in Cate Haste, *Keep the Home Fires Burning: Propaganda in the First World War*, London: Allen Lane, 1977, p.32.

5 Quoted in Carruthers, *Media at War*, p.53.

6 Carruthers, *Media at War*, p.54.

taken or losses suffered, but also for the jaunty assessment of troop morale and general well-being that they sustained.[7]

Almost one hundred years later, Australian media coverage of the war in Afghanistan takes us back into the world of Eye-witness. For much of the period of the Australian Defence Force's (ADF) commitment in Afghanistan, independent observers have been *personae non gratae*. The military has crafted its own reports from the front lines that it has then offered to the media, in the form of press releases and occasional briefings. This official account of the war has promoted the improved security the ADF has brought to its operational area, the mentoring and training it has provided to Afghan National Security Forces (ANSF), the roads it has constructed and the health centres and schools it has built. Meanwhile it has carefully downplayed the brutality and destructiveness of the war, drip-feeding the public a nutritious diet of positive news from Afghanistan. The Australian public's access to objective information about and understanding of the longest military commitment in the nation's history has been correspondingly impoverished. Just how impoverished was hinted at in Ross Southernwood's December 2012 review of Chris Masters' *Uncommon Soldier* (2012). In his appraisal of Masters' study of the making of the modern Australian warrior, Southernwood, a reviewer of numerous military titles, revealed that 'Until reading this book I was under the impression the Australian Army's role in Afghanistan was mainly a defensive one – keeping secure areas safe and generally helping society continue operating as normally as possible in its region of influence, Uruzgan province, from its base at Tarin Kot … [W] hat I didn't know was just how proactive and aggressive the Australians are in the fighting.'[8] ADF Public Affairs (PA) has evidently done a good job in promoting its version of the war as a species of armed social work. If a knowledgeable reviewer is so ignorant about the basic parameters of the Australian mission in Afghanistan, one might assume that the disinterested man or woman in the street is virtually in the dark.

If the mainstream media have been dependent on the ADF for access to news from Afghanistan, the public has been, and remains, almost entirely reliant on the media for its information about what its troops are doing there and its apparent ignorance about the war reflects a critical failure of coverage. As we will see, the media have to bear their share of the responsibility for

7 Carruthers, *The Media at War*, p.53.

8 Ross Southernwood, 'Review of *Uncommon Soldier: Brave, Compassionate and Tough, the Making of Australia's Modern Diggers*', by Chris Masters, in *The Sunday Age*, Melbourne Inside, 30 December 2012, p.14.

this failure, but one must also acknowledge that journalists cannot report on events that they cannot access. Only since 2011 have the numbers of Australian reporters embedded with the ADF reached levels comparable with those of many of our coalition counterparts and comparator militaries, while their freedom of movement in Afghanistan still falls short of that enjoyed by the Dutch, Canadian, British and US media. This book will not only contend that Australia's Department of Defence (DoD) and the ADF have gone out of their way to restrict the media's access to the troops and their missions in Afghanistan, it will also explore how, why and with what effects they have done so. Accordingly, if in December 2007 Richard Tanter could ask then Prime Minister Kevin Rudd 'Why are we in Afghanistan?', in 2013, as Australian forces prepare to withdraw from Uruzgan and hand over responsibility for security in the province to their Afghan colleagues, it seems more pertinent to inquire 'What did we do there and why do we know so little about it?'[9] How is it possible in the network society of the twenty first century that the Australian public should have been so ill informed for so long about what its troops have been doing in Afghanistan, and why has this situation been allowed to persist?

This book will seek to answer these questions by considering what was unique about the organisation, focus and channels of Australian coverage of the war and by identifying and appraising the effects of the political, economic and cultural forces that shaped them. It will do this, in part, by comparing Australia's history of military-media-government relations, its arrangements for media access to and reporting on the troops in Afghanistan and the role and status of the ADF within Australian society, with that of the Dutch – with whom we shared responsibility for security in Uruzgan – and the Canadians, a fellow Commonwealth force with a comparable commitment of troops to the mission. The book will examine who among the media went to Afghanistan, where they were permitted to travel, what they were allowed to see and what they were able to report. It will analyse how, in the three countries, differing organisational cultures within the military, the media and the government shaped contrasting professional norms and practices and how these affected the media's access to and capacity to cover the conflict. It will consider why in some instances these professional cultures changed, sometimes dramatically, and why in others they remained largely untouched. The book will investigate why, in Afghanistan, the Dutch

9 Richard Tanter, 'Memo to Kevin Rudd: Why are we in Afghanistan?' *Arena Magazine*, No. 92 (December-January 2007/08), p.9.

and Canadian militaries opened themselves up to unprecedented media scrutiny while during the greater part of its commitment the ADF made it more difficult than ever for the media to access Australian forces and the battlefield. It will compare and contrast the military's centrality in Dutch, Canadian and Australian narratives of national identity and consider how this informed the differing reporting of and responses to the Afghan war. As such, the book will demonstrate not only *how* the coverage of the war differed between the three countries, but *why*.

That said, my principal focus is on the Australian experience of the war in Afghanistan as reflected in the reported actions and recorded opinions of the military, the media, the government and the public. In the book I will endeavour to set the military-media relations that shaped coverage of the Afghan War within a deeper historical and cultural context. To that end I will consider how the Vietnam War continued to cast a long shadow over Australian military-media relations, crucially shaping the coverage of the war in Afghanistan, and will examine why, when US attitudes towards the media underwent wholesale revision through the 1990s, the ADF held fast to the antagonisms of old. I will consider the relationship between the military and the government and analyse how the rise in political micro-management of the military – illustrated here by Operation Relex and the Children Overboard affair – damaged relations between politicians and the armed forces. I will examine how political bipartisanship on the war stifled broader media and public debate about its aims and prosecution. I will analyse why the media's focus on the war has been most commonly articulated through the narrative of death, how the reporting of ADF fatalities has furnished the principal prism through which the public have experienced and apprehended the war and how this has distorted its understanding of how, by whom and for what the war is being fought. The book will offer the first analysis of Australian public opinion polling on the war and consider why public opinion has been so little understood and so determinedly ignored by the government, the military and the media. I will also examine the economic, logistical and conceptual challenges the media confronted in their endeavours to cover the war, how the collapse of the traditional media funding model re-shaped reporting of the war, the origins and effects of domestic editorial reluctance to pursue the story, how the peripheral nature of the ADF's involvement in Afghanistan sent the media stars elsewhere and how all of these combined to diminish national coverage of the ADF and its exploits.

INTRODUCTION

The war in Afghanistan has not only been the nation's longest military commitment, it has also been the worst reported and least understood conflict in Australian history. This book sets out to demonstrate how and why this has happened. When the Australian media should have been bearing witness to the most pressing international security issue of the decade, they were forced to sit on their hands while their role and functions in Afghanistan were handed over to ADF Public Affairs, Eye-witness *redux*. Returned to centre stage, Eye-witness has assuaged the public's fears and stoked its patriotic fervour: this book seeks to explain how he got there and to determine what the chances are of killing him off once and for all.

Chapter 1

MISTAKING THE LESSONS OF VIETNAM

Cultural Baggage

The ADF has a deep-seated mistrust of the motivations and professional practices of the fourth estate.[1] Time after time, the military claim, they 'see the media not getting it right, having a spurious agenda and more often than not causing trouble.'[2] The media's coverage of their work, the ADF argue, is so poor that the job of keeping the public informed about its activities would be better performed by its own personnel in Public Affairs.[3] As the years have passed, the ADF's frustration and hostility have hardened into an 'institutional aversion to media' and a 'lingering bias' against its organisations and practitioners.[4] The feeling is mutual. The fourth estate has

1 For more on the history of Australian military-media relations see Fay Anderson and Richard Trembath, *Witnesses to War: The History of Australian Combat Reporting*, Melbourne: Melbourne University Press, 2011. For a particular focus on relations during World Wars 1, 2, the Vietnam War and the fighting in Afghanistan see, respectively: John F. Williams, *ANZACS, The Media and the Great War*, Sydney: University of New South Wales Press, 1999; John Hilvert, *Blue Pencil Warriors: Censorship and Propaganda in World War II*, St Lucia: University of Queensland Press, 1984; Trish Payne, *War and Words: The Australian Press and the Vietnam War*, Melbourne: Melbourne University Press, 2007; Kevin Foster (ed), *What are we doing in Afghanistan? The Military and the Media at War*, Melbourne: Australian Scholarly Publishing, 2009.

2 Chris Masters, *Uncommon Soldier: Brave, Compassionate and Tough, the Making of Australia's Modern Diggers*, Sydney: Allen and Unwin, 2012, p.336. 'When Australian soldiers are questioned about what most pisses them off, the media usually makes the list' (Masters, *Uncommon Soldier*, p.113).

3 For a detailed analysis of this survey of ADF opinion, and more information about the sample, see Kevin Foster and Jason Pallant, 'Familiarity breeds contempt? What the Australian Defence Force thinks of its coverage in the Australian media, and why', *Media International Australia*, No. 148 (August 2013), pp.22–38.

4 Lieutenant Colonel Jason Logue, *Herding Cats: The Evolution of the ADF's Media Embedding Program in Operational Areas*, Canberra: Land Warfare Studies Centre (Working Paper No. 141), June 2013, p.2.

complained long and loud about the ADF's lack of transparency and its apparent determination to impede the media's access to conflict zones and the Australian forces serving in them. In 2009 one senior defence correspondent argued that 'it is time for some brutal honesty between the military and the media. Both parties need either a statement of principles founded on mutual mistrust … a declaration of open season, or a genuine effort at mutual understanding and greater access.'[5] The former Chief of Army, General Peter Leahy, has expressed the view that 'the relationship between the government, the military and the media is broken' and that the time has come 'to hit the reset button.'[6]

The fractious relationship between the military and the media can be traced back through the Second World War all the way to the Western Front and Gallipoli.[7] Yet in the contemporary context it was the conflict in Vietnam that played the key role in entrenching the military's antagonism towards the fourth estate as the Australians fell in behind their US allies in blaming the media for their defeat in South East Asia. Indeed, long before Saigon fell to the North Vietnamese on 30 April 1975, it was already axiomatic within US military circles that the responsibility for its defeat in South-East Asia rested squarely with the media. During the Paris peace negotiations that ended the war, General Maxwell Taylor, former US Ambassador to South Vietnam, claimed that the communists 'bombarded our domestic opinion with continuing propaganda from Paris and Hanoi, often using for that purpose the "free world" media … The press – not all, but the vast majority – was opposed to our Vietnam policy and very vocal. The television also. Allowing television on the battlefield after our troops got there created an impossible situation at home.'[8] While the Pentagon proposed that the most

5 Ian McPhedran, 'War! What War?' in *What are we doing in Afghanistan? The Military and the Media at War*, ed. Kevin Foster, Melbourne: Australian Scholarly Publishing, 2009, p.73.

6 Peter Leahy, 'The Government, the Military and the Media: Hurry, Hit the Reset Button', in *The Information Battlefield: Representing Australians at War*, ed. Kevin Foster, Melbourne: Australian Scholarly Publishing, 2011, p.6.

7 See Anderson and Trembath, *Witnesses to War*, pp.43–208; Ian Jackson, '"Duplication, Rivalry and Friction": the Australian Army, the Government and the Press during the Second World War', in *The Information Battlefield: Representing Australians at War*, ed. Kevin Foster, Melbourne: Australian Scholarly Publishing, 2011, pp.74–85.

8 Quoted in Tiffen, 'News coverage of Vietnam', 1983, p.186. Robert Elegant claimed: 'South Vietnamese and American forces actually won the limited military struggle. They virtually crushed the Viet Cong in the South, the "native" guerrillas who were directed, reinforced, and equipped from Hanoi; and thereafter they threw back the invasion by regular North Vietnamese divisions. None the less, the War was finally lost to the invaders after the US disengagement because the political pressures built

effective means of securing victory lay in 'calling up reserves ... bombing the North more heavily ... mining Haiphong harbor; destroying bridges to China ... attacking "sanctuaries" ... invading the North and stopping "infiltration" from that area', the media's focus on the human costs of such a strategy, and the political and social divisions it would inflame, ensured that neither politicians nor the public would lend their support to it.[9] Proponents of the oppositional media thesis, the conviction that, in Robert Elegant's words, the media 'was instinctively "agin the Government" – and, at least reflexively, for Saigon's enemies', contended that free to travel where they wished, witness what they would and write as they pleased, US and international reporters proffered an increasingly critical analysis of the military's aims, strategies and performance that eventually turned the politicians and the public against the war: 'By harnessing public squeamishness, the media had served to limit strategic options to the point at which victory became untenable'.[10] As a consequence of this, Elegant proposed: 'For the first time in modern history the outcome of a war was determined not on the battlefield, but on the printed page and, above all, on the television screen'.[11] Encouraged by such forceful advocacy, senior officers in the US, Britain, Australia, and throughout the NATO militaries, came to share a common set of convictions about the media's culpability for what had happened in Vietnam that critically shaped their attitudes towards and relations with the fourth estate for the next quarter of a century: 'The press was not to be trusted; biased journalism had, by itself, turned the American public against the Vietnam effort ... and, if given half a chance, newspeople, especially ratings-hungry television people, would portray the military in a bad light.'[12]

According to Daniel Hallin, the conviction that 'television turned the American public against the war is accepted so widely across the American political spectrum that it probably comes as close as anything to being

---

up by the media had made it quite impossible for Washington to maintain even the minimal material and moral support that would have enabled the Saigon regime to continue effective resistance'. Robert Elegant, 'How to lose a war', *Encounter*, Vol. 57, No. 2, 1981, p.73.

9 Jeffrey P. Kimball, 'The Stab-in-the-Back Legend and the Vietnam War', *Armed Forces and Society* Vol. 14, No. 3, (Spring 1988), p.438.

10 Elegant, 'How to lose', p.73; Carruthers, *The Media at War*, p.100. Kimball notes that 'A nearly pure form of the [oppositional media] theory is represented in the writings and statements of Richard Nixon, Ronald Reagan, William Westmoreland, U.S. Grant Sharp, the John Birch society, writers for National Review and Accuracy in Media' (Kimball, 'Stab-in-the-Back', p.438).

11 Elegant, 'How to lose', p.73.

12 Peter Braestrup, 'Foreword', *Hotel Warriors: Covering the Gulf War*, by John J. Fialka, Washington: Woodrow Wilson Center Press, 1991, p.xi.

conventional wisdom about a war that still splits the American public'.[13] Yet studies have not only demonstrated that the belief that 'the media were adversaries to American policy in Vietnam or a decisive factor in the outcome in the war' is false; they have also shown that television exercised far less influence over US and international public opinion than conventional wisdom would have us believe.[14] While it may have been the case that by the middle of the 1960s many Americans were spending a great deal of their time watching their television sets: 'This did not necessarily mean, however, that their owners were paying close attention to them.'[15] In a 1969 study sponsored by the National Association of Broadcasters: 'Of 232 viewers who were asked, "What do you recall from tonight's broadcast," 51 percent failed to recall a single story out of an average of nineteen that had appeared. Of the 49 percent who could remember at least one, the commentary … at the end of the program, in theory the most influential in terms of public opinion, was the least remembered.'[16]

Nor, as was claimed by proponents of the oppositional media thesis, did a nightly diet of blood and gore shift the attitudes of the American public regarding the war. Empirical analysis of public opinion and focus group data showed that coverage tended to reinforce viewers' existing opinions about the war rather than change them, while images of blood and gore were not nearly as commonplace as has been assumed.[17] Despite the large number of journalists in Vietnam and the assumption that hordes of them trooped across battlefields from the delta to the DMZ, Henry Allen of the *Washington Post* argued that at most times: 'No more than forty reporters were where bullets were flying,' while during the Tet offensive that number scarcely doubled.[18] Technical constraints and editorial caution ensured that the footage these reporters captured and screened remained mostly inoffensive. Camera teams in Vietnam were a three-person operation – cameraman, soundman and a reporter, the latter two yoked together by a cable. Because the camera was cumbersome and difficult to operate from a

---

13 Daniel Hallin, *The 'Uncensored War': The Media and Vietnam*, Berkeley: University of California Press, 1989, pp.105–6.

14 Hallin, *Uncensored War*, p.x.

15 Michael Mandelbaum, 'Vietnam: The Television War', *Daedalus*, Vol. 111, No. 4 (Fall 1982), p.159.

16 William Hammond, 'The Press in Vietnam as Agent of Defeat: A Critical Examination', *Reviews in American History*, Vol. 17, No. 2 (June 1989), p.315.

17 For a more detailed discussion of television's tendency to reinforce existing opinions see Hallin, *Uncensored War*, pp.106–8.

18 Quoted in Thomas Rid, *War and Media Operations: The US Military and the Press from Vietnam to Iraq*, New York: Routledge, 2007, p.56.

prone position, and because most of the combat up until the Tet offensive took place in the jungle, the mountains or the delta, with a good deal of that happening at night, television showed little of the fighting. When it did capture combat it tended to show it 'from a distance or to depict its aftermath ... There was considerable commotion ... but little of the violence characteristic of Vietnam.'[19] The tepid nature of the resulting coverage was reinforced by a combination of military circumspection and editorial diffidence. While the military were determined to keep US dead off the small screen, ostensibly in deference to the sensitivities of the bereaved, they were assisted by the networks, who, with one eye ever-fixed on the bottom line 'cut film that showed too much violence rather than lose viewers to another channel.'[20] As a result, 'only about 22 per cent of all film reports from South East Asia in the period before the Tet offensive showed actual combat, and often this was minimal – a few incoming mortar rounds or a crackle of sniper fire.'[21] Lawrence Lichty observed that between August 1965 and August 1970, 'of some 2,300 reports that aired on evening television news programs no more than 76 showed anything approaching true violence – heavy fighting, incoming small arms and artillery fire, killed and wounded within view.'[22]

Regardless of its objective inaccuracy, the conviction that the media had lost the war in Vietnam bred a hostility to the press that 'soaked deep into the military's cultural tissue.'[23] Through the 1980s and 1990s the prejudices of senior officers who had first-hand experience of the war were 'transmitted down the line' to the point where they constituted a key component of the military's 'organizational wisdom ... no official document articulated let alone demanded an emotional bias against the fourth estate', as no such edict was necessary: 'that bias was deeply entrenched in military culture.'[24] Hatred of the media rapidly became what scholars of organisational communications call a tacit or routine knowledge asset, part of the organisation's conventional wisdom, absorbed not through explicit direction but via the more natural processes of group socialisation and corporate enculturation.[25]

---

19 Hammond, 'Press in Vietnam', p.315.
20 Hammond, 'Press in Vietnam', p.316.
21 Hallin, *Uncensored War*, p.129.
22 Hammond, 'Press in Vietnam', p.315.
23 Rid, *War and Media Operations*, p.62.
24 Peter Braestrup, *Battle Lines*, New York: Priority Press, 1986, p.69; Rid, *War and Media Operations*, p.61.
25 This terminology is taken from the work of the Japanese management scholar Ikujiro Nonaka, see 'A Dynamic Theory of Organizational Knowledge Creation', *Organization Science*, Vol. 5, No. 1 (1994), pp.14–37.

The belief that the media had stabbed the military in the back was not only widely dispersed within the organisation it was also stubbornly enduring. When former Special Forces officer and Vietnam veteran Henry Gole invited journalists to the Army War College's media days for discussions with students, he noted that despite the passing of decades, 'Some 20 years after their experience in Vietnam, student attitudes towards the media were overwhelmingly negative and seemingly permanent, at least in that generation of embittered officers.'[26] When Colonel John Shotwell of the US Marine Corps arranged similar sessions at the Amphibious Warfare School he observed that as a result of the 'depth of suspicion' between the parties, discussions rapidly degenerated into 'fingerpointing antipathy': 'Officers who'd never once had to confront either a reporter or an armed opponent blamed the media for losing the war for us in Vietnam, impugned their morals, and maligned their loyalties.'[27] Writing in the early 1990s, Bernard Trainor proposed that 'today's [US] officer corps carries as part of its cultural baggage a loathing for the press … Like racism, anti-Semitism, and all forms of bigotry, it is irrational, but nonetheless real.'[28] And, being real, it has had concrete outcomes. Despite the fact that the principal lesson the US military took from Vietnam was wrong – the belief that a free press had lost it the war – Thomas Rid notes that this 'became a defining feature of the US military's public affairs policy for the next quarter century. The lesson, translated into practical advice for future operations, was that the press needed to be treated like an adversary and that media access to the battlefield should be strictly denied.'[29]

The lessons of Vietnam were refined by the British experience in the Falkland Islands in May and June 1982, where the campaign to reclaim the islands after an Argentine invasion was underpinned by strict controls over the media.[30] The geographical isolation of the Falkland Islands meant that the only means of getting there once Argentina's invasion had cut them off

---

26 Henry Gole, 'Don't Kill the Messenger: Vietnam War Reporting in Context', *Parameters* (Winter 1996–97), p.151.

27 John M. Shotwell, 'The Fourth Estate as a Force Multiplier', *Marine Corps Gazette*, (July 1991), p.72.

28 Bernard Trainor, 'The Military and the Media: A Troubled Embrace', *Parameters*, (December 1990), p.2.

29 Rid, *War and Media Operations*, pp.62–3.

30 For more on media coverage of the Falklands War see, inter alia: Valerie Adams, *The Media and the Falklands War*, London: Macmillan, 1986; Derrik Mercer, Geoff Mungham and Kevin Williams, *The Fog of War: The Media on the Battlefield*, London: Heinemann, 1987; Kevin Foster, *Fighting Fictions: War, Narrative and National Identity*, London: Pluto Press, 1999.

from their pre-existing means of access, was courtesy of the Royal Navy. This gave the Ministry of Defence the whip hand in its dealings with the media, enabling it to weed out potentially hostile correspondents and dictate the ground rules for those who were granted passage. As Derrik Mercer noted, 'hardly ever have circumstances been more propitious for a censor than they were for the British in the Falklands.'[31] It was these ground rules that caught the eye of the Pentagon and provided the model for its dealings with the US media over the next twenty years. Their key provisions – 'permit only a handful of journalists to accompany the sea-borne forces into battle; ensure that reporters were never without a military minder, and that they relied exclusively on military communications equipment to transmit copy back home' – were first applied by the Americans during Operation Urgent Fury, the invasion of Grenada, in October 1983.[32] In their endeavours to faithfully replicate the British experience in the South Atlantic, the US military set about ensuring that access to Grenada would be courtesy of the military alone, aggressively policing both the land and the surrounding waters. Four journalists who made it ashore were arrested by US forces and transported to the invasion force's flagship, the USS *Guam*. Six more who had chartered a boat in an effort to reach the islands were intercepted and also taken to the *Guam*.[33] When the shooting was over the first media contingent granted access to the islands was a pool from the major networks whose representatives were escorted around the key sites of the conflict by a posse of zealous public affairs personnel and permitted to gather material which the military vetted. While the media waited for a flight out to Barbados – from where they were scheduled to transmit their material in time for the evening news bulletins – President Reagan made a live address to the nation, carried by all the major networks, announcing victory in Grenada and the safe evacuation of the nearly 1000 US citizens marooned by the fighting. The networks followed the live cross from the oval office with the only visuals available at that point, footage shot by the US Army showing 'young American students making the "V" sign and smiling at the cameras as they walked up the ramp of the "rescue" aircraft.'[34] While the US media

31 Mercer, Mungham and Williams, *The Fog of War*, p.39.

32 Carruthers, *The Media at War*, p.120.

33 For more on this see Peter Young and Peter Jesser, *The Media and the Military: From the Crimea to Desert Strike*, Melbourne: Macmillan, 1997, pp.129–31. For a first-hand account see Vice Admiral J. Metcalf III, USN (retd) 'The Press and Grenada, 1983', *Defence and the Media in Time of Limited War*, ed. Peter R. Young, London: Frank Cass, 1992, pp.168–174.

34 Young, *Media and Military*, p.132.

raged against the restrictions that had been imposed on them and the bad faith shown by the Pentagon, the government and the military exulted.[35] As Peter Young noted, Grenada:

> was a lovely war from the public information point of view ... The images were of a war that had been fought without dead bodies, without fighting or blood, and without suffering or civilian casualties. Only a guaranteed showing of success and an emotive pictorial rationale of the reasons the United States went to war appeared on the television screens of America and the world.[36]

In public information terms the first Persian Gulf War may have seemed no less lovely. Here the Americans applied 'the lessons learned from Vietnam, the Falklands, Grenada and Panama' on a grand scale.[37] After Saddam Hussein's invasion of Kuwait on 2 August 1990 and the subsequent build-up of US forces in Saudi Arabia in Operation Desert Shield, more than a thousand of the world's media descended on the Arabian peninsula where they registered with the US led Joint Information Bureau (JIB) in Dhahran. When Operation Desert Shield became Operation Desert Storm on 17 January 1991 and the fight to liberate Kuwait and punish Iraq began in earnest, 192 of the more fortunate or more enterprising journalists, most of them Americans, in small Media Reporting Teams (MRTs), accompanied the troops in the forward areas providing pooled dispatches for their colleagues in the rear.[38] Their movements closely monitored by military Public Affairs Officers (PAOs), their copy vetted and then transmitted by the military, as traffic allowed, the MRT journalists were entirely at the mercy of their uniformed minders.[39] Indeed they were little better off than the 'hotel warriors' back in the air-conditioned comfort of Riyadh and Dhahran, sitting through the barrage of official briefings, the smart-bomb footage and the military hard sell.[40] The comprehensive control over the media that the military enjoyed in the First Gulf War, in particular their capacity to regulate access and impede communications, seemed to provide

---

35 See Young, *Media and Military*, pp.132–4.

36 See Young, *Media and Military*, p.133.

37 Philip Taylor, *Munitions of the Mind: A History of Propaganda from the Ancient World to the Present Day*, Third Edition, Manchester: Manchester University Press, 2003, p.287

38 There is some dispute about the exact number of MRT journalists: Susan Carruthers offers 160, John J. Fialka is the source for 192, see Fialka, *Hotel Warriors*, p.15.

39 For an analysis of the MRT experience see Carruthers, *Media at War*, pp.132–5.

40 For more on the experience of the hotel warriors and the differing pools see Fialka, *Hotel Warriors*.

'a classic example of how to project a desired view of conflict in the new informational environment that had emerged during the 1980s.'[41]

Yet this was not the media management triumph that it first appeared. The reporters on the ground saw and experienced the failures of the system close up. One of the MRT journalists, John J. Fialka of the *Wall Street Journal*, noted how, 'Within hours of the launching of the largest military attack since World War II, the Army's system for supporting the reporters who were covering it collapsed.' Though reporters were on hand to witness and record 'one of the best U.S. Army stories ever', the system for returning their copy to the JIB for vetting and onward transmission to the US broke down completely: 'The Army-designed pony express system of couriers and its teams of reporter escorts were hopelessly understaffed, underequipped, and poorly trained and motivated for the job. The upshot: As the battles raged, we (couriers, escorts, journalists) and news copy, film, and videotapes spent a lot of valuable time lost in the desert.'[42] Despite political triumphalism in the White House and the claim by Assistant Secretary of Defence for Public Affairs, Pete Williams, that the information management arrangements in Washington and the Gulf 'gave the American people the best war coverage they ever had', Peter Braestrup condemned the media's Gulf War experience as 'high-cost, low-benefit horde journalism.'[43] He counselled 'Both Washington policymakers and senior Army officers' that they 'should not embrace the notion that handling the media Gulf War-style is the way to do things next time ... "Next time" will be different.'[44]

'The Fourth Estate as a Force Multiplier'

As Braestrup's remarks indicate, by late 1991 it was clear that the game had already changed. For both government and the media one of the key lessons from the First Gulf War was that 'the new informational environment that had emerged during the 1980s' and the lessons of Vietnam that had shaped it, no longer applied. While the military were busy corralling the media and feeding them scraps of good news, they were regularly wrong-footed by a sophisticated Iraqi information campaign. This sated the news-hungry media with a surfeit of incident that temporarily gave the Iraqis control over

41 Taylor, *Munitions of the Mind*, p.287.
42 Fialka, *Hotel Warriors*, pp.11, 12.
43 Quoted in Bruce Cumings, *War and Television*, London: Verso, 1992, p.117; Braestrup, 'Foreword', p.xiii.
44 Braestrup, 'Foreword', p.xiii.

the 'information initiative.'[45] Where US and British military commanders focused on the degradation of Iraqi infrastructure, the precision bombing of bridges and government buildings, Iraqi 'minders' directed the small number of western news crews who had remained in Baghdad to sites demonstrating the human cost of the bombardment. On 23 January 1991, US bombers attacked what was purportedly a biological weapons production facility in Abu Ghraib. When western journalists were bussed to the compound some hours later, though the factory had been destroyed, the signboard that identified the complex as a 'Baby Milk Plant', helpfully inscribed in English as well as Arabic, had remarkably survived. Peter Arnett's report questioning official claims about the nature of the plant earned a rebuke from the White House Press Secretary, Marlin Fitzwater, who condemned Arnett's employer, CNN, as a 'conduit for Iraqi disinformation.'[46] Three weeks later when a US Air Force (USAF) F-117 dropped two precision-guided bombs on a command and control bunker in al-Firdos, suspicions about the loyalty of western reporters in Baghdad turned into open hostility. Though both the CIA and the Defence Intelligence Agency (DIA) had repeatedly 'validated the target' as a military facility, on the night of 13 February it was being used as a civilian air-raid shelter and was occupied by hundreds of old people, women and children.[47] When news of the tragedy broke, the Iraqi information ministry hastily transported the international press corps to the site, where CNN, the BBC and ITN 'filmed scenes of charred human remains being removed from the ravaged building ... The footage was revelatory, as grief-stricken survivors unwrapped bundles of molten human flesh.'[48] On the BBC's *Newsnight*, Jeremy Paxman observed: 'Until today it had seemed such an uncannily sanitised war: clever bombs that wrecked real estate but somehow seemed to leave people unscathed'.[49] In Washington and London the official response to the media coverage was incandescent. However, it was not the loss of life that so exercised politicians and their myrmidons in the press but the BBC's decision to offer such graphic and sympathetic coverage of the enemies' suffering. The *Daily Mail* dubbed the BBC the 'Baghdad Broadcasting Corporation', while the *Sun*, echoing

---

45 Rid, *War and Media Operations*, p.84.

46 Quoted in Johanna Neuman, *Lights, Camera, War: Is Media Technology Driving International Politics?* New York: St Martin's Press, 1996, p.217. For more on this incident see Rid, *War and Media Operations*, pp.84–6.

47 Rid, *War and Media Operations*, p.86.

48 Carruthers, *Media at War*, p.139.

49 Philip Taylor, *War and the Media: Propaganda and Persuasion in the Gulf War*, Manchester: Manchester University Press, 1992, pp.208–9.

Churchill's accusation during the Second World War, denounced it as 'the enemy within.'[50] On the other side of the Atlantic the barbs were sharper still. Republican Congressman R. Lawrence Coughlin attacked Peter Arnett as 'the Joseph Goebbels of Saddam Hussein's Hitler-like regime.'[51] Over the course of the First Gulf War the US had to dedicate considerable time and resources to countering the Iraqis' propaganda triumphs. Far from demonstrating the defeat and humiliation of the fourth estate, the conflict provided an object lesson in why the US military needed to enlist the media as an ally and stop treating them as an enemy. The war thus set in train the most comprehensive reform of US military-media relations since Vietnam.

The *Gulf War Air Power Survey* (1993), a five-volume study commissioned by the United States Air Force in the wake of Operation Desert Storm, laid the ground for the wholesale revision of the lessons of Vietnam when it concluded that a principal message from the First Gulf War was that 'press coverage is an unavoidable yet important part of military operations.'[52] This was a point graphically reinforced by CNN's Pentagon correspondent, Jamie McIntyre, when he advised the military that in future operations: 'Wherever commanders go, they should plan for CNN. Like the weather, we'll always be there – just another feature on the battlefield terrain.'[53] After eight months of negotiations with network bureau chiefs, the Pentagon issued a directive adopting nine principles dictating the media coverage of future fighting, the most important of which stated that 'open and independent reporting' would be 'the principal means of covering a conflict.'[54]

To this end the Pentagon embraced the US Marine Corps' approach to media relations, 'the most sophisticated attitude on public affairs in the entire US military at the time.'[55] The strategy was outlined in Colonel John M Shotwell's 1991 *Marine Corps Gazette* article, 'The Fourth Estate as a Force Multiplier.'[56] The article set out how, during the First Gulf War, under Shotwell's direction, the Marines had provided logistical support to media who accompanied their forces into battle. By facilitating access to stories and providing the means of transmitting them back to the US, the Marines 'helped build and maintain the support of the American public' for the Corps

50 Taylor, *Munitions of the Mind*, p.295; Carruthers, *Media at War*, p.139.
51 Peter Arnett, *Live from the Battlefield*, London: Corgi, 1995, p.420.
52 R.L. Olson, *Gulf War Air Power Survey, Volume Three: Logistics; Support*, Washington DC: Government Printing Office, 1993, p.135.
53 Quoted in Rid, *War and Media Operations*, p.87.
54 Rid, *War and Media Operations*, p.86.
55 Rid, *War and Media Operations*, p.87.
56 Shotwell, 'The Fourth Estate', pp.70–79.

and the campaign.[57] As a result of its expertise in handling public affairs, 'the Marines garnered most of the publicity' during the First Gulf War, 'skewing the coverage of the ground war, in which they performed a much smaller, supporting role to the Army.'[58] The diminution of the Army's role and influence was a direct result of their failure to move their information management strategy and practices beyond the lessons learnt in Vietnam. While 'Army commanders only grudgingly accepted journalists assigned to them and, at times, could not conceal their deep-seated hostility towards the press', the Marines 'never seemed to get enough media people in the field', and reaped the benefits of a more conciliatory and proactive relationship with the fourth estate.[59]

The *Gulf War Air Power Survey* was further notable in identifying the other key driver leading military-media relations out of the post-Vietnam postures of disdain and hostility, namely, the growing recognition that, like Saddam Hussein, future adversaries were going to employ their own sophisticated information operations aimed at undermining public support for the military or dismantling multi-national alliances by exploiting existing fault-lines.[60] The US and their NATO allies were given an object lesson in such information operations, and an insight into their consequences, during their intervention in Kosovo in 1999 where greater force of arms, even victory on the battlefield, afforded them little advantage when divorced from a corresponding triumph in the information dimension.

In March 1999 NATO launched Operation Allied Force, a bombing campaign intended to end the killing and expulsion of Kosovo's ethnic Albanian population and force Serbian President, Slobodan Milosevic, to the negotiating table. Because the operation was exclusively airborne there were no NATO ground forces with whom reporters might embed, and so no media on the spot to relay the alliance's version of events as they occurred. This failure to consider the conflict's information dimension was deftly exploited by the Serbs. On 14 April 1999, US Air Force F-16s bombed a convoy evacuating refugees from advancing Serb forces near the village of Djakovica, mistaking it for a Yugoslav armoured column. Dozens were killed and scores more wounded. Serb authorities moved swiftly to

---

57 Shotwell, 'The Fourth Estate', p.71.

58 Fialka, *Hotel Warriors*, pp.26–7.

59 Fialka, *Hotel Warriors*, p.27.

60 For a discussion of Saddam Hussein's thraldom to the Vietnam Myth, his conviction that US public support for Operation Desert Storm would crumble at the sight of casualties from Iraq, as it had in Vietnam, see Carruthers, *Media at War*, pp.131–2.

capitalise on the blunder, offering western journalists in Belgrade free and timely transport to the site of the bombing. The resulting images of 'mangled tractors and minibuses ... burned and bloodied corpses ... limbs scattered among destroyed vehicles' and their accompanying reports made headlines across the world.[61] Over the next five days CNN presented more than sixty reports on the Djakovica attack and both the *New York Times* and the *Los Angeles Times* featured the disaster on their front pages – the latter under a headline proposing that 'Convoy Deaths May Undermine [NATO's] Moral Authority.'[62] After initial denials, it took NATO five days to muster a coherent response to the disaster, by which time it had ceded the information advantage to the Serbs and paid the price in damaged legitimacy and rising public disapproval of the campaign.[63]

Three weeks later, acting on flawed intelligence, NATO missiles slammed into the Chinese Embassy compound in Belgrade, killing three and wounding fifteen.[64] This time the international media were on hand to witness the debacle as it unfolded and this became the single most reported event of the war. Once again it took NATO days to present a plausible public explanation for what had happened. In the meantime the Serbs took full advantage both on the battlefield and in the information environment. As former NATO spokesman Jamie Shea noted, during the five days that the Djakovica bombing dominated the news, while the western media and their publics were focused on the deaths of a handful of unfortunate refugees, Serb militias drove more than 200,000 civilians out of Kosovo.[65] Likewise, in the wake of the Chinese Embassy bombing, Serb spokesmen took to the airwaves to claim that it was their people, not the Kosovars, who were the victims of terror and indiscriminate assault.

So complete was the Serbs' command of the information agenda that they were able to leverage practical military gains from it. When, after the

---

61 Rid, *War and Media Operations*, p.98.

62 Joel Havemann, 'Convoy Deaths May Undermine Moral Authority', *Los Angeles Times*, 15 April 1999, p.1.

63 Of the 23,000 bombs dropped by NATO during Operation Allied Force, Jamie Shea claims that only 30, or 0.0013 per cent failed to hit the intended target. See Dr Jamie P. Shea, 'The Kosovo Crisis and the Media: Reflections of a NATO Spokesman', *Lessons from Kosovo: the KFOR Experience*, ed. Larry Wentz, Washington: Department of Defence Command and Control Research Program, 2002, p.157. Whatever the veracity of Shea's claims, it is a mark of the deftness of the Yugoslav information campaign that it was able to make such effective propaganda capital out of so minuscule a sample.

64 NATO had been led to believe that the building housed the Yugoslav Federal Protectorate for Supply and Procurement.

65 See Shea, 'The Kosovo Crisis', p.162.

Djakovica attack, NATO cancelled daytime sorties and then abandoned the bombing of Belgrade in the wake of the Chinese Embassy incident, General Wesley Clark, NATO's Supreme Allied Commander Europe, conceded that 'The weight of public opinion was doing to us what the Serb air defence system had failed to do: limit our strikes.'[66] As a result of such experiences, commanders and planners realised that, like their adversaries, 'the US military needed to engage in what doctrine would call counter propaganda activities.'[67] And they could only do that, they discovered, by integrating public affairs into strategic planning, by bringing the media into the fold, working with them, harnessing their broadcasting power and tolerating their intrusive inspection.

Once again the US Air Force was ahead of the curve. Its 1998 doctrine on information operations heralded a revolution in military thinking about the nature and deployment of information: 'Conventional wisdom holds that release of information will be detrimental to military operations. However, commanders should consider the possible advantages of releasing certain information to demonstrate US resolve, intent, or reparations.'[68] Implicit in this proposal was a call to the military to shift its approach to information management from defence to attack, to move beyond the anxious oversight of news shaped for domestic consumption and recognise that 'the relevant audiences important to the commander are not limited to soldiers and the American public, but are also international as well as local to the operation.'[69] Once information is regarded as a weapon, as well as a shield, the military can use it to maintain morale at home, build alliances abroad and intimidate and dishearten their enemies, obviating the need for any actual fighting: 'Making these audiences aware of United States military capabilities and United States resolve to employ these assets can enhance support from allies and friendly countries and deter potential adversaries.'[70]

---

66 Wesley K. Clark, *Waging Modern War: Bosnia, Kosovo, and the Future of Combat*, New York: Public Affairs, 2001, p.444.

67 Rid, *War and Media Operations*, p.87.

68 United States Air Force, *Information Operations*, Air Force Doctrine Document 2–5, (Washington: USAF), 1998, p.16. In 2001, the newly revised *Doctrine for Joint Operations* (2001), the paramount document in the US military's doctrinal hierarchy, endorsed the centrality of the media as one among a number of weapons at a commander's disposal. See US Department of Defense, *Doctrine for Joint Operations*, Joint Publication 3–0 (Washington: Department of Defense, 2001), III.

69 Department of the Army, *Public Affairs Tactics, Techniques and Procedures*, Field Manual 3–61.1, Maryland: Department of the Army, 9. 1.

70 Rid, *War and Media Operations*, p.126. Sun Tzu's *The Art of War*, and its advocacy of the efficacy of demoralising one's opponent rather than beating him in battle, was

Yet without a media contingent 'at the tip of the spear', with the freedom and the technical means to tell the story, counter enemy propaganda and allay US public scepticism about their military's veracity, all of this sophisticated planning and the good intentions that underlay it would come to nothing. In late 2002, as the US prepared for a second invasion of Iraq, the Assistant Secretary of Defence for Public Affairs, Victoria Clarke, persuaded her boss, the Secretary of Defense, Donald Rumsfeld, that the military needed to take the media with them into battle. From the outset Clarke made it clear that the media operation was not an entertainment option for the couch surfers of America, but that it had 'an integrated strategic function in the overall war plan and had been designed to achieve five specific objectives: to pre-empt and counter Iraqi disinformation; to encourage dissent and defection among Iraqi civilians and fighting men; to publicise the successes of the US invasion; to manage the public's expectations about what might be achieved in Iraq; and to achieve and maintain information dominance.'[71] Though Rumsfeld thought the embedding of the media was 'a big gamble', he considered it 'probably one worth taking' and he signed off on the program.[72]

A bigger challenge was convincing the combatant commanders, in particular the Commanding General, Tommy Franks. Struggling to pull a war plan together, Franks had little time to consider the needs of the media; he 'was not only busy, he did not like the press to begin with.'[73] A Vietnam veteran, he also brought to the campaign an approach to the security of information unhindered by the latest thinking on media operations: 'When I heard the term "embedded media," it sounded dangerous', he noted. 'Assigning newspaper and magazine writers and broadcast correspondents to combat units could present problems: transportation, support, and liability. And there were concerns about operational security, in this age of satellite phone and Internet video cameras.' Whatever the shortcomings in Franks' grasp of the new technology, once Victoria Clarke and the General's media director, Jim Wilkinson, had briefed him on the proposed media operation Franks was an enthusiastic convert: 'I saw it as a winner.' What persuaded Franks was his recognition that having the reporters immersed in the military environment would generate empathy between the military, the

---

clearly a powerful influence on the formulation of information operations theory.

71 Rid, *War and Media Operations*, p.133.

72 Rid, *War and Media Operations*, p.133.

73 Rid, *War and Media Operations*, p.133. Franks told his media director: 'I don't give a rat's ass what you do with 'em [the press], just keep them out of my hair'. Tommy Franks, *American Soldier*, New York: Harper Collins, 2004, p.644.

media and the public: 'If the media were actually living and marching with the troops … they would experience war from the perspective of the soldier or marine.' This would ensure that the American people not only got 'to see the professionalism of their sons and daughters in uniform,' but that seeing the fighting from their perspective they would identify with and more deeply commit to them.[74]

With the necessary military and command support in place, on 10 February 2003, as the US armed forces geared up for the invasion of Iraq, Clarke's office in the Pentagon issued the Public Affairs Guidance (PAG) provisions that laid out the responsibilities of the military and the media around access to the area of operations, freedom of movement within it, and the review and transmission of copy. The guidelines required the military to facilitate 'long term, minimally restrictive access to U.S. Air, Ground and Naval forces.'[75] In pursuit of this policy, an array of responsibilities and prohibitions were imposed on the military. They were required to 'ensure the media are provided with every opportunity to observe actual combat operations.'[76] They had to provide seats on 'priority inter-theater airlift' to make sure that reporters could get to the fighting.[77] While the military had the right to direct PA officers to accompany the media, 'the absence of a PA escort is not a reason to preclude media access to operations.'[78] Once at the front, the document proposed that the media would be free to pursue the action at their own risk: 'The personal safety of correspondents is not a reason to exclude them from combat areas.'[79] And that went for *all* correspondents: 'Gender will not be an excluding factor under any circumstance.'[80] Having facilitated the access the media needed to gather their copy, the military then had to assist its free and timely transmission: 'No communications equipment for use by media in the conduct of their duties will be specifically prohibited.'[81] Nor would their copy be subject to

---

74 Franks, *American Soldier*, p.640.

75 Office of the Assistant Secretary of Defense for Public Affairs, *Public Affairs Guidance (PAG) on Embedding Media During Possible Future Operations/Deployments in the U.S. Central Commands (CENTCOM) Area of Responsibility (AOR)*, Washington: Department of Defense, 2003, 2. A. For further information on how the policy was sold to politicians, the military hierarchy and then implemented see Rid, *War and Media Operations*, pp.129–43.

76 Defense, *PAG*, 3. G.

77 Defense, *PAG*, 2. C. 2.

78 Defense, *PAG*, 3. F.

79 Defense, *PAG*, 3. G

80 Defense, *PAG*, 3. H.

81 Defense, *PAG*, 2. C. 4.

censorship other than in clearly defined circumstances: 'There is no general review process for media products.'[82] As a result, 'The standard for release of information should be "Why not release" vice "Why release". Decisions should be made ASAP, preferably in minutes, not hours.'[83] The adoption of these guidelines not only made sound operational sense, it also endorsed the military's commitment to the core democratic values advanced by the allies in their invasions of Iraq and Afghanistan: 'Our ultimate strategic success in bringing peace and security to this region will come in our long-term commitment to supporting our democratic ideals. We need to tell the factual story – good or bad – before others seed the media with disinformation and distortions.'[84] Accordingly, the policy explicitly forbade any attempt by the military to 'prevent the release of derogatory, embarrassing, negative or uncomplimentary information.'[85]

By contrast, Australian media management policies in force from the days of Vietnam seem dedicated to the reverse of the PAG: keeping the media at arm's length from the military, denying them freedom of movement, impeding their access to troops in the field, detailing PA officers to shadow their every move, subjecting copy to security review, delaying or obstructing the transmission of unsympathetic coverage, seeking to ensure thereby that derogatory, negative or embarrassing information about the ADF would never see the light of day. Where the US military's attitudes towards and relationship with the media underwent a fundamental transformation between the First and Second Gulf Wars, the ADF's was marked by consistency and continuity with the entrenched animosities of the past.

---

82 Defense, *PAG*, 3. R.
83 Defense, *PAG*, 3. Q.
84 Defense, *PAG*, 2. A.
85 Defense, *PAG*, 4.

Chapter 2

THE 'FEEL FREE TO FUCK OFF' APPROACH TO PUBLIC RELATIONS

Trust Overboard

The most striking feature of the ADF's media operations practices in Afghanistan has been their continuing fidelity to the lessons of Vietnam and their underlying assumption that the fourth estate is the enemy. Where Tommy Franks, and just about everybody below him in the US military, recognised that the best means of promoting its aims in Iraq and showcasing the professionalism of the men and women tasked with their attainment was via largely unfettered media access to the troops, until the full scale implementation of a media embedding program in 2011 the ADF remained dedicated to keeping the media on a short leash, restricting their access to the troops and controlling their copy. Where the PAG made the military responsible for ensuring that the media could access the theatre of battle, cover events and speedily transmit their copy, the most recent agreement governing the ADF's interactions with the media on the battlefield, the *Statement of Understanding For Accredited Media (Ground Rules)*, issued by the Department of Defence in January 2009, places the burden of compliance squarely on the shoulders of the media. It is the media who must accept that they may not be able to report from or name certain locations, that they 'will be escorted at all times,' 'must adhere to the direction and advice of the military escort officer at all times,' and must 'consult with the escort officer or the Defence's [*sic*] Director General Public Affairs (DGPA) or his staff in relation to stories directly arising from this access to ADF elements.'[1] Failure to comply with any of these regulations will not only bring immediate sanction but may result in ongoing exclusion from all ADF personnel and

1 Department of Defence, *Statement of Understanding For Accredited Media (Ground Rules)*, Canberra: Department of Defence, 1 January 2009.

operations: 'Violations of any of the conditions will result in the Correspondents' removal from the location and access to ADF staff and may have implications for future access to ADF elements on operations.'[2] The accompanying *Operationally Sensitive Information Brief* likewise contains a list of the information that 'is not to be visually recorded', and a second list of information that 'shall not be released.'[3] It is, of course, entirely appropriate that the ADF should seek to protect information about 'Restricted military areas, facilities and installations,' 'intelligence or Special Forces personnel and equipment,' 'Interiors of vehicles and aircraft,' and 'The flight line at Kandahar airfield and military aircraft operating on or near it.'[4] Yet what is striking about these documents is their failure at any point to consider Defence and the ADF's responsibility to keep the public informed about what it is doing with their resources and in their name, and the onus this would place on them to facilitate the media's access to, freedom of movement and association within, and expeditious transmission of material from the area of operations. These documents reinforce the view, prevalent within Defence and the ADF, that the media are on the battlefield not by right but at the military's grace and favour, and that by extension the public's right to know extends only as far as the military is prepared to allow it.

This position is further illuminated in the Department of Defence's *Defence Instructions (General) Public comment and dissemination of official information by Defence personnel*, which were last updated and released on 5 October 2007. The instructions, like the *Operationally Sensitive Information Brief*, are overwhelmingly focused on what cannot be said, or on outlining the coordination, clearance and authorisation procedures for what can. Permissive statements – 'Public comments must be as open as possible to maintain and strengthen Defence's credibility and reputation' – are invariably offset by cautionary or prohibitive clauses – 'While Defence encourages Defence personnel to engage with the public, the information they provide must be coordinated, agreed and authorised.'[5] The keynote here is oversight, lines of responsibility and the chains of command that enforce them. While it is important to recognise the differences of purpose between the *Defence Instructions*, the *Statement of Understanding For Accredited Media (Ground*

---

2 Defence, *Statement of Understanding.*

3 Department of Defence, *Operationally Sensitive Information Brief*, Canberra: Department of Defence, 1 January 2009.

4 Defence, *Operationally Sensitive.*

5 Department of Defence, *Defence Instructions (General) Public comment and dissemination of official information by Defence personnel*, Canberra: Department of Defence, 2007, Appendix C, 7.

Rules), and the PAG – the former shapes the interface between Defence personnel, the media and the public in the domestic context, the latter two govern military-media relations on the battlefield – what is most notable about them is their contrasting attitudes to information and how these shape their relations with its principal purveyors and consumers, the media and the public. The Pentagon recognises the power of information as a force multiplier and a weapon of war, and takes pains via the PAG to project an appearance of candour. By contrast, the Australian documents express the conventional military view of information as a volatile element whose release and distribution is to be carefully managed for fear of the harm it might do. As a number of media commentators have noted, these views are underpinned by and lay bare 'a culture of contempt' for politicians, the public and the media that neither the Department of Defence nor the ADF feel any need to explain or disguise.[6]

In Australia, relations between the Department of Defence, the ADF, their civilian and political masters, the media and the public have never been easy.[7] However the Children Overboard Affair in October 2001, when senior government ministers, including the Defence Minister, Peter Reith, falsely claimed that asylum seekers had thrown their children into the sea in an effort to secure rescue and passage to Australia, further 'strained the relationship between Defence and successive ministers.'[8] Relations between Defence and the Minister immediately prior to the incident were already unusually tense. In 2000, public comment arrangements in the Department of Defence had been brought into line with other government portfolios when the uniformed leadership were 'forced ... to cede to the Minister, and executive government as a whole, much more power over defence public information.'[9] As Brian Humphreys, the former Director General of Communication Strategies for the Department of Defence and one of

6 Paul Daley, 'Defence versus Parliament: the next great debate', *The Sunday Age*, 1 March 2009, p.19.

7 See Anderson and Trembath, *Witnesses to War*; Williams, *ANZACS, The Media and the Great War*; Hilvert, *Blue Pencil Warriors*; Jackson, 'Duplication, Rivalry and Friction, pp.74–85; Payne, *War and Words*; Foster (ed), *What are we doing in Afghanistan?*

8 Deborah Snow and Cynthia Banham, 'Calling Shots in Defence', *Sydney Morning Herald*, Weekend Edition, 28 February – 1 March 2009, p.7. For more on the Children Overboard affair see Senate Select Committee, *Report into a Certain Maritime Incident*, Canberra: Commonwealth of Australia, 2002, and David Marr and Marian Wilkinson, *Dark Victory*, Sydney: Allen and Unwin, 2002.

9 Brian Humphreys, 'The Australian Defence Force's Media Strategy: What it is and Why, and Why it Needs to Change', in Foster, *What are we Doing in Afghanistan?* p.41.

the architects of the new arrangements, noted, the armed forces needed a reminder of who was in charge:

> At that time I was stunned by some in the Department of Defence who showed open disregard for the role of the Minister. Back then it was not unusual for Minister's office staff to experience audible sighs when calling into Defence headquarters to ask for something. This was a dramatic departure from the culture in other government departments, where a call from the Minister's office was a cue to drop everything else. In Russell, though, many in Defence were candid in their belief that they worked for the Governor General and that the Minister was someone to tolerate rather than respect.[10]

However, the reforms intended to re-assert the accountability of the armed forces to their civilian governors only served to illustrate the susceptibility of such high-minded ideals to political sharp-practice and the invidious position in which this placed the military. In August 2001, when the Norwegian cargo ship *Tampa* rescued 438 mainly Afghan Hazara asylum seekers from their crippled boat, the KM *Palapa 1*, Prime Minister John Howard refused to allow the ship to enter Australian territorial waters and sent an SAS boarding party out to the cargo vessel to ensure that his orders were followed. In the political and media storm that these actions unleashed, a special task force appointed by the Cabinet decided that 'there would be total control of information about the *Tampa* operation by the government through ministerial offices. None of the officials involved in Canberra or on Christmas Island would be allowed to talk to the press.'[11]

While the *Tampa* crisis was underway, the government launched Operation Relex, directing Royal Australian Navy (RAN) vessels to blockade the Indian Ocean between Indonesia, Christmas Island and Ashmore Reef in an effort to prevent further incursions by asylum seeker vessels. This radical policy was matched by an equally extreme approach to public affairs, in which the government took 'extraordinary steps to keep information about Operation Relex from the public. Even before detailed planning for the blockade began, Peter Reith had imposed far tighter control of information flowing from the military.'[12] At a meeting with Admiral Chris Barrie, Chief of the Defence Force (CDF), 1998–2002, and the secretary of the Defence

---

10 Humphreys, 'The Australian Defence Force's Media Strategy', p.41. Russell is the Canberra suburb where Defence Headquarters is located.

11 Marr and Wilkinson, *Dark Victory*, p.65.

12 Marr and Wilkinson, *Dark Victory*, p.133.

Department, Allan Hawke, 'Reith put before them a sweeping plan to give his office control over the release of all military information to the public.'[13] While David Marr and Marian Wilkinson concede that the existing arrangements by which the military briefed the press were far from candid:

> Reith's new proposal amounted to a change of culture. The military would now have to clear all media releases with Reith's press secretary, Ross Hampton ... So tight were these new Defence Instructions (General), that the media was now barred from Defence seminars and conferences except by special clearance. Any approaches by the media had to be reported to senior officers. One provision even barred military officers from providing any information to the public 'which could place in doubt their political impartiality or acceptance of the obligation to implement the policy of the elected government.'[14]

The military were not happy, though they had little opportunity to express their displeasure as the public commentary restrictions ensured that: 'There would be no military briefings of the press and journalists would not be allowed to quiz military officers about Relex. Even the commanders of Relex', among them the Chief of the Defence Force, 'were gagged. Every press enquiry to the military about the operation was to be bounced back to the minister's office. Though this was only a policing operation, the level of censorship would be tougher than the media was used to in wartime.'[15]

As such, when on 6 October, HMAS *Adelaide* was sent to intercept the *Olong*, a boat from South Sumatra bound for Christmas Island, designated as Suspected Illegal Entry Vessel (SIEV) 4, the frigate's Commander, Norman Banks, and many of the crew had a clear view of what transpired when the boat's engines stopped and the vessel began to take on water. As the *Olong* began to sink, Banks saw passengers jumping into the sea and sent a boarding party from HMAS *Adelaide* to steady the vessel and dissuade those aboard from further abandonment. At this moment: 'Banks was interrupted by a telephone call from Brigadier Mike Silverstone at Northern Command Headquarters in Darwin. The brigadier was an army man but Banks answered directly to him in Operation Relex.' Silverstone needed an update on the situation because Defence Minister Reith was about to be interviewed on television. 'Banks gave Silverstone some brief facts. He would later recall telling Silverstone some of the passengers were throwing

13 Marr and Wilkinson, *Dark Victory*, p.133.
14 Marr and Wilkinson, *Dark Victory*, p.134.
15 Marr and Wilkinson, *Dark Victory*, pp.134–5.

themselves into the water and threatening to throw in their children.'[16] Soon afterwards Banks was 'stunned' to find that the Prime Minister, the Ministers for Defence, Immigration, Foreign Affairs, and others, were alleging that SIEV 4's passengers had thrown their children into the sea and that these assertions were now splashed across the media in the early days of a federal election campaign.[17] Reith had gone even further, claiming that 'we have a number of people, obviously RAN people who were there who reported the children were thrown into the water.'[18] However disturbed Banks was by 'the serious "misinformation" in the media coverage', under the media directions governing Operation Relex nobody in the military – from the Able Seamen who dived into the water to rescue men, women and children as SIEV 4 began to sink, to the ship's Commander, right up to the CDF – was able to comment on what had actually happened and so correct the record.[19] All defence-related media enquiries pertaining to the incident had to be directed to the minister's Press Secretary, Ross Hampton, who, 'with the improved levers of power given to the Minister's office ... was able, with the support of his superiors ... to bring Defence information to a grinding halt' while peddling the government's official line.[20] Worse still, when the military pointed out to the minister's office that his claims were false, the minister's staff blamed the military for failing to correct their own earlier accounts and for sowing confusion, while Reith himself 'castigated' the CDF.[21]

The whole episode badly damaged whatever trust had built up between the military and the government, driving a more cautious approach to public information in the ADF. Some years later, former Defence Minister Joel Fitzgibbon noted that the Children Overboard affair 'produced a more risk averse culture and a determination [in the ADF] to put up barriers between

16 Marr and Wilkinson, *Dark Victory*, pp.184, 185.
17 Marr and Wilkinson, *Dark Victory*, p.197.
18 Quoted in Marr and Wilkinson, *Dark Victory*, p.203.
19 Marr and Wilkinson, *Dark Victory*, p.197.
20 Humphreys, 'The Australian Defence Force's Media Strategy', p.42.
21 Marr and Wilkinson, *Dark Victory*, p.208. Marr and Wilkinson offer the following explanation of how the assertion that children were thrown overboard from the *Olong* originated. As Silverstone spoke to Banks 'he hurriedly scribbled some notes in his diary: the boat's steering was disabled; it was dead in the water; the passengers were threatening a mass exodus; they were wearing life jackets, although some had discarded them. He wrote, "men thrown over side. 5, 6 or 7." When Banks hung up Silverstone added the word "child" to the note believing, he would say later, that Commander Banks told him a child about 5, 6 or 7 years old had been thrown over the side'. Marr and Wilkinson, *Dark Victory*, pp.184, 185.

both politicians and media organisations.'[22] The conviction among the ADF's senior commanders that many of the politicians they served were without principle, 'that "public information" was a dirty word' and that that they should keep a low profile and so avoid the potential for compromise, resulted in the establishment of a 'thicket of procedures and clearance requirements' around interactions with the media and the public.[23] By 2009 'self-serving obfuscation' had become an 'ingrained habit' in Defence and an editorial in the *Sydney Morning Herald* noted that 'To outsiders – who include the public, the media, and most members of Parliament – the Defence Department has become increasingly tight with even routine information over recent decades.'[24] This 'tightness' reflected both a literal and a figurative closing of the uniformed ranks in the face of perceived enemies, among whom the ADF numbered not only hostile powers, but also the politicians tasked with their management. Put simply, politicians and public servants deputed to manage members of the armed forces regularly ran into a wall of resentment and resistance. According to former Defence Minister, Dr Brendan Nelson, it was 'fair to say that at times the uniformed side of Defence finds it difficult to respond to directives that come from civilians in the form of the government and minister of the day.'[25] The same qualities that underpinned the forces' effectiveness in a fight, that bound them together against their enemies, also set them against the system they notionally served: 'One of the great values which is enmeshed in the defence force … is that of mateship, protecting and defending your mate, but … that culture can actually work against the best interests of not only Defence but indeed the country that it serves.'[26]

Through Gritted Teeth

If the Children Overboard affair gave the military good cause to mistrust the motives and behaviour of their political masters, it served to reinforce the views it had long held about the fourth estate. But how did the military come to harbour such negative opinions about the media in the first place,

---

22 Cynthia Banham and Jonathan Pearlman, 'It's war: minister takes aim at defence', *Sydney Morning Herald*, Weekend Edition, 28 February – 1 March 2009, p.1.

23 Humphreys, 'The Australian Defence Force's Media Strategy', p.43.

24 Snow and Banham, 'Calling Shots in Defence', p.7. Editorial, 'Need-not-to-know doctrine', *Sydney Morning Herald*, 27 February 2009, np.

25 Cynthia Banham and Deborah Snow, 'They don't follow orders: Nelson opens fire on top brass', *Sydney Morning Herald*, 26 February 2009, p.1.

26 Banham and Snow, 'They don't follow orders', p.1.

and why have they been so enduring? What did the media do to the military that marked them as hostile and how did this earn them their undying enmity? On the basis of the printed evidence, the ADF's allegations of media antagonism towards the military make no sense. Looking back at more than a century of Australian coverage of the nation's military, Tom Hyland points out that 'the media's default position with the defence force has been compliant' – if not reverential. As a consequence of this posture the media 'have largely created and sustained a consistently positive image of the ADF in action' and 'bestowed on the military a repository of enormous goodwill.'[27] This is clearly reflected in its ritualised coverage of Anzac Day with its standard forms and stock figures – the dawn service, the solemn silence, ageing heroes proudly marching, the reunions, the two-up games and the remembrance of lost comrades.[28] While the Anzac myth originated in British journalist Ellis Ashmead-Bartlett's dispatches for the London press from Gallipoli, it was taken up as a national cause and crafted by Australia's Official War Correspondent, C.E.W. Bean, who dedicated the rest of his career to the memorialisation of the Australian serviceman. 'In both world wars,' Richard Trembath notes, Australian 'journalists were expected to be publicist, historian, propagandist and military cheerleader.'[29] Despite some discontent, and occasional acts of rebellion, the vast majority embraced these roles with enthusiasm. Bean's successor, the Official War Correspondent in the Second World War, Kenneth Slessor, observed that 'Every correspondent wants to help the effort to win the war, and wouldn't mind colouring his dispatches to suit the plan,' while Alan Moorehead recognised that his principal responsibility in reporting the war was to maintain morale: 'you must give the public good news.'[30] A central feature of that good news was the celebration of the nation's forces.

Despite the media's faithful cheerleading on its behalf, the Australian military has held onto its suspicion of and hostility towards the fourth estate – a position that the experience of Vietnam only served to harden and deepen. This antagonism towards the media arose, in part, from a broader tendency to evaluate the Australian experience of the Vietnam War in the light of, and as if it was identical to, the US experience. As Jeffrey Grey has noted:

---

27 Tom Hyland, 'The Media Never Lose', *The Information Battlefield: Representing Australians at War*, ed. Kevin Foster, Melbourne: Australian Scholarly Publishing, 2011, p.41.

28 For more on this see Sharon Mascall-Dare, 'An Australian Story: Anzac Day Coverage Investigated', *The Information Battlefield*, pp.162–180.

29 Anderson and Trembath, *Witnesses to War*, p.136.

30 Young, *Media and Military*, p.40.

'American popular culture is so pervasive, especially in the English-speaking world, that our "memories" of the war are shaped and coloured by American responses to the American experience.'[31] Informed by such a perspective, the Australian military have long spoken darkly about the media's 'betrayal' of the armed forces in Vietnam and how this contributed to a public backlash against the troops: 'The most widespread and persistent belief attached to Australian Vietnam veterans is that none received a "welcome home" upon their return to Australia. Allied to this is a perception, rather better grounded, that soldiers returning from Vietnam received a hostile reception, or at best were greeted with complete indifference even by their families.' Grey argues that 'All of these views are inaccurate to a greater or lesser extent.'[32] They are inaccurate because what is being 'remembered' here is not authentic Australian experience but the concoctions of Hollywood, and while these 'often have little to do with the way in which American soldiers actually fought and experienced the war; they have even less to say to Australians.'[33]

For the US military the key culprit in the great Vietnam swindle was the media who, they alleged, had single-handedly turned the politicians and the people against the war and the men fighting it. Likewise in Australia, the conviction that the media were hostile to the military, that they 'maligned the troops after so wholeheartedly supporting them' and thereby played a central role in stirring up public resentment against them, has gained widespread acceptance.[34] Yet as Rodney Tiffen has reminded us: 'It is a fundamental mistake ... to think the debate about American media coverage of the [Vietnam] war can be simply translated to Australia.'[35] The resourcing, professional practices and intended purposes of the Australian media in relation to the Vietnam War were completely different to those of their US counterparts.

The commitment of Australian forces to Vietnam came at a time when Australian newspapers and their readers were enjoying improved and more-timely access to overseas news. In the face of this new accessibility, the nation's metropolitan dailies began 'to re-assess their foreign news

---

31 Jeffrey Grey, 'In every war but one? Myth, history and Vietnam', *Zombie Myths of Australian Military History*, ed. Craig Stockings, Sydney: New South Press, 2010, p.211.

32 Grey, 'In every war', p.199–200. For a representative sample of such views see Paul Ham, *Vietnam: The Australian War*, Sydney: Harper Collins, 2007, pp.560–573.

33 Grey, 'In every war', p.211.

34 Ham, *Vietnam*, p.415.

35 Rodney Tiffen, 'The War the Media Lost: Australian News Coverage of Vietnam', *Vietnam Remembered*, Updated Edition, ed. Gregory Pemberton, Sydney: New Holland Publishers, 2009, p.118.

coverage.'[36] Yet instead of laying the foundations for a new sense of the Australian media's connectedness with the world, this re-assessment underscored its parochialism and reinforced its detachment from global events: 'While an increase in available overseas material encouraged newspapers to report foreign news and perspectives, its initial effect was to blind newspaper executives in Australia to the need for an Australian input.'[37] The consequences of this insularity were evidenced in the media's failure to commit sufficient resources to adequately cover the war in Vietnam: 'Just as Australia's military commitment was disproportionately smaller than America's, so was Australia's journalistic commitment ... The number of Australian correspondents in Vietnam at any one time never numbered more than a handful, while during peaks of newsworthiness there were several hundred from the United States.'[38] One such peak was in 1968, the year of the Tet offensive, the siege of Khe Sanh and the cessation of the bombing of North Vietnam. Throughout these key events in the war's history while dozens of US journalists reported from Saigon, Hue and other key sites, John Brittle vainly endeavoured to persuade his employers at the *Adelaide Advertiser* to send him to Vietnam. They refused all entreaties, Brittle reflected, because 'they did not think it was worthwhile.'[39] Brittle was not alone in his isolation. Some Australian newspapers failed to muster a single visitor to the war: 'The *Sydney Morning Herald*, which had sent more correspondents to World War II than any other Australian newspaper, did not manage to send one to Vietnam.'[40] Despite the fact that 'some [Australian] papers sent correspondents for lengthy periods, none ever had a permanent Vietnam correspondent.'[41]

For the duration of the conflict 'The most constant source of material for Australian newspapers came from the international news agencies.'[42] With a few exceptions, the Australian media had determined to pursue a softer, more personal angle on the nation's commitment to the war. When Pat Burgess covered the conflict for Fairfax, he told Trish Payne that his employers 'didn't want news, they were going to rely on the agency for news ... they only

---

36 Payne, *War and Words*, p.16.
37 Payne, *War and Words*, p.17.
38 Tiffen, 'The War the Media Lost', p.126.
39 Anderson and Trembath, *Witnesses to War*, p.231
40 Anderson and Trembath, *Witnesses to War*, p.231
41 Tiffen, "News Coverage", p.166. Trish Payne corroborates: 'No Australian newspaper retained a reporter in Vietnam for the duration of Australia's participation in the Vietnam War', Payne, *War and Words*, p.16.
42 Tiffen, 'News Coverage', p.166.

wanted airmailers ... a feature type story.'[43] Television reporters faced even greater obstacles in their efforts to cover the war. Television broadcasting had only begun in Australia in 1956. By the early 1960s television news was still in a 'primitive' state and none of the commercial channels had developed the 'independent capacity to gather overseas news.' Indeed, 'For much of the period of Australia's military involvement in Vietnam, TV news was barely capable of giving timely and pertinent coverage from Canberra, let alone Saigon.'[44] The Australian Broadcasting Corporation (ABC) was the only Australian broadcaster with correspondents permanently based in Asia. While its reporters in Singapore enjoyed the relatively easy access that proximity to the conflict brought, their coverage of events was hampered by technical shortcomings. With the processing of film still done back in Australia 'the possibilities for sophisticated editing and the integration of material from different sources were far more limited.'[45]

The military offered the media a show of cooperation in Vietnam, but with the government's connivance they conspired to keep the correspondents at arm's length: 'A telegram from Austforce, Vietnam, to the Department of the Army in Canberra stated that their senior officers "had been advised on a confidential basis that they should as far as possible avoid contact with press representatives without making it obvious that they are doing so."'[46] The reporters recognised that 'they were at best tolerated and at other times actively discouraged' by the men in uniform.[47] Peter Couchman of the ABC noted that 'reporters were sort of welcomed through gritted teeth ... you always got the impression that you were a bit of a nuisance.'[48] Others put it more pithily. Tim Bowden notes in his biography of Neil Davis that: 'Unlike the Americans and other allied groups fighting in South Vietnam, the Australians did not welcome foreign correspondents; they had a deep-seated distrust of the press. It was known in the trade as the "feel free to fuck off" approach to public relations.'[49]

Expected to support the cause and burnish the military brand by concentrating on 'home-towners' or cheery colour pieces, reporters who showed

43 Payne, *War and Words*, p.17.
44 Tiffen, 'The War the Media Lost', p.118.
45 Tiffen, 'The War the Media Lost', p.119.
46 Anderson and Trembath, *Witnesses to War*, p.237.
47 Anderson and Trembath, *Witnesses to War*, p.237.
48 Anderson and Trembath, *Witnesses to War*, p.237.
49 Tim Bowden, *One Crowded Hour: Neil Davis Combat Cameraman, 1934–1985*, Sydney: Angus and Robertson, 1987, p.141. For a further explanation of the origins of this description of the Australian 'policy' see Anderson and Trembath, *Witnesses to War*, p.238.

any inclination to pursue more investigative angles, to question why the Australians were in Vietnam, what they might reasonably do there, or to criticise what they saw among their own people, were obstructed and implicitly, if not more directly, invited to fuck off again. Creighton Burns, who covered the war for *The Age*, and later edited the paper, recalled that the military's attempts to impose censorship and impede the reporter in his work in Vietnam were 'horrific … you couldn't talk to an Australian soldier without the presence of an officer there.'[50] Veteran correspondent, Denis Warner, who had covered Korea and the Second World War, responded with fury to these efforts to restrict his professional practice, describing them as 'the most blatant attempt to impose censorship at source that I have ever encountered in any Army in any war at any time.'[51]

It wasn't only government and military restrictions that impeded the media's coverage of the war. Those correspondents who made it to Vietnam found that a further – if not the principal – constraint on their reporting originated with their employers. Keith Smith of the Australian Associated Press (AAP) discovered that he 'was expected to self censor and not send material that was critical of the government's position.'[52] John Mancy and Alan Ramsey, also of AAP 'were told to stick to reporting stories and not to carry out investigative pieces or editorialise.'[53] The ABC imposed 'strict guidelines' dictating 'what its news division staff could say and could not say', which resulted in the prohibition of 'any form of commentary.'[54] The government's determination to formalise media restrictions was demonstrated in October 1968 when the Defence Minister, Allen Fairhall, issued draft guidelines which 'required that any Australian journalists quoting Australian soldiers had to submit their copy for approval to military officials in Vietnam.'[55] Earlier in the year the government had signalled its dismay at perceived media hostility to its policies in Vietnam. When the Prime Minister, John Gorton, was asked if he would look into Vietnamese communist denials that they were responsible for the deaths of three Australian journalists killed in a Vietcong raid on Cholon, he declined to do so, in

50 Fay Anderson, 'The New and Altered Conventions of Reporting War: Censorship, Access and Representation in Afghanistan', in Foster, *What are we Doing in Afghanistan?* p.127.

51 Quoted in Payne, *War and Words*, p.5.

52 Anderson and Trembath, *Witnesses to War*, p.233.

53 Anderson and Trembath, *Witnesses to War*, p.234.

54 Anderson and Trembath, *Witnesses to War*, p.234.

55 Payne, *War and Words*, p.4.

the process taking a swipe at 'press coverage in Vietnam which … does not support as it might, the efforts of Australians in that area.'[56]

While Fairhall's 'guidelines' were not well received by the fourth estate, they were hardly unexpected. The government had consistently demonstrated a 'penchant for heavy-handed intervention' into the operations of the media, best illustrated in the 'humiliating control' it exercised over the ABC.[57] Earlier in the decade the Prime Minister, Sir Robert Menzies, had personally blocked the making of a film about US-Canadian relations on the grounds that such an intrusion might upset our allies, while in 1963, at the behest of the French, the government vetoed the broadcast of a BBC interview with French opposition figure George Bidault. The effects of such intrusive micro-management on the coverage of the war in Vietnam were depressingly predictable. The pressure brought to bear on ABC journalists 'to do stories favourable to government policy', was matched by the determination of editors to block the publication or broadcast of any material that contradicted it.[58] The Australian combat cameraman, Neil Davis, who, via Visnews, furnished the Australian networks with a substantial proportion of their film coverage of the war, believed that 'his Vietnam footage was cut much more drastically in Australia than anywhere else in the world', particularly at the ABC. On the basis of what viewers saw of Vietnam on television, he told Tim Bowden, 'You'd think it was a war without violence, that it was all sweetness and light. Just our Australian boys patrolling and keeping the dreaded Communists in check. The hierarchy of the ABC's news department believed that news programs were a family affair, and they didn't want the wife and kids watching blood and guts over seven o'clock dinner – even in black and white.'[59] As a consequence, the Australian public's exposure to and understanding of the war were deeply deficient.

The media's failure to commit adequate resources to cover the war in Vietnam was matched – and significantly shaped – by a corresponding 'cognitive failure among media managements,' a failure to think beyond the bounds of their traditional relationship with the government and the people.[60] The Australian media were, as Tiffen notes, 'more a dependent than an independent variable in the political process' in Australia, more accustomed

---

56 Payne, *War and Words*, p.8. The dead Australian journalists were Michael Birch, Bruce Cantwell and John Piggott: Frank Palmos survived.

57 Tiffen, 'The War the Media Lost', pp.120, 119.

58 Tiffen, 'The War the Media Lost', p.120.

59 Tim Bowden, *One Crowded Hour*, p.186.

60 Tiffen, 'The War the Media Lost', p.126.

to accepting and passing on the government's position than questioning or contesting it.[61] As a result, throughout the war 'There was a striking coincidence between government rhetoric and most editorial comment.'[62] The Brisbane *Courier-Mail*'s response to Prime Minister Holt's announcement in March 1966 of the trebling of the Australian troop commitment in Vietnam, was to dedicate the first three paragraphs of its editorial to a direct quotation from the Prime Minister's speech to parliament.[63] On those rare occasions when dissenting views on Vietnam did appear they 'were accompanied by considerable nervousness and reluctance among news executives' – not that they needed to worry given that such opinions 'were more often than not either ignored or denigrated'.[64] Notably: 'The coverage of anti-war dissent in Australia was consistently negative, with rarely any suggestion that it deserved serious consideration.'[65] Government interference, military coercion and editorial diffidence thus combined to ensure that 'the performance of the Australian media' in its coverage of the Vietnam War 'was overwhelmingly timid,' evidenced in 'less independent probing, less willingness to devote adequate resources to reporting the war, and a far more restricted range of opinion and analysis.'[66] As a consequence, Tiffen claims, the media 'failed' in their main political roles – to serve as 'an agent of disclosure' and to provide 'a forum for diverse commentary and analysis.'[67]

'Carton Avoidance' and Cultural Change

Though the Australian military suffered numerous setbacks at the hands of the Viet Minh, it clearly triumphed over its own media in Vietnam, playing its part in ensuring that coverage of the war occupied a narrow range between 'general support' and vociferous partisanship.[68] As a result of these outcomes, the military regarded its experience of working with the media

61 Tiffen, 'The War the Media Lost', p.125. Tiffen notes that 'with little opportunity for independent gathering of evidence, the news media were reduced to passive conveyors of official views'. Tiffen, 'News Coverage', p.172.

62 Tiffen, 'The War the Media Lost', p.126. Tiffen notes that: 'When Australia committed troops on 29 April 1965, and again when Prime Minister Holt trebled the commitment in March 1966, the decision received overwhelming editorial support'. Tiffen, 'The War the Media Lost', p.126.

63 *Courier-Mail*, 10 March 1966.

64 Tiffen, 'News Coverage', p.167; Tiffen, 'The War the Media Lost', p.125.

65 Tiffen, 'News Coverage', p.184.

66 Tiffen, 'News Coverage', p.184.

67 Tiffen, 'The War the Media Lost', p.125.

68 Tiffen, 'News Coverage', p.184

in Vietnam as a vindication of the benefits of limited contact and strict control. Where the Americans learned from the First Gulf War, Kosovo and elsewhere that the lessons of Vietnam were wrong, that the media were not the enemy but an ally, and a handy force multiplier at that, the ADF hung onto and reinforced the lessons it learned in Phuoc Tuy. To some extent this can be accounted for by the relative paucity of the ADF's contemporary operational exposure. Where the Americans, the British and many NATO forces have had sufficient opportunity to trial new ways of working with the media since Vietnam, to experience for themselves the failures of the post-Vietnam model and to arrive by trial and error at something better suited to a new world of communications technology, information operations and their changing needs, the ADF has been starved of equivalent opportunities. Though Australian journalists were present in the area of operations during the ADF commitment to Cambodia between 1991 and 1993, 'the deployed force operated under a highly restrictive UN media policy' denying them the opportunity to test the media operations lessons learned from the UK and US experiences.[69] Likewise, when 23 Australian journalists accompanied members of the ADF's Media Support Unit to Somalia during Operation Solace in early 1993, the opportunities to trial new policies were limited by the brevity of the media's stay in the area of operations, where they remained for only a fortnight. The 'turning point', according to Jason Logue, came in 1999, during Operation Warden, when the ADF was deployed to East Timor as the lead member of a 22-nation coalition.[70] Faced with this new level of responsibility and the massive international interest in the events in East Timor as the Indonesians prepared to depart the country after the Timorese overwhelmingly voted for independence, it was clear that 'the ADF's existing policy concerning media on operations needed immediate revision.'[71] However, the changes implemented as a result of the experience in East Timor reflected the ADF's continued mistrust of the fourth estate. While a 'key lesson from Operation Warden was the understanding that the media were permanent actors in the modern battlefield', the resulting decision to disband the Media Support Unit and create the 1st Joint Public Affairs Unit (JPAU), whose focus was 'on capturing, compiling and releasing ADF-developed imagery product', reflected the ADF's determination to compete against

69 Logue, *Herding Cats*, p.11.
70 Logue, *Herding Cats*, p.11.
71 Logue, *Herding Cats*, p.12.

rather than cooperate with the media in the gathering and dissemination of words and images from the front lines.[72]

The ADF's attitudes towards the media are not just the product of a relative lack of operational experience, they are a key shaping influence on that experience, reflecting entrenched cultural values within the armed forces that are resistant to reform. As the former CDF General Peter Cosgrove observed, the military has long preferred to give the fourth estate a wide berth: 'Throughout the modern history of the Australian Defence Force … with perhaps a few exceptions, the military has kept the media very much at an arm's length.'[73] While, on occasions, as in Vietnam, government has encouraged such behaviour, media evasion requires no official approval as it reflects one of the ADF's key cultural norms. Chris Masters found that his early efforts at interviewing and filming the troops in Afghanistan were hampered by a culture of 'carton avoidance', by the 'unwritten rule that the soldier who appears on camera has to buy beers' for his colleagues.[74] Keen to talk to one soldier, who, injured in an IED attack, had insisted on returning to duty with his comrades, Masters had to wait: the soldier 'needed group permission' before he could 'say his piece.'[75] While this ADF custom 'may well have a worthy genesis, reflecting a suspicion of "big noting" and "bunging it on"', Masters notes, 'it does not help when trying to tell their story, a story they universally conceded was not getting through to the broad public and their own families back home.'[76] An aversion to close contact with the fourth estate has evidently 'soaked deep' into the Australian military's 'cultural tissue'. It will take a dedicated effort from the armed forces to correct this condition, to prepare the ground for the rehabilitation of its relations with the media and so ensure that its story can be told.

Even if the ADF was prepared, or eager, to reform its relations with the media, it seems to lack the organisational means to direct and drive the cultural change that this would demand. The Department of Defence is one of the nation's largest employers, with a workforce in excess of 100,000

---

72 Logue, *Herding Cats*, p.12.

73 General Peter Cosgrove, 'Inconvenient Truths: The Military and the Media', *The Information Battlefield: Representing Australians at War*, ed. Kevin Foster, Melbourne: Australian Scholarly Publishing, p.2.

74 Chris Masters, 'The Media's Left and Right of Arc', *The Information Battlefield: Representing Australians at War*, ed. Kevin Foster, Melbourne: Australian Scholarly Publishing, 2011, p.37. Masters notes that among the troops 'There is a cultural resistance to the limelight, to being seen as a big noter'. Masters, 'The Media's Left and Right of Arc', p.37.

75 Masters, 'The Media's Left and Right of Arc', p.37.

76 Masters, *Uncommon Soldier*, p.115.

personnel. It has a presence in every state and territory, manages over 3 million hectares of land, and operates advanced fleets of aircraft, ships, submarines and other fighting vehicles. Its 'assets and inventory amounts to $73 billion, and its annual budget of $26.5 billion is equivalent to around 1.8 per cent of our gross domestic product.'[77] Jointly managed, under a diarchy, by a civilian Secretary and the uniformed CDF, the Department has long been regarded by politicians, the media and expert commentators as dysfunctional. A sprawling congeries of entrenched practice and uniformed fiefdoms resistant to civilian oversight, beyond the capacity of any Minister to manage let alone reform, it is 'a source of profound frustration to the government.'[78] A 2011 report from the Australian Strategic Policy Institute (ASPI) described the Department's current state of operation and organisation as 'beyond intolerable,' noting its 'manifest inefficiency and clouded accountability.'[79] Because the Department lacks a governance infrastructure commensurate with its size and complexity, neither the Minister, nor the CDF, nor the Secretary is able to 'impose a regime of performance management and accountability over the organisation.'[80] While the ASPI report recognised that the Department was desperately in need of 'stronger central strategic control,' it conceded that because of its Byzantine structures and the 'seriously dysfunctional' state of 'authority and accountability across much of Defence,' the Department's ministers 'are caught in an invidious situation from the day they take up the job with limited ability to hold Defence officials to account.'[81] Even were they able, Dan Oakes notes, there is little incentive for them to do so: 'ministers are typically reluctant to hunt out who is responsible for mistakes because an antagonistic relationship with Defence is more likely to result in the replacement of the minister, rather than the secretary of the department or chief of the Defence Force.'[82] With a dysfunctional department and an emasculated leadership it is little wonder that it has been so difficult to organise and effect change within the Department, particularly change that encourages greater openness.

---

77 Mark Thomson, *Serving Australia: Control and Administration of the Department of Defence* (Canberra: Australian Strategic Policy Institute, 2011), p.5.

78 Thomson, *Serving Australia*, p.1.

79 Thomson, *Serving Australia*, p.2.

80 Thomson, *Serving Australia*, p.2.

81 Thomson, *Serving Australia*, pp.2, 11, 19.

82 Dan Oakes, 'Defence in "beyond tolerable state" says analyst', *The Age*, 27 June, 2011. The coming and going of five Defence Ministers since 2006 eloquently attests to the challenges that the position brings.

By contrast, the US military were able to bring off a spectacular turnaround in the culture of hostility that marked its relations with the media. As the Pentagon came to realise that in the rapidly transforming information environment of the new millennium the attitudes towards the media that the US military had brought with them out of the Vietnam War were hindering their strategic and operational efficiency, they set about shifting the organisation's perceptions of the press. They were able to do this because they had both the ways and the means of instituting deep-rooted organisational change. Weber observed that reliant on routine, repetition and established processes, bureaucracies are inherently resistant to change. Military organisations offer a prime case in point, with their organisational culture held in place by 'rigid adherence to rules, clear chains-of-command, and a hierarchical rank system.'[83] Yet militaries face a unique challenge to their inherent cautiousness. The imperative to adapt to the fluid operational environment of the battlefield and the ever-accelerating pace of technological and informational innovation requires that they do not resist change but embrace it. The US military has responded to this challenge by developing a comprehensive cycle of review, evaluation, simulation and reform. Military campaigns, one's own and others', are observed and analysed, performances appraised, new methods trialled, new processes developed and disseminated, before the whole process of review begins again. Thus the organisation's institutional memory is endlessly refreshed, new doctrine, the precepts, principles and practices that teach and conserve the military's explicit knowledge base, is developed, amended and renewed by the latest experiences and the tacit knowledge they generate.

Like all modern militaries, the ADF pursues a similar process of perpetual self-review and improvement of its practices on the basis of 'lessons learnt'. Jason Logue's Working Paper (No. 141) for the Land Warfare Studies Centre, *Herding Cats: The Evolution of the ADF's Media Embedding Program in Operational Areas*, published in July 2013, represents just such a contribution to this process as it relates to the evolution of the ADF's media operations practices. In the paper, Logue argues for the continuation and expansion of the embedding program developed by the ADF in Afghanistan. While he acknowledges that 'there are numerous risks associated with the program, the greater risk', he argues, 'lies in *not* granting access to the media.'[84] However convincing his arguments, Logue's advocacy for continued contact

83 Rid, *War and Media Operations*, 2007, p.15.
84 Logue, *Herding Cats*, p.viii.

between the armed forces and the media seems doomed to fall on deaf ears. Though the ADF has no shortage of dedicated public affairs personnel, like Logue, it does not have a leader capable of resisting political and military hostility to push through the sort of cultural change his recommendations entail. Further, Defence Public Affairs has no overarching communication plan, no explicit statement of its precepts, principles, practices, nor, more pertinently, of the attitudes and aims dictating its relations with the media – in short, it has no doctrine. In the absence of any distilled expression of the organisation's explicit knowledge about the media, and the opportunity this would create for debate, review and revision, the ADF's views about and interactions with the fourth estate continue to be defined by ingrained cultural attitudes, the assumed or unconscious knowledge that shapes the organisation's conventional wisdom. Often unexpressed, though widely held to be true, these opinions are stubbornly resistant to change. This was demonstrated by the comments of Lieutenant Colonel Darren Huxley DSC, the Commanding Officer of Mentoring Task Force 2, who deployed to Afghanistan in 2010 to 2011. Invited by Logue to contribute to his Working Paper by commenting on his experience of the embedding program, Huxley noted:

> From a command perspective, I believe it is always a balancing game when we invite strangers (and that's what embedded journalists are) into our house. Perhaps they will play by the rules and respect the effort that went into preparing for the mission and the difficulty of the task we are trying to execute or maybe they are just exploring the opportunity for their own profile and professional gain. Obviously, in a liberal democracy, it is absolutely correct for us to be open to scrutiny, but it will never be easy to depart from a view that media embeds are generally looking for failure on which to report.[85]

In the face of such entrenched beliefs among such senior commanders about the aims and professional practices of the media, it is hard to see Logue's modest proposal gaining the traction it needs to ensure its implementation.

Logue isn't the only one whose hopes for practical and policy change within the ADF run counter to its prevailing culture. On 24 February 2010 the former Defence Minister, John Faulkner, addressed the C.E.W. Bean Foundation Dinner in Canberra proposing a new contract between the

---

85 Logue, *Herding Cats*, p.45.

government, the military, the media and the Australian public.[86] He called on the military to follow his own example, to exercise greater openness in their dealings with the press and the public, to accept the scrutiny and criticism that this brings, to live up to their democratic responsibilities, and to finally come clean with the Australian people:

> In a democracy, power supposedly belongs to the people, and is exercised only on their behalf. Democratic governments like ours can only say we act on **behalf** of the community when we act with their **consent**. And that consent, ladies and gentlemen, is not genuine if gained with coercion, or with deception. Nowhere is this more important than it is when it comes to a nation's military actions. When the Australian Government commits Australian forces, we put Australian lives at risk, and exercise potentially – often actually – lethal force in the name of the Australian community. It is essential therefore that the community knows not only the reasons but also the costs of such action.[87]

As heartening as this speech was in its recognition of and refusal to tolerate the ADF's failure to deal openly with the media or honestly with the public, it also represented a cry of desperation, a statement of political intent with no bureaucratic or organisational means to give it effect. Translating political edict into operational practice is, as Faulkner knows, easier said than done. Vietnam is alive and well up at Defence HQ in Russell, where it not only provides a veneer of legitimacy to the ADF's continuing restrictions on media freedom but also validates the bureaucratic inertia opposed to broader cultural change. The lessons of Vietnam might be false but for thirty-five years they have worked like a charm for the ADF, so why revise them now?

---

86 For more on the C.E.W. Bean Foundation see www.npc.org.au/cew.

87 Senator John Faulkner, '2010 C.E.W. Bean Foundation Dinner Address', accessed July 6, 2011, www.senatorjohnfaulkner.com.au/file.php?file=/news/KSBKDMDOTF/index.html. Emphasis in original.

Chapter 3

MILITARY-MEDIA RELATIONS IN THE NETHERLANDS, CANADA AND AUSTRALIA

The Four Respects

The consequences of the ADF's continuing faith in the lessons of Vietnam are clearly embodied in its management of military-media relations during the war in Afghanistan and the nature and scope of the reporting they enabled. What made both the practices and purposes of the ADF's media management regime distinctive is best reflected by way of comparison – but comparison with whom? Historical parallels between Australian information management practices and those of their traditional comparator militaries, Britain and the US, provide illuminating insights into the origins and effects of the ADF's failure to move with the times. However, in the case of Afghanistan, more pertinent, and more revealing comparisons can be made with two of Australia's other coalition partners, the Dutch and the Canadians, whose roles in Afghanistan were broadly similar and whose force commitments were roughly equivalent in size. Until the withdrawal of the bulk of the Dutch and Canadian forces in August 2010 and December 2011, there were, respectively, around 1500, 1600 and a little-under 3000 Australian, Dutch and Canadian troops in Afghanistan.[1] Further, from

---

1 The ADF had a shifting force commitment that, from 2007 onwards, stabilised at around 1,500 personnel. For more detail on Australia's role in Afghanistan see the Fact Sheets on Afghanistan, released by the Defence Minister on 17 October 2010: www.defence.gov.au/defencenews/articles/1017/1017.htm By comparison the British commitment was steady at 9,500 while the US had 90,000 personnel in Afghanistan, rising to a peak of 130,000 during the surge of 2010. For exact figures see www.isaf.nato.int/troop-numbers-and-contributions/index.php. For a more independent view see the Nautilus Institute's *Australia in Afghanistan Briefing Book*, www.globalcollab.org/publications/books/australian-forces-abroad/afghanistan.

2006–10 the Dutch and the Australians shared responsibility for security in Uruzgan province, and a base outside its capital, Tarin Kot. From here they worked cooperatively, but mostly separately, protecting various Provincial Reconstruction Team (PRT) initiatives, stabilising security in the province, mentoring and training Afghan National Security Forces personnel, interdicting the Taliban, attacking areas where they exercised control and frustrating their efforts to re-assert power over others.[2] Canadian Forces (CF) served in the adjoining province of Kandahar in 2002, Kabul from 2003–2005, and Kandahar again from 2006 until the Canadian Infantry Battle Group withdrew in July 2011, followed by the remainder of Canadian personnel in December 2011. Over these periods the Canadians fulfilled similar roles to the Dutch and Australians in Uruzgan, protecting their PRT projects, mentoring and training the ANSF, clearing mines, decommissioning weapons, and due to their greater force of arms – they had a squadron of Leopard tanks on the ground – taking a more central role in large scale offensives against the Taliban.[3]

While each nation's forces were engaged in cognate operations, facing similar risks in pursuit of common strategic goals, when one looks at how they organised the media coverage of their commitment in Afghanistan, in particular the uses they made of embedded reporters, it is sometimes hard to believe that they were fighting on the same side in the same war. When one contrasts Dutch and Canadian policies shaping military-media interaction with those employed by the Australians, comparing each nation's performance across a range of factors reflecting its readiness to facilitate and enhance the open communication of its aims and operations – the establishment of a transparent process for the allocation of embed places, the militaries' readiness to tolerate objective scrutiny of their performance, the militaries' facilitation of access to their troops in the field, the freedom of movement enjoyed by the media once there, the relative reliance of the differing publics on official sources for news about the war, and a broader preparedness among the militaries to participate in dialogue with the media in the development, fine-tuning and reform

2 For more information on the Dutch deployment see www.defensie.nl/english/tasks/missions/afghanistan Chris Masters notes the subtle differences of culture between the ADF and the Dutch military and their view of their roles in Afghanistan. See Masters, *Uncommon Soldier*, pp.106–10.

3 For detailed analyses of the Canadian deployment, and the political manoeuvring leading up to it see Peter Piggott, *Canada in Afghanistan: The War So Far*, Toronto: Dundurn Press, 2007; Janice Gross Stein and Eugene Lang, *The Unexpected War: Canada in Kandahar*, Toronto: Penguin, 2007.

of these policies – Australia's performance compares poorly on virtually every count.

In their study of Dutch embedded journalism in Afghanistan, *Eyes Wide Shut?* (2008), Ulrich Mans and his colleagues examined seven factors that had determined the nature and quality of media access to Dutch forces and their operations in Afghanistan – media management policy, selection of reporters, timing of their visits, facilitation of access, freedom of movement, control over content, and sanctions.[4] These provide a useful analytical framework for examining Dutch, Canadian and Australian approaches to military-media relations in Afghanistan and a common basis on which comparisons between the practices of the three might be made.

Dutch participation in Afghanistan was politically contentious from the outset. Originally sold to the public as a 'reconstruction mission,' there was considerable disquiet within the coalition government about Dutch force projection.[5] As a result, the military's every move in Afghanistan was closely scrutinised by the responsible authorities. For example, in December 2003 NATO requested that the Dutch send combat aircraft to support International Security Assistance Force (ISAF) operations in and around Kabul. The Dutch Government debated the request and, in January 2003, agreed to send 6 AH-64D Apache helicopters to augment the firepower of the Kabul Multi-National Brigade (KMNB). At the same time the Government directed the Ministerie van Defensie (MvD) to post 'liaison officers to the staff of the KMNB and to the ISAF headquarters to evaluate the deployment of the helicopters against the mandate and the rules of engagement.'[6] With such detailed oversight of the actions of its forces, the governing coalition could only proceed with the commitment in Afghanistan in the context of the full and free flow of information from the war zone, hence the media were afforded open and largely unencumbered access from the earliest days of the Dutch deployment.

---

4 For more on this see Ulrich Mans, Christa Meindersma and Lars Burema, *Eyes Wide Shut? The Impact of Embedded Journalism on Dutch Newspaper Coverage of Afghanistan*, The Hague: The Hague Centre for Strategic Studies, 2008, pp.7–8.

5 Joseph T. Jockel, 'The Dutch Army in Afghanistan', *The Dorchester Review*, 20 October 2011. See www.dorchesterreview.ca/2011/10/20/the-dutch-army-in-afghanistan/ accessed 15 February 2013.

6 Netherlands Institute of Military History, International Security Assistance Force (ISAF), Mission Overview, The Hague: Ministry of Defence, 2009, 9. See www.defensie.nl/english/nimh/history/international_operations/mission_overview/48178809/international_security_assistance_force_(isaf) accessed 14 February 2013.

The principles and practices dictating Dutch military-media relations in Afghanistan were formalised in a code of conduct or *gedragscode*, which was part of an over-arching communications strategy, the *Communicatieplan*.[7] This document frames a clearly stated strategic goal: 'to showcase the importance and the developments of the mission and its specific assignments in a professional manner, to reach the public, visitors, politicians and others that are involved.'[8] To ensure that each of these groups was as well informed as they could be without compromising the safety of the military or the news gatherers, the *Communicatieplan* rested on four principles of 'respect' intended to underpin the planning and inform the behaviour of media organisations, journalists, the MvD and its Public Information Officers (PIOs), namely 'respect the security, respect the individual, respect the home front, respect the coalition.'[9]

While the MvD and the military were keen to talk up Dutch successes in Uruzgan they also recognised how difficult it would be to sustain an exclusively upbeat account of the deployment or to conceal from the media, and the general populace, the challenges its personnel faced in a complex operation like Afghanistan. Consequently, from the first days of the commitment the MvD made it a high priority to ensure that the public and the families of the servicemen and women were given a realistic picture of what the mission entailed and the hazards it brought. The Director of Communications at the MvD, Dr Joop Veen, recalled that once it was clear that the operation in Uruzgan was going ahead and would represent a major commitment of forces and materiel, 'we also knew it would be a risky operation. The chance that Dutch soldiers would be killed or would be badly hurt was very real in that mission. We knew that beforehand and we said to ourselves if we don't make visible from the beginning of the mission what the military are doing over there, then you have a gap between the perceptions here in the Netherlands and what is happening over there.'[10] In order to avoid the development of any such gap in perceptions, the military's PIOs were explicitly cautioned to guard against the emergence of 'two separate worlds' in their presentation of the conflict, to avoid an overly positive or negative account of the war that independent media coverage would then contradict.[11] As Commander

7 The Dutch *Communicatieplan* is available (in Dutch) at www.communicatieplan.info/wp-content/uploads/2008/02/communicatieplan_mindef_uruzgan_2006.pdf

8 Quoted in Mans, *Eyes Wide Shut?* p.15.

9 Quoted in Mans, *Eyes Wide Shut?* p.16.

10 Author interview with Dr Joop Veen, 21 June 2012.

11 Quoted in Mans, *Eyes Wide Shut?* 15. Dutch PIOs are now known as Public Affairs Officers, PAOs.

Robin Middel, former Spokesman for the Chief of Defence and Head of Operations in the Directorate of Information and Communications at the MvD conceded, it was not feasible to maintain an uninterrupted flow of good news from Afghanistan: 'It's not possible for me, especially at a distance, to tell a soldier "you have to tell a good story all the time" ... It is not possible to let the guys only tell the good stories ... if I tell a good story and the guys tell otherwise, it's a problem.'[12]

The overriding aim of the Dutch embed policy was to furnish the Dutch public with a comprehensive account of its military personnel at war and so avoid any possible gap between domestic understandings of the conflict and conditions on the ground. As Joop Veen noted, in order to 'bridge that gap we decided to have embedded journalism, we decided to have combat camera teams permanently over there in the field.'[13] Though the Dutch military were keen to facilitate media access to its troops from the earliest months of their deployment to Afghanistan, in August 2006, many Dutch journalists were ambivalent about the embed policy from its inception. Though some saw it as a welcome development, affording reporters 'structural access and greater insight into the military domain' than they had enjoyed before, many felt that to accept the assistance of the MvD was to enter a Faustian pact.[14] Reporters were not uniformly enthusiastic about the degree of control that the military proposed to exercise over their access and movement but they also conceded that the embedding program was 'better than nothing.'[15] The most trenchant criticism of the program came from freelancers who claimed that reporters who travelled, ate and bunked with the men they were supposed to report on could produce only 'semi-journalism.'[16] Later, others felt that as a result of the program Dutch journalists had grown so accustomed to military assistance that they developed a 'bunker mentality' and would not venture beyond military areas to seek the wider story.[17] Notably, this is a complaint that the Canadians came to echo, though for different reasons.

The MvD offered Dutch reporters free transport to Afghanistan from the military airbase at Eindhoven, free accommodation and personal safety equipment, and made available three embed places of two weeks duration on a rolling basis. Robin Middel noted that the two-week turnaround time for

12 Author interview with Middel, 23 September 2010.
13 Author interview with Dr Joop Veen, 21 June 2012.
14 Quoted in Mans, *Eyes Wide Shut?* p.18.
15 Quoted in Mans, *Eyes Wide Shut?* p.18.
16 Quoted in Mans, *Eyes Wide Shut?* p.18.
17 Quoted in Mans, *Eyes Wide Shut?* p.18.

reporters was decided upon in an effort to ensure that the reporters retained their objectivity: 'we thought if you stay longer ... you will get too much involved in what the troops are doing, you get too much ... part of the family.'[18] The selection process for embed places was open and transparent. As Hans de Vreij of Radio Netherlands observed, there were 'Never any problems with the defence ministry' around arranging trips to Afghanistan.[19] To put this in context, Kim Sengupta, Defence and Diplomatic correspondent for London's *Independent*, described the British process as a 'bizarre Stalinist exercise which no one could quite understand', while Thomas Harding of the *Daily Telegraph* observed that in the early days of the British commitment to Iraq and Afghanistan, 'dealing with the MoD [Ministry of Defence], getting the embed itself' was 'More stressful than dealing with the Taliban or the Iraqi militia, more stressful than dealing with the army, more stressful than dealing with your news desk.'[20]

The MvD did not actively select or nominate particular journalists for deployment. In theory, any journalist from any Dutch news organisation could ask to go. The MvD did, however, seek to maintain a balance between print, television and radio reporters, defence, political and development coverage, harder and softer news, thus ensuring breadth of coverage. Robin Middel noted that alongside the development reporters and the defence correspondents 'we took the less serious media in, we took radio reporters in and ... one of the more popular Dutch DJs, [who] made a broadcast every day for 3 hours from the camp. All that kind of experiments we had and we never had a problem.'[21] The media did not recall these experiments quite so fondly. In a meeting with Middel, Peter ter Velde, defence correspondent for Dutch television broadcaster NOS, recalled that he and other journalists expressed their disapproval at the inclusion of entertainment reporters in the embedding scheme:

> we were more or less satisfied with the way it worked but we told them you also send a lot of journalists who are not really familiar with wars and stuff, and also the mission became more infotainment than real hard news. And of course that was in the interests of the MoD [*sic*]. We have a nice program with music and stuff from Uruzgan so they also

---

18 Author interview with Middel, 23 September 2010.

19 Author interview with de Vreij, 22 September 2010.

20 Author interview with Kim Sengupta, 12 October 2010; Author interview with Thomas Harding, 11 October 2010.

21 Author interview with Middel, 23 September 2010.

send that kind of people too, it was actually a war zone. And I didn't agree on that one, I still don't agree that they did that kind of stuff.[22]

Over time, certain national news organisations, *NRC Handelsblad*, *Volkskrant*, Radio Netherlands, NOS, and a small cohort of defence reporters took a special interest in the war, developed close relations with MvD officials in The Hague and as a result tended to rotate through Afghanistan on a more regular basis.[23]

The timing of visits to Afghanistan was the responsibility of the MvD. Reporters submitted their requests for embeds to the MvD's Public Information Department. The department then liaised with the PIOs in Uruzgan who were responsible for the overall coordination of visits as they were affected by planned operations and developments on the ground. The Commander in Uruzgan ultimately determined whether it was possible for journalists to join specific operations at particular times. It was the role of the MvD and its PIOs in theatre to facilitate media access to all aspects of the Dutch mission in Afghanistan – even Special Forces, with whom Peter ter Velde embedded on more than one occasion.

The Dutch military's facilitation of media access and the political imperative to maintain full and balanced coverage of the deployment put special pressure on the PIO, who was, in the opinion of the Hague Centre for Strategic Studies, 'the key figure in the Dutch embed scheme.'[24] The variable success of the Dutch embedding program resulted, in no small part, from the effectiveness of the PIOs. In the early days of the campaign, Jaus Müller recalled, the PIOs were not well attuned to the reporter's needs: 'in the first years those officers were really hard line military people, so it was quite difficult to cooperate with them and they were not helping you. They were always his master's voice, the voice of the general leading the mission and they were not always that cooperative.'[25] Not all PIOs were so doctrinaire. Hans de Vreij noted that 'the quality of press information officers ... differed hugely; some PIOs ... saw me as a problem whereas others would see me as an opportunity.'[26] Robin Middel noted that one of

---

22 Author interview with ter Velde, 23 September 2010.

23 Dutch journalists who have reported regularly from Afghanistan include Peter ter Velde of NOS TV, Steven Derix and Jaus Müller of *NRC Handelsblad* and Hans de Vreij of Radio Netherlands.

24 HCSS, 2008, p.25.

25 Author interview with Müller, 22 September 2010.

26 Author interview with de Vreij, 22 September 2010. See also author interview with Müller, 22 September 2010.

the key lessons learned by the military in Afghanistan that would shape future media management practice was the importance of ensuring 'the professionalisation of Press Information Officers … We have to prepare them more to make sure that they see where the risks are, but more where the chances are.'[27]

The PIO was the first point of contact for reporters, advising them of available stories, coordinating their activities and reviewing their copy. While the PIO was understandably keen, indeed expected, to promote the military and present its achievements in a positive light, s/he was also subject to a range of competing pressures which made the job a constant balancing act – to give due attention to reconstruction stories, to cultivate good working relationships and maintain professional credibility with military colleagues and reporters – in all to serve the MvD, to serve the story, to assist the media and to respect the public. It is hardly a surprise that while the PIOs could please some of their constituencies some of the time, they could never please all of them all of the time. An occasional point of friction was the right, or otherwise, of more senior officers in the field to overrule a PIO's decision about media access. When conflicts of this kind arose, Robin Middel noted that where there was no compelling operational argument against the media's inclusion, the PIO's decision generally stood, and that he had, on occasions, had to ring commanders in Uruzgan to reinforce the PIO's case.

One of the PIO's key responsibilities was to manage the reporters' movements. The Dutch reporter was free to go wherever he or she wished on base, and to visit PRT projects and accompany Dutch military patrols off it, subject to local conditions and the Commander's approval. There was, technically, a requirement that a PIO accompany him or her at all times and that all interviews were on the record, but Dutch journalists indicated that this regulation was rarely, if not barely, observed. Jaus Müller of the Dutch daily *NRC Handelsblad* noted, 'I could talk to everyone … Everything was totally open.'[28] The reporters' open access to the troops played a key role in breaking down the natural suspicion between the media and the military and contributed to a frank and balanced portrayal of the soldiers' experiences. Peter ter Velde recalled that on one occasion when he and his cameraman were dropped at a patrol base in the Chora Valley, the troops, clearly nervous about having the media there, kept their distance:

27 Author interview with Middel, 23 September 2010.
28 Author interview with Müller, 22 September 2010.

> After a few hours the platoon commander came and sat next to me and said …
>
> 'I really don't like it that you're here.'
>
> 'Yeah … I said, I understand … this is your platoon, you don't know us, you don't know what we want, you don't know if you can trust us, you don't know if we're going to make stories in which we will screw you completely. This is the life you live here day and night … suddenly you have two intruders in your group, so I understand why you don't like the idea of us being here. So let's talk.'[29]

ter Velde made it clear to the troops that they could trust him not to misrepresent them or their task, that he would offer a frank reflection of their experiences. To that end he warned them that if he witnessed anything untoward he would also report that: 'in the first chat with the platoon commander, I always say "listen … I want to show what you guys are going through, I want to show your work. I will never screw you. I will never screw you. If you tell me things in trust I will not publish them, but I want to give an honest picture of what you are doing. If I see irregularities I will publish them too," so they completely understand.'[30]

Dutch journalists were also free to disembed from the military, to leave the base to cover accessible stories in civilian areas before re-embedding and returning to the security of the base. Jaus Müller's experience reflected how important it was for reporters to break free from the embrace of the military in order to gain an insight into what the locals really thought of the troops' presence:

> I went to a bakery one time and the mission of that moment was to figure out what the response was, the local response [to] the military. So, well, we went into this bakery. I went alone and after that 10 soldiers came in. But they were completely armed. I mean there was this huge body armour and hand grenades all over the place and I don't know how many guns. So there was this baker and he was just shaking in his bakery, and it was like 'what the hell's happening in here?' So I asked him, 'what do you think about the Dutch forces?' And he was like … 'great, nice, welcome!' and of course that's not objective … What else would you say? [31]

29 Author interview with ter Velde, 23 September 2010.
30 Author interview with ter Velde, 23 September 2010.
31 Author interview with Müller, 22 September 2010.

Peter ter Velde regarded the opportunity to disembed as less a choice than a responsibility to ensure that the Dutch public had access to a balanced account of what its troops and development partners were doing in Afghanistan and whether the goals they had set themselves were being realised: 'if you travel with the military you have a one-sided story and only if you also got unembedded then you got the other side of the story and it's the only way it works… I think in order to show what's going on here you have to do both.'[32]

The main bone of contention between Dutch reporters and the MvD was over control of content. The MvD, like the British, insisted on and enforced a process of universal copy review.[33] All material had to be submitted to a PIO to ensure that there were no inadvertent breaches of operational security. Journalists adopted a range of positions on this: some accepted it as a reasonable condition of privileged access, some welcomed the clear parameters it brought, while others virulently opposed the principle that their copy was not their own. Hans de Vreij did not regard censorship as a problem: 'for me it was totally normal. I found it quite naïve and I still find it quite naïve of journalists to think that they can go along with the military, attend meetings, hear deep background stuff and not submit their material to a censor'.[34] Jaus Müller, on the other hand, felt strongly about control of copy: 'I think it's bad, I think it's, it's almost like a censor. It's a principle, it's a principle of handing over your material and get[ting] comment and then publish it, it's totally weird. So I wasn't happy with it and we argued a couple of times.'[35] In practice, nearly all accepted that censorship was not a substantive issue, that there was rarely a case that could not be resolved through discussion or appeal.[36]

In the event of a reporter publishing or broadcasting forbidden or contested material, the MvD had no formal provision for sanctions against those who contravened its directives. Individual infractions were dealt with on a case-by-case basis. Some journalists stated that when they had been asked to excise material for reasons they did not believe were justified they had refused to do so. Without a formal sanctions regime, the military and the journalist simply had to put the episode behind them, learn from it,

32 Author interview with ter Velde, 23 September 2010.

33 Author interview with Sengupta, 12 October 2010.

34 Author interview with de Vreij, 22 September 2010.

35 Author interview with Müller, 22 September 2010.

36 Some journalists noted the inconsistency of the policy in that while material produced in the field was subject to review, reports written on the aircraft on the way home, in other foreign bureaux, or back in the Netherlands, that might reveal more sensitive information, were not.

perhaps refer it to their superiors in the Netherlands for future resolution, and move on.

The Kandahar Bureau

When the Canadian media followed their troops to Kandahar in early 2002 they did so in the context of a recent history of strained relations with the armed forces. A series of military scandals through the 1990s – the torture and murder of a Somali teenager by members of the Airborne Regiment in 1993, violent hazing rituals in 1995 and repeated allegations of sexual assault in 1998 – had been exposed and aggressively pursued by the media. As a result of the ensuing investigations the military lost public respect and political support, its personnel numbers nosedived and its budget was slashed. While the decision to commit troops to Afghanistan offered CF and the Department of National Defence (DND) an opportunity to rebuild their relations with politicians and the Canadian public, it soon became clear that this would also require a fresh approach to military-media relations and the substantial revision or development of new policy documents to articulate them. When, in late 2001, the Canadian Government agreed to commit forces to Afghanistan, 'Public Affairs doctrine had not been updated since the late 1980s, and there existed no official policy for dealing with media in-theatre.'[37] In response, for eighteen months, from December 2001 to June 2003, the military worked on a detailed agreement governing its interactions with the fourth estate, which would eventually evolve into the *Canadian Forces Media Embedding Program* (CFMEP).[38] The first iterations of this document drew heavily on the Public Affairs Guidance devised by Victoria Clarke for the US military in Iraq in February 2003 and its provisions were consciously broad. As Dominique Price notes: 'The body of the main document was intended as a guide to public affairs procedure, but more so to instruct commanding officers, under whose ultimate discretion the embed program would operate in-theatre. The instruction was intentionally generic, in order to ensure the commander had room to adapt to the circumstances in theatre.'[39] From the time it came into operation in September 2003, when Canadian Forces re-deployed to Kabul, the CFMEP was regularly reviewed

37 Dominique L. Price, *Inside the Wire: A Study of Canadian Embedded Journalism in Afghanistan*, Unpublished MA Thesis, Carleton University, Ottawa, 2009, p.39.

38 The final iteration of the CFMEP-JTFA, dates from April 2010. It was available on the Canadian Department of National Defence website but, given the cessation of Canadian combat operations in Afghanistan, the link has since been disabled.

39 Price, *Inside the Wire*, pp.41–2.

and revised in consultation with the media.[40] Notably, from its inception the CFMEP was not only intended to address operational security requirements, media needs and furnish commanders with sufficient latitude to adjudicate and deal with information management problems as they arose, one of its principal goals was to serve the public, to ensure that relevant policies were in place 'to inform Canadians about the role, mandate and activities of the Canadian Forces (CF) on deployed operation.'[41]

In its efforts to facilitate this the agreement made provision for the embedding of 30 journalists with CF at any one time.[42] Between February and August 2002, during the first rotation of its forces in Kandahar, CF hosted between twenty and thirty Canadian reporters. For the sixteen-month period between January 2006 and mid-April 2007, 230 journalists embedded with CF, 'an average of 80–90 embeds per [six-month] rotation,' reflecting the exponential increase in public interest in the deployment and thus ensuring a wide array of opinions from a diversity of sources discussing Canada's involvement in the war.[43] After a few teething problems the selection process for embeds settled into a transparent and orderly routine. Reporters intending to visit Afghanistan let the military know the sorts of stories they were hoping to cover – combat, political, reconstruction, women and so forth. Public Affairs personnel in Ottawa endeavoured, as far as they were able, to arrange access to appropriate patrols, projects or people and the journalists were then allocated a spot on a relevant flight.[44] The timing of media visits to Afghanistan was largely dictated by the availability of places and the matching of reporters to the particular issues, events or people they had expressed an interest in covering. Technically, any Canadian reporter – and any foreign reporter for that matter – could embed with CF provided a spot was available, though the prohibitive cost of insurance largely restricted participation to the national media.[45] The CF required the media to make their own way to Kandahar and furnish their own protective equipment.

---

40 The original document was written by Don Roy, a strategic planner with military public affairs. For a history of its evolution see Price, *Inside the Wire*, pp.37–43. The commitment of CF to Kabul in July 2003 put these reporting arrangements under some strain. See Price, *Inside the Wire*, pp.49–53.

41 CFMEP, April 2010, p.1.

42 This number was later reduced to 16.

43 Sharon Hobson, *The Information Gap: Why the Canadian Public Doesn't Know More About its Military*, Calgary: Canadian Defence and Foreign Affairs Institute, 2007, p.12. In the first ten weeks of 2007 the Dutch facilitated 370 external visitors to Afghanistan, a significant proportion of whom were reporters. See Mans, *Eyes Wide Shut?* pp.25–6.

44 Author interview with Gloria Galloway, the *Globe and Mail*, 18 October 2010.

45 Author interview with Galloway, 18 October 2010.

While some Canadian reporters spoke approvingly of the CFs readiness to facilitate their access to operations and projects once they got to Afghanistan – Gloria Galloway of the *Globe and Mail* thought that the PA officers she had worked with were 'terrific' – others were less complimentary.[46] Stephen Thorne of the Canadian Press (CP) described the PAOs he had dealt with in Kandahar and Kabul earlier in the campaign as 'a real pain in the ass.'[47] These comments not only demonstrate how heterogeneous were the reporters' experiences of working with the CF in Afghanistan, they also hint at the evolution of this experience, and how, after a rocky beginning, it evolved to the point where, for a period of time, the military and the media could meet and work on close and cooperative – if not always equal – terms. Canadian military-media relations during the deployment to Afghanistan can be divided into four distinct periods which we might think of as phases of pre-, developing, mature and post-cooperation. Through these periods, reporters struggled with, firstly, an increasing and latterly a decreasing degree of access to, freedom of movement among and cooperation from the military and their political masters.

In the immediate aftermath of the September 11 attacks, as the Canadian government weighed its response to the US's request for support in its forthcoming invasion of Afghanistan, the Privy Council Office assumed responsibility for all government and military communications, and 'the transparency policy' that the DND had adopted in 1998, was 'overridden.'[48] While this decision was no doubt driven by the immediate sense of national peril that the attacks occasioned, it is also clear that a decade of scandal within the military had given Canada's politicians cause for anxiety about the sort of publicity the nation's forces attracted and a solid motive for directing the public's attention elsewhere. As a consequence of the Privy Council Office's intervention, 'The government effectively shut down any information flow on the military by hiding behind "national security" concerns.'[49] When the first members of the 3rd Princess Patricia's Canadian Light Infantry Regiment (3PPCLI) arrived in Kandahar in late February

46 Author interview with Galloway, 18 October 2010.

47 Author interview with Stephen Thorne of the Canadian Press, 20 October 2010.

48 Hobson, *The Information Gap*, p.5. For more on the transparency policy see Defence Administrative Orders and Directives DAOD 2008-0, Public Affairs Policy www.admfincs.forces.gc.ca/dao-doa/2000/2008-0-eng.asp

49 Hobson, *The Information Gap*, p.5. Analysts interviewed by David Pugliese of the *Ottawa Citizen* noted that 'The amount of information the Canadian Forces has released since the Sept. 11 terrorist attacks pales in comparison to what other countries … have disclosed'. David Pugliese, 'Canadian Forces Pass Up Spotlight', *Ottawa Citizen*, 6 March 2002.

2002, this official nervousness about the release of information had evidently transmitted down the line and the media who accompanied the force complained that the PAOs and their superiors regarded them with suspicion. The first embedding agreement that Mitch Potter of the *Toronto Star* saw was presented to him in Kandahar, not prior to his departure, and was 'written in the language of the first Gulf War.'[50] In keeping with the first Gulf War theme, Potter recalled that 'there was generally a spirit of mistrust from the military towards the journalists, just a baseline feeling that we were people that had to be dealt with and nobody was too enthusiastic about it. It was more about limiting us than anything else.'[51] As a result, the first weeks of the Kandahar deployment 'were frustrating to reporters, who were given little access and even less information.'[52] There were exceptions. Stephen Thorne of CP had established a good relationship with Lieutenant Colonel Pat Stogran, Commanding Officer of 3PPCLI and was able to accompany the troops on a number of combat operations, most notably their assault on the 'Whale's Back', in eastern Afghanistan.[53]

When CF redeployed to Camp Julien in Kabul in 2003, media access to the troops remained highly restrictive: 'According to *National Post* reporter Chris Wattie, entry to Camp Julien was repeatedly delayed, and once inside, access to troops was minimal and depended largely on the commanding officer's discretion.'[54] In a speech to the Royal Canadian Military Institute in January 2004, Wattie claimed that this strategy of obstruction had its origins at the highest levels of government: 'Certain elements in the Prime Minister's Office, Privy Council Office, and Director General Public Affairs, both civilian and uniformed, opposed embedding from the beginning. Documents were delayed, our arrival on base was pushed back several times, and approvals were slow to arrive. After more than a week of stalling, the reporters actually organized a revolt, telling DGPA in Ottawa that unless we were embedded the next day, we were leaving the country.'[55] Wattie's discomfiture arose, in part, from the fact that at the same time as he and his colleagues from the Canadian Broadcasting Corporation (CBC), Canwest,

---

50 Quoted in Hobson, *The Information Gap*, p.8.

51 Quoted in Hobson, *The Information Gap*, p.8.

52 Quoted in Hobson, *The Information Gap*, p.8. See also Mitch Potter, 'Kandahar, Inside and Out', *Toronto Star*, 10 February 2002.

53 Thorne won the 2002 Ross Munro Media Award for these reports. The award is given to the 'Canadian journalist who has made significant and outstanding contributions to the general public's understanding of issues related to Canadian defence and security', www.cdfai.org/russmunro.htm

54 Price, *Inside the Wire*, p.52.

55 Quoted in Hobson, *The Information Gap*, p.10.

the CP and Canadian Television (CTV) arrived in Kabul, the document which set out the military's obligations to afford media access to Canadian personnel, the CFMEP, was in the process of being approved by the Judge Advocate General back in Ottawa.

In the vacuum, the officer responsible for making the embedding program work, Lieutenant Colonel Omer Lavoie, recalls that 'the public affairs team in-theatre quickly realized it would need to shift away from the American model, not as a reflection of ideology but of circumstance.'[56] The original intention, to embed reporters with units on tactical operations for a fixed duration, was not popular with the journalists and, due to the strictly limited resources of the Canadian media and the nature of the CF's deployment, would not work. Instead, reporters were placed with individual rifle companies on specific missions as space in vehicles allowed, on a rotational basis.

Despite these endeavours by staff on the ground to arrive at some sort of *modus vivendi* with the media, the higher command, still smarting from a decade of adverse publicity, was nervous about any negative exposure and quick to react badly to bad news. Stephen Thorne, who had enjoyed such good and mutually rewarding access to the troops in Kandahar, complained that correspondents were excluded from reporting on operations in the northern Spring of 2004 and that the obstacles placed in their way came straight from the top of the military. He alleged that the then head of ISAF and future Chief of the Defence Staff (CDS), Lieutenant General Rick Hillier, with the assistance of other senior Canadian military personnel, 'shut down all media access to raids involving Canadian troops after a suicide bomber took out a Canadian jeep last Jan. 26 [2004,] killing one.' According to Thorne, Hillier's actions 'gave the impression that the military was willing to cooperate as long as things went smoothly but, as soon as things went wrong or contrary to the military – never mind the public – interest, then the cooperation would be withdrawn.'[57] Hillier, we will come to see, later underwent and led a significant change in attitude towards the media: Thorne's attitudes to the military underwent no such reciprocal conversion. Despite Thorne's dismay and the fact that 'the larger issues about CF capabilities and Afghanistan prospects were not covered in any great depth' in the media, Sharon Hobson notes that 'the public affairs officers dealing with the program were happy with what they had

56 Quoted in Price, *Inside the Wire*, p.51.
57 Quoted in Hobson, *The Information Gap*, p.11.

accomplished,' confident that the nature of the reporting they had enabled had led to a 'growth of understanding in the media' about what CF were doing in Afghanistan.[58]

When CF returned to Kandahar in February 2006, the government and the high command were aware that they were taking on a far more dangerous mission than their previous deployments, and did their best to prepare the Canadian public for potential casualties. This had a galvanising effect on the fourth estate: 'The prospect of increased risk and potential combat brought the media to Afghanistan in droves.'[59] Based at Kandahar Airfield, CF sought to use its presence in one of the war's major transit points to aid its media strategy, deploying journalists on patrols with force elements as soon as they arrived. However, as Dominique Price observes, 'units were unprepared to offer seats to reporters, and too few opportunities were initially made available for the unexpected level of demand.'[60] As a result, the PA team in theatre were forced to improvise, to set up alternative story opportunities and invite the reporters to do likewise: 'Military-media interaction on base took on a "bid and ask" quality, with reporters in negotiation with PAOs over seats and media opportunities.'[61] In the face of the changed circumstances on the ground, PA officer Captain Robert Frank notes that 'the public affairs team made several amendments to embed policy in order to improve organization and management: the number of embed positions was cut in half, down from 30 to 15; a maximum embed stay of six weeks was implemented; and, a process was put in place for news organizations to formally request embed extensions.'[62] These innovations, alongside the gradual bedding down of the CFMEP, met with a generally 'enthusiastic' response from the press.[63]

From soon after the return of CF to Kandahar in 2006, Canadian reporters enjoyed fewer restrictions on their freedom of movement and freedom of association with the troops than their Australian or Dutch compatriots and as a consequence, in Sharon Hobson's view, 'were given tremendous access to the soldiers they were covering.'[64] Not only were reporters actively encouraged by PAOs to accompany forces on patrol, they were also free to disembed, to come and go between military and civilian stories as the security situation permitted, their nerves would allow and their assignments

58 Hobson, *The Information Gap*, p.11.
59 Hobson, *The Information Gap*, p.12.
60 Price, *Inside the Wire*, p.55.
61 Price, *Inside the Wire*, p.56.
62 Price, *Inside the Wire*, p.56.
63 Hobson, *The Information Gap*, p.12.
64 Hobson, *The Information Gap*, p.12.

demanded. Indeed, the Canadian military *encouraged* its reporters to go off base to pursue a more rounded picture of events in Kandahar. From 2006–2007 Toronto's *Globe and Mail* retained an office in Kandahar City and a full-time correspondent, Graeme Smith, for whom coverage of Canadians in combat was only ever a part of his assignment.

While Mitch Potter of the *Toronto Star*, acknowledged the 'extraordinary access' to the troops that he enjoyed when he was embedded in the northern Spring and Autumn of 2006, he also recognised that this was as good as it was ever going to get: 'that was the peak of the willingness of the Canadian military to give unlimited access ... I think a lot of people feel that that has been reeled back a little bit.'[65] Potter was quite correct. Once the date for the final withdrawal of CF from Afghanistan was locked in, reporters found the military far less accommodating than before. Stephen Thorne and Murray Brewster, senior correspondents with CP, both argued that with much of the good PR work done and with a greater sensitivity to the potential political ramifications of bad news as the troops' departure loomed, there was increased micromanagement of coverage from Afghanistan by the Prime Minister's Office, and so less readiness to assist roving reporters.[66]

It was not only the politicians who narrowed their focus in the latter years of Canada's commitment. As the Kandahar deployment became more hazardous and the CF suffered more and more casualties, reporters grew increasingly risk averse. While some were less prepared than before to venture beyond the wire, others were directed by their editors to stay on base to cover casualties and ramp ceremonies, to staff what became known as the 'death watch.' Early in 2006, Captain Doug McNair, a PAO with the Canadian Expeditionary Force Command (CEFCOM), recalled that a senior public affairs officer with the troops was 'concerned about the development of what he called a "bureau mentality" ... He was saying that "this is the Kandahar bureau for these guys. They have an office, they have phones, they have Internet, and they're sitting around declining opportunities to go outside the wire in the company of soldiers and develop an understanding of what's really going on."'[67] The media's obsession with combat and casualties was, the government and the military felt, giving the Canadian people a misleading impression of the broader detail of the deployment and what it was achieving, the progress that was being made by PRTs, in the digging of wells, the

---

65 Quoted Hobson, *The Information Gap*, p.12.

66 Author interviews with Murray Brewster of the Canadian Press, and Thorne, on respectively 19 and 20 October 2010.

67 Quoted Hobson, *The Information Gap*, p.14.

building and opening of schools, the agricultural revitalisation projects that had been completed. Not unreasonably, the media pointed out that reports of combat and casualties were the stories their readers and viewers were most keen to follow, and that the digging of a well or the completion of a health centre was not 'news'.

Whatever its focus, Canadian reporters, unlike their Dutch colleagues, retained control over their copy. Briefed about forbidden topics and warned off operationally sensitive issues, they were free to write and shoot whatever else they were able to witness. The CF did reserve the right to sanction reporters for breaches of the policy, rescinding their embedded status and excluding them from Kandahar Airfield when such infractions occurred. Stephen Thorne recalled 'a couple of times when [Canadian PAOs] kicked me off the base ... and then once I got kicked off the base by the US commander' – for doing what he regarded as a routine part of his job, photographing the return to Kandahar Airfield of the bodies of four US Engineers killed in an explosion.[68] More often, where problems arose, as with the Dutch, the reporters and the PA personnel on the ground, or their editors and more senior PA officers in Ottawa, did their best to resolve disputes, and where appropriate amended the embedding agreement to reflect changed conditions.

Embedding Trials

Stephen Thorne's run-in with the US commander reflects at least one of the difficulties faced by reporters, and the military, on a multi-national mission where each nation has a different understanding of what can and cannot be reported. Gloria Galloway of the *Globe and Mail* noted that the freedoms enjoyed by Canadian reporters at Kandahar Airfield 'drove the Americans nutty.'[69] Yet it wasn't only the Americans who were driven to distraction by the liberties accorded to Canadian correspondents. In late 2006 the Australian Broadcasting Corporation reported that four Canadian journalists embedded with CF were removed from their embeds after complaints from allied forces that the Canadian policy on embedded journalists was 'too liberal.' The Canadian Department of National Defence later confirmed that 'Australia was one of the nations that did the most complaining.'[70]

---

68 Author interview with Thorne, 20 October 2010.

69 Author interview with Galloway, 18 October 2010.

70 www.abc.net.au/news/newsitems/200612/s1819811.html.

The ADF's discomfiture at the media freedoms enjoyed by others hardly comes as a surprise given the history of its relations with its own media. The Australian policy on covering the war in Afghanistan – which we might think of as a joint Department of Defence-ADF project – can be accused of many things, though liberality is not one of them. Indeed, in the absence of any publicly available doctrine detailing the goals shaping Australian coverage of the fighting in Afghanistan and the means by which they might be achieved, it is a moot point whether Defence and the ADF actually had a media policy. As the former Director General of Communication Strategies for the Department of Defence, Brian Humphreys, noted in 2009, the ADF, like the Department of Defence, 'has no formal strategy for media relations ... While there are tactical public information plans, a general policy direction and a number of informal strategies, there is no considered and documented media strategy.'[71] Late in 2010 the Department appointed a Director General for Strategic Communication, with a small supporting staff, but no explicit communications strategy and no policies driving its fulfilment have yet emerged from this bureaucratic re-deployment.[72] The 2009 Defence White Paper *Defending Australia in the Asia Pacific Century: Force 2030* makes no mention of strategic communication, media operations or media policy, though the ADF's Directorate of Joint Effects does have an Information Operations section.[73] Likewise, the 2013 *Defence White Paper* dedicates a number of paragraphs to information management as it relates to cyber-security, but as with the 2009 document makes no mention of strategic communications or media operations.[74]

It's not as if the ADF need to re-invent the wheel here. As noted, the Dutch *Communicatieplan* can provide some useful pointers. If accessing a decent translation is a problem, the ADF can always turn to the British who have an exemplary model of such a document. The *Defence Communications Strategy* is a five-page document outlining the strategy's principal aim, the

---

71 Humphreys, 'The Australian Defence Force's Media Strategy', pp.31–2.

72 The foundation Director General Strategic Communication was the former Director General Public Affairs, Brigadier Alison Creagh.

73 The White Paper does address the need for Information superiority (pp.81–4), and examines the current state of the ADF's Information and Communications Capability (pp.119–121) and how it might be expanded. Yet in both cases these are regarded mainly as hardware issues and the domain of critical infrastructure upgrades. The White Paper remains silent on matters of Information and Media operations. See Department of Defence, *Defending Australia in the Asia Pacific Century: Force 2030*, Canberra: Department of Defence, 2009.

74 See Department of Defence, *Defence White Paper 2013*, Canberra: Department of Defence, 2013.

communications priorities and principles this engenders, how these can be achieved, who has responsibility for ensuring their attainment and how success will be measured.[75] Its aims and purposes are stated with commendable clarity and economy in its opening paragraph: 'The Defence Communications Strategy aims to maximise the effect of our communications efforts in order to improve understanding and support for Defence and enhance the reputation of the Armed Forces collectively, each Service individually, the Ministry of Defence [MoD] and its various component parts and MOD civil servants.'[76] In Australia the inability, or unwillingness, of Defence and the ADF to generate such a document has been a critical failure with ongoing detrimental consequences for military-media relations and the free flow of public information. In the absence of doctrine of the kind that drove the renewal of relations between the military and the fourth estate in the US in the years between the first and second Gulf Wars, the ADF's responses to the media continue to be shaped by the routine knowledge laid down long ago and crucially reinforced in Vietnam. The effect of this has been to reproduce and further entrench established patterns of mutual suspicion, hostility and mistrust.

On the basis of the available evidence, one might argue that the ADF's failure to produce such a policy is less a mark of neglect than a reflection of its information management priorities. Defence and the ADF have persistently regarded the coverage of the war as a straightforward public affairs challenge to which they have responded with a narrative of 'positive progress.'[77] This narrative is most persistently promulgated through the Department of Defence's media releases, which, when they are not reporting on ADF casualties, offer an undiluted stream of positive news from Afghanistan.[78] This is articulated through news of advances in Afghan National Army (ANA) capacity and operational effectiveness, daring raids on the enemy by the Special Operations Task Group (SOTG), new infrastructure and the spread of stable governance this implies. There are dozens of examples to choose from, the following are representative: MSPA 081/18 'Two bomb makers captured in Afghan-led SOTG operation' (25 March 2010); MSPA 083/10 'Three IEDS disarmed by MTF-1 protecting Mirabad villagers'

75 The Defence Communications Strategy could formerly be found at www.mod.uk/DefenceInternet/AboutDefence/CorporatePublications/PolicyStrategyandPlanning/DefenceCommunicationsStrategy.htm. It has since been taken down.

76 Defence Communications Strategy, 1.

77 Hyland, 'The Media Never Lose', p.43.

78 The Department of Defence's media releases can be accessed at: www.defence.gov.au/media/index.cfm.

(25 March 2010). Then, after Defence stopped allotting its media releases a serial number, 'Afghan led security operation in Uruzgan completes first phase' (4 August 2011); 'A+ for effort – new girls' school opens in Tarin Kot, Afghanistan' (1 August 2011).

The celebration of military progress and the civilian development it has enabled has ensured that the official Australian portrait of events in Afghanistan glows with what Hugh White has termed a 'perennial airbrushed optimism.'[79] Disinterested observers with a more intimate knowledge of the realities on the ground have proven less sanguine about the efficacy of ADF operations. When Jeremy Kelly travelled through Uruzgan late in 2012 he was struck by the gap between the ADF's 'mission accomplished' rhetoric and what he found there:

> Australian military officials are quick to list achievements by its development arm: three times as many healthcare facilities since 2006 and a rise in the number of schools from 34 in 2006 to 205 now. They are impressive numbers, but they don't tell the whole story. In Chora, only one of the 32 schools supposedly open actually has students attending ... The rest are 'just for teachers taking a salary' ... Meanwhile, in the western district of Deh Rawood, government and foreign officials were shocked last year when they found land surrounding three vacant schools, all built with foreign money, was being used to grow opium and cannabis.[80]

White himself has consistently proffered a more downbeat assessment of the ADF's progress and effectiveness, claiming that on the evidence of the current situation in the country one can only conclude that 'Australia's military operation in Afghanistan has failed.'[81]

In the light of the ADF's commitment to the promotion of its aims and achievements and the media's apparent reluctance to offer an objective channel for their broader dissemination, it is no surprise that the Australian military followed the 'slow road to media embedding' and took almost a decade to implement a basic program.[82] In late 2010, nine years after Australian forces first arrived in Afghanistan, the Department of Defence claimed that 'Following a review of embedding policy and a trial deployment

---

79 Hugh White, 'The Defence Minister', *The Monthly*, November 2010, p.10.
80 Jeremy Kelly, 'Afghans just waiting for hell to break loose', *The Weekend Australian*, 29–30 December 2012, p.13.
81 Hugh White, 'Afghanistan mission a total failure', *The Age*, 5 February, 2013, p.11.
82 Logue, *Herding Cats*, p.14.

in 2009,' the ADF 'now conducts an embedding program.'[83] Yet in 2010, just as there was no trace of the 'embedding policy' referred to above, nor was there any evidence of the system, routine or procedures that one ordinarily associates with a 'program' dictating how a correspondent might apply or qualify for an embed place. Despite this, between 2010 and the end of 2011 many more Australian reporters were able to go to Afghanistan than had previously been the case and increasing numbers embedded with the ADF: 'The 2011 media embed program was significantly expanded beyond 2010 and was almost cumulatively greater in media agency access during a single 12-month period than all the preceding years combined.'[84] But there was still no transparent process for selecting who went and no publicly available information about Defence or the ADF's priorities in the allocation of places. While Defence noted that 'The ADF embed program offers access to the MTF for two representatives from a single media agency for up to 21 days,' there was no information about what might dictate the timing of embeds or how they might relate to specific operations.[85] That the ADF was offering any embeds at all was a notable advance on the pre-2009 situation. However the scarcity of Australian embed places – 'Each MTF rotation will host a minimum of two embed cycles' – should be set beside the Canadian average of 80–90 embed cycles per rotation when its system was working at its height.[86] While the Canadians had almost twice as many troops as the Australians in Afghanistan they offered their media 40 or 45 times as many embed opportunities per rotation. A difference of this magnitude seems to say more about the priority the CF and the ADF accord to public information than it does about their relative capacity to absorb and facilitate the media.

During 2011 Lieutenant Colonel Jason Logue took a more prominent role in the organisation and direction of the embedding program, and both preparation and access began to improve. Logue arranged 'meet and greet' functions at which officers about to deploy could meet defence correspondents for a mutual get-to-know-you-and-what-you-do session in a relaxed and informal setting. At the end of 2011 Logue issued the first call for 'Expressions of Interest' from reporters who wished to participate in a newly

83 Author correspondence with Captain (now Major) Chris Linden of the Ministerial Support and Public Affairs Branch of the Department of Defence: email attachment, 22 November 2010.

84 Logue, *Herding Cats*, p.21.

85 Author correspondence with Linden, 2010: 1.

86 Author correspondence with Linden, 2010: 1.

constituted embedding program which would see a near permanent media presence in the country through 2012.[87] More than 70 responded; so many, Logue claims, that 'the 2012 embed program sometimes exceeded the administrative capacity of tactical supporting elements.'[88] As of 2012, the ADF offers six different means of media access to the troops in Afghanistan:

> **Media embed:** The media embed program is a logistically supported ADF program that sponsors access to an area of operations by representatives of accredited media agencies for a fixed period. A small number of placements are reserved for emerging journalists nominated by media agencies, those beginning their career with a likely future covering Defence issues.
>
> **Documentary embed:** The documentary embed is an ADF program that provides logistic support and sponsors access to an area of operations by individuals or teams producing a documentary or feature for a fixed period or series of fixed periods over the deployment of a major troop rotation.
>
> **Regional media embed:** The regional media embed is also logistically supported and is an ADF program that sponsors access for a fixed period to an area of operations by representatives of selected and accredited media agencies representing publications and programs based in the region from which the major component of deployed personnel originates. A single regional media embed is deployed for each major rotation of personnel.
>
> **In-country media embed:** An in-country media embed is a partially supported ADF program that sponsors access to an Australian area of operations by accredited media who have made their own way to the operational region for a fixed period. In-country embeds are only accepted if the media embed program allows and the tactical commander agrees. These media embeds are accredited through the parent coalition headquarters.
>
> **Media participation in VIP visits:** Media participation in VIP visits occurs under a supported ADF program that sponsors access

87 See Defence Media Release, '2012 Australian Defence Force Media Embed Program, request for expressions of interest', 21 December 2012, news.defence.gov.au.

88 Logue, *Herding Cats*, p.14.

> to an Australian area of operations by representatives of accredited media agencies who accompany visiting dignitaries (military or civilian) on short visits. Participants in this program have little scope to conduct activities outside the defined program for the visit.
>
> **Media participation in arts/cultural tours:** Media participation in arts/ cultural tours occurs under a fully supported ADF program that sponsors access to an area of operations by representatives of accredited media agencies who accompany visiting arts/cultural activities such as Forces Entertainment tours or the Australian War Artist program. Participants in this program have little scope to conduct activities outside the defined program for the visit.[89]

Via these access mechanisms Defence aims to provide 'a maximum of two separate agencies attached as media embeds to tactical elements at any one time with a third coming into or out of the theatre of operations. In addition, a single documentary or in-country embed may be attached during this period if tactical commanders believe he/she can be appropriately supported.'[90]

Those reporters granted access to the ADF in Afghanistan sign up to a set of *Ground Rules* in which they agree not to provide visual images or write about a specific list of forbidden topics – damage sustained by insurgent attacks, the interior of vehicles and aircraft, plans for future operations, troop strength, etc.[91] This is all perfectly legitimate and no reasonable reporter would object to its provisions. But there is no sense of how these restrictions fit into a broader communications policy or help articulate its aims.

---

89 Logue, *Herding Cats*, pp.14–15. Media access arrangements in 2010 substituted Media participation in arts/cultural tours with the following: 'NATO Sponsored Defence is actively engaged with NATO to facilitate Australian media access through their Media Opinion Leaders – Afghanistan (MOLA) and Trans-Atlantic Opinion Leaders – Afghanistan (TOLA) activities. Defence routinely recommends Australian journalists and academics to NATO for inclusion in these structured visits that NATO conducts and funds'. (Author correspondence with Linden, 2010: 2).

90 Logue, *Herding Cats*, p.16. Logue's claim that 'This level of media embedding is well beyond that undertaken by the ADF's coalition partners in terms of the journalist-to-troops ratio' is disputable (Logue, *Herding Cats*, p.16).

91 The specific exclusions are listed in the *Operationally Sensitive Information Brief* (ENCLOSURE 13 to ADMINIST 01/09 Jan 09) that all reporters are required to sign.

Reporters who have embedded with the ADF in Afghanistan have offered mixed views on the ADF's readiness to facilitate access to operations. Some have praised the energy and understanding of PA officers who have done everything in their power to ensure access to operations or Forward Operating Bases (FOB) for the media.[92] Others have complained bitterly about command interference in their plans and movements and the inability of the PA officers to exercise any leverage in these disputes.[93] Notably, many Australian reporters seem to have had a mixed experience with the ADF. Nick Butterly of the *West Australian* noted that on his first embed, in 2010, he was 'incredibly lucky to have been partnered with the media liaison officer I was given. He was keenly interested in newspapers and always wanting to push the bounds of the embed as far as we could.' He went on to observe that he had 'since heard some horror stories of other reporters being saddled with media liaison officers who saw their jobs purely in terms of shutting down awkward stories and pedalling positive ones.'[94] Mark Burrows of Nine News seems to have encountered both help and hindrance from his liaison officers during his two embeds, in 2010 and 2011 with the ADF. Noting that 'In 2010 my escort "got" what I wanted and was acutely aware I needed stories with an edge', he is conspicuously silent about his 2011 liaison officer. His dissatisfaction with the latter is implied in his conclusions about the two embeds: 'It's been my experience over two embeds that, if the escort and Commanding Officer can trust the journalist, that faith will be returned in spades. Conversely, if trust is absent, the stories will suffer.'[95]

The role and preparedness of escort officers have been matters of some concern for the ADF, as they were for the Dutch military. Indeed, Logue notes that 'simply calling them "escort officers" poses problems as it immediately implies that the person is a minder watching the media embed's every move, rather than a facilitator between the media embed and the tactical elements.' Logue recommends the adoption of the term 'liaison

---

92 Thom Cookes of the ABC and Hugh Riminton of Network Ten spoke highly of the efforts of their PA escorts to facilitate access for them. For Riminton, see Logue, *Herding Cats*, pp.53–5.

93 Ian McPhedran of News Limited laid out his discontents in the '"Embedding" Trial Report' he wrote to the then CDF, Air Marshal Angus Houston, after his trial embed in August 2009. For a full transcript of the report see www.abc.net.au/mediawatch/transcripts/0935_report.pdf. Notably, Sally Sara of the ABC, who was also part of the trial embed, has remained silent about her experiences.

94 Logue, *Herding Cats*, p.48.

95 Logue, *Herding Cats*, p.50.

officer' reflecting his or her role as a translator or facilitator.[96] Whatever the nomenclature, until these officers demonstrate their readiness to help rather than hinder the embed, reporters will continue to regard them as impediments and overseers.[97]

A number of senior officers showed an admirable openness to the media and did their utmost to facilitate coverage. 'Unlike some of his colleagues', the Commanding officer of [Mentoring and Reconstruction Task Force] MRTF1, Lieutenant Colonel Shane Gabriel, believed that it was important for the fourth estate to bear witness from the front lines: 'The media has a right to be there. We have nothing to hide.'[98] Likewise, when Chris Masters and his film crew arrived at Patrol Base Wali, the officer commanding, Major Jason Groat, emerged from his command post to make it clear to the reporters that 'We are welcome inside at any time and have an open invitation to every daily briefing.'[99] Major General Angus Campbell, Commander Joint Task Force 633 (JTF 633) during 2011, with overall responsibility for operations in Afghanistan, offered a less enthusiastic, more calculating assessment of why the military should engage with the media. Noting that 'As Australians we live in a democracy', he concedes that 'There is an expectation, a reasonable one in our society, to engage with media. We have no choice but to do so.' He asserts that media reporting of Defence is sometimes 'underwhelming' and that 'for some, the value in media embedding may not be readily apparent', and can scarcely conceal his discomfort at the fact that the defence force 'are required to engage with the media, to enable the media and to interact with the media.' Yet he rationalises this unwonted propinquity with the fourth estate by pointing out what the ADF stand to gain, or hold onto, by cooperating with the media: 'Put simply, war is sustained through public support which, in turn, is enabled through regular and consistent contact with the media. It is simply unreasonable to not engage because to not do so will damage the campaign.'[100] In short: none of us like it, but grit your teeth, lie back and think of victory. Two cheers for democracy!

---

96 Logue, *Herding Cats*, p.31.
97 See McPhedran, 'War! What War?', pp.72–3.
98 Masters, *Uncommon Soldier*, p.200.
99 Masters, *Uncommon Soldier*, p.227.
100 Logue, *Herding Cats*, p.44. JTF 633 was the combined Task Force providing Australian Defence Force elements assigned to Operations Catalyst, Kruger and Slipper. It also supported whole of government efforts in Iraq, the Middle East Area of Operations and Afghanistan.

When Paul McGeough and photographer Kate Geraghty of Fairfax travelled to Tarin Kot in January 2013 to report on the current state of affairs in Uruzgan, they ran into a more customary ADF welcome. On their arrival they were 'met on the tarmac by several Australian military officers' who told them 'You have no permission to be here.' Determined to avoid the restrictions routinely imposed on reporters by the ADF, McGeough and Geraghty had decided to seek accreditation for their assignment from an Afghan agency and had travelled to Uruzgan independent of the ADF. Apprised of this strategy, McGeough alleges, the ADF set out to 'derail the Fairfax assignment', and so 'block independent reporting in the province', by holding a meeting with spokesmen 'from a raft of government agencies in southern Afghanistan' where the Afghans were pressured to withdraw any offers of assistance they may already have made to the Fairfax journalists. Farid Ayil, a spokesman for the Uruzgan Chief of Police, Matiullah Khan, corroborated McGeough's account, claiming that 'The [ADF] guy went around the table getting everyone to say they had refused.' When it became clear that the Chief of Police had not refused and had determined to host the journalists, the unnamed ADF officer 'demanded to know why we were taking you' and presented 'a litany of reasons' to back his arguments for excluding the reporters: 'the Fairfax team was in Oruzgan to "write wrong stories"; it had travelled to Tarin Kowt "without permission"; and it had entered Afghanistan "without a letter from the Australian government"'.[101] Though the journalists had not written a word or captured a single image from Uruzgan to this point, in the eyes of the unnamed officer, the fact that they were intending to work beyond ADF oversight was clear evidence of their hostility towards the military and a legitimate basis for excluding them.

As one moved up the ranks at JTF 633, the pressures determining the level of media facilitation that the task force's most senior officers were prepared to approve became more overtly political. As JTF 633's former commanding officer Major General John Cantwell recalled, he too, like the men below him, was responding to directions from his superiors: 'My Australian military and political masters are hypersensitive to any possible misstep or misbehaviour by our troops, so every potentially negative episode, big or small, costs many hours in reports, investigations and follow-up action.'[102]

101 Paul McGeough, 'How the ADF tried to control the real story of Oruzgan', *The Saturday Age*, 16 March 2013, p.9.

102 Major General John Cantwell with Greg Bearup, *Exit Wounds: One Australian's War on Terror*,Melbourne: Melbourne University Press, 2012, p.280.

While there is no evidence that the minister or his staff oversaw, approved or vetoed the media's applications for access to Afghanistan, political considerations clearly played a major role in shaping military decisions about PA priorities on the ground. Accordingly, in the absence of any official policy dictating the legitimate extent of media access, the Australian reporter's access to and freedom of movement in Afghanistan was determined by an uncertain and shifting combination of factors – the political pressures of the day, the commander's goals, the PA officer's powers of persuasion, and the reporter's readiness to play by the ADF's rules.

For Australian reporters who make it to Afghanistan, according to the regulations that do exist, there is no such thing as an off-the-record interview with ADF personnel. *The Statement of Understanding for Accredited Media* notes that 'the correspondent will be escorted at all times,' and must 'adhere to the direction and advice of the military escort officer at all times' or face removal from the area of operations.[103] In reality the escort system worked in a variety of different ways. Some reporters relied on their PA escorts for advice and direction, others ignored them, some dispensed with their services altogether.[104] Some advised their PA escorts that in interviews they would ask the questions and tolerate no intrusions from the PA. On some bases the regulations were rigorously enforced, reducing agile reporters to creative opportunism. Karen Middleton recalls garnering candid insights from a British officer at Kandahar Airfield when her PA minder was asleep.[105] A number of journalists have noted that it was easier to secure off-the-record comments once they were beyond the wire.[106] Others were given total freedom to talk to whom they wanted.[107]

---

103 Department of Defence, Statement of Understanding for Accredited Media (Ground Rules), Canberra: Department of Defence, nd, np. Chris Masters enjoyed virtually unlimited, and mostly unsupervised access to the troops when making his documentary for the ABC, *A Careful War* (2010), although this marked the exception rather than the rule.

104 Compare the experiences of Kathy McLeish, Chris Masters and Thom Cookes. Masters notes that the PA officer who accompanied him on his 2010 trip to Afghanistan was known by the troops as the FONC – the friend of no cunt. See Masters, *Uncommon Soldier*, p.219.

105 See Karen Middleton, 'Who's Telling the Story? The Military and the Media', *The Military, the Media and Information Warfare*, eds Peter Dennis and Jeffrey Grey, Canberra: Australian Military History Publications, 2009, p.157.

106 On his 2009 'sponsored visit', Hyland noted that it was easier to talk to the troops once you had moved off base and beyond the wire: Masters noted the same phenomenon.

107 When Masters was filming his ABC documentary, *A Careful War*, he was free to talk to anybody who was prepared to be interviewed.

There is no provision for or experience of Australian reporters moving between embedded and disembedded status. Reporters are expected to remain under the direction of the responsible commander. Should the correspondent elect to forfeit the protection of the ADF the embed would be considered at an end. The review of copy is also a grey area. Despite Defence's assertion that it 'does not exert editorial control over reporting by journalists during [their] visits other than ensuring that operational security is not breached,' the process for ensuring that there are no breaches of operational security is the moot point here.[108] Jason Logue notes that the ADF currently exercises '100 per cent review of all media embed participant material before filing' and observes that 'Australia is the only nation in ISAF that still requires this level of oversight.'[109] In practice the system works a little less rigidly in that while some reporters have had their work routinely screened, others have not.[110] When photojournalist Adam Ferguson requested an embed with the ADF in 2010 he was told that 'a military public affairs minder' would accompany him at all stages and that a 'more senior public affairs person would vet [his] images.'[111] Finally, the *Ground Rules* make provision for the removal of correspondents who contravene the regulations. Logue notes that since committing to its media embedding program 'the ADF has only had to deal with one significant operations security breach' and that on investigation it was found that 'the fault lay with an ADF officer assigned to escort the media embed, who was ignorant of the operations security requirements and actively facilitated the media's coverage of a certain aspect of operations in Afghanistan.'[112] I am not aware of any Australian reporters having been thrown off base or out of an embed.

This comparison not only reveals the distinguishing features of Dutch, Canadian and Australian information management systems and demonstrates why certain arrangements resulted in satisfactory outcomes for all parties while others left one or other feeling aggrieved, it also identifies the critical components, inherent and contextual, enabling fruitful relations between the military and the media. The success of the Dutch system can be traced back to the highest levels of government. Driven by the

---

108 Author correspondence with Linden, 2010: 1.

109 Logue, *Herding Cats*, p.33.

110 Tom Hyland did, Thom Cookes and Nick Butterly did not.

111 Adam Ferguson, 'The long and the short of covering a war', *The Walkley Magazine*, Issue 64, October–November 2010.

112 Logue, *Herding Cats*, p.18.

political imperative to inform the people about what its men and women were doing in Afghanistan, the military observed the directions of their political masters and collaborated with the media to ensure that a balanced picture of the Dutch engagement in Uruzgan emerged. Relations with the media remained cooperative, if not always harmonious, because they were founded on doctrine that both parties had had a hand in developing and fine-tuning, that clearly set out each party's rights and responsibilities and provided a baseline for dispute resolution. In Canada, given the military's recent embroilment in one demoralising scandal after another, there was political trepidation about the potential for adverse publicity arising from too liberal an approach to information management – a trepidation that faded but never entirely disappeared. Despite this, the military and the media gradually worked through their mutual suspicion and, again, with the assistance of directing, mutually supported doctrine, arrived by trial, error, conflict and conciliation at a working relationship that, for a couple of years at least, delivered the media 'excellent access' to the troops and mutual benefits for both parties. In Australia, by contrast, there was neither political leadership driving an open information policy nor the military doctrine needed to manage the operation of such a system. For the greater part of the conflict, while the government was focused on minimising and managing any bad news, the ADF barely moved beyond the entrenched antagonism towards the fourth estate that it had brought into the war. In the absence of information management doctrine to which both parties had contributed and in which both could invest, there was little or no common ground on which fundamental issues might be raised or minor disputes resolved. The ADF's principal media operations goals were focused on promoting the actions of its personnel in Afghanistan and defending its reputation from a media cohort they believed was intent on finding fault and besmirching the military brand. When the ADF did, finally, embrace a media embedding program, it did so not because it believed in greater transparency or the public's right to know but because it had become politically impossible to continue to resist meaningful scrutiny. In the event, Logue proposes, a virtue can be made out of this unpalatable necessity, in that the experience in Afghanistan suggests that 'an appropriately managed media embed program, sustained over time, reinforces credibility for the organisation and its message.'[113] For almost a decade the media, desperate for access, were left to batter at the gates and bewail their exclusion or meekly follow the

113 Logue, *Herding Cats*, p.19.

directions of their military minders. Despite the belated introduction of the embedding program and the facilitation of more informal contacts between officers and media correspondents, there was no appetite in government or the upper echelons of the military for a bolder approach, for some trial and error and the lessons they might teach. The access that was finally made available, though welcome, was too late for reporters who had already suffered through years of obstruction at the hands of the ADF.

Chapter 4

BUS TOURS, DOGS AND PONIES: COVERING THE ADF IN AFGHANISTAN

Media Hosting

Australian media management practices in Afghanistan underwent a long and painful evolution that brought them to their most developed arrangement, the one in effect throughout 2012 and 2013, where a minimum of two media agencies were on the ground at any one time with a third one going into or coming out of Afghanistan. Given where the Australians started this represents commendable progress, though it still falls short of the access enjoyed by US, British, Dutch and Canadian reporters. To some extent, arrangements for the Australian media have been shaped by the size, scope and nature of the ADF's commitment in Afghanistan. So what has the ADF actually been doing there, and what did this demand in the way of force commitment?

As at December 2012, Australia contributed around 1550 troops to NATO's International Security Assistance Force mission of whom a little over 1200 were deployed in Uruzgan province with the remainder in Kabul, Kandahar and elsewhere in Afghanistan and the Gulf States.[1] Its two principal force commitments were the 730 personnel comprising the Mentoring Task Force (MTF), and the 300 or so men from the Special Air Services Regiment and the Commando Regiments who make up the Special Operations Task Group (SOTG). While the SOTG's principal role was 'to

1 Troop numbers fluctuate slightly as personnel rotate. The figures quoted here are sometimes specific, and sometimes reflect an average over a particular period. These numbers will fall gradually through 2013 as the ADF withdraws its forces. By February 2013 the total number of troops had already fallen to a little below 1100.

conduct population-centric, security and counter-network operations,' namely to target the insurgent networks in the province, to hunt down, kill or capture the Taliban's bomb makers and local force commanders, the Mentoring Task Force provided three Operational Mentoring and Liaison Teams (OMLTs), four Mentoring Teams (MTs), and a range of Manoeuvre, Engineer and Logistics support to the ANA.[2] Those soldiers in the OMLTs 'live with, train and provide support to their Afghan National Army colleagues at patrol bases in Uruzgan province, focused on the main population centres,' where their main task was to prepare the Afghan National Army's 4th Brigade or Kandak to take over security in the province before the proposed withdrawal of Australian forces in late 2013.[3] By the beginning of 2013 Australian forces had handed over to the ANA and the Afghan National Police (ANP) all of the Forward Operating and Patrol Bases that they had set up, withdrawing their men and material to Camp Holland, the main base outside Tarin Kot.

Though Australia has made much play of the fact that it was, at its fullest extent, the eleventh largest contributor of troops to ISAF, 'its reach and influence is still tiny.'[4] Its troop commitment was a fraction of that of its senior partners, making it one of the 'minor players in the Afghanistan experiment.'[5] At the height of its 2010 'surge' the United States had 130,000 personnel in Afghanistan, well above its long-term average of 90,000. It too is now drawing down its forces and has reduced its numbers to 68,000. The British have maintained a force of 9,500 while the Germans contributed

---

2 www.defence.gov.au/op/afghanistan/info/factsheet.htm The Mentoring Task Force (MTF 2010–present) was, previously, the Mentoring and Reconstruction Task Force (MRTF 2009–2010), and before that the Reconstruction Task Force (RT 2006–2009).

3 www.defence.gov.au/op/afghanistan/info/factsheet.htm For a detailed account of Australia's commitments in Afghanistan see the Fact Sheets prepared by the Department of Defence in preparation for the October 2010 Parliamentary debate on the war in Afghanistan. They can be accessed here www.defence.gov.au/defencenews/articles/1017/1017.htm For a more up to date account see www.defence.gov.au/op/afghanistan/info/factsheet.htm Due to the rising incidence of 'Green on Blue' attacks, where Afghan soldiers turn their guns on coalition forces, ADF personnel are now less likely to live alongside their Afghan colleagues. See Colin Crosier, 'Walls separate diggers from Afghans', *The Age*, 14 November 2012, www.theage.com.au/national/walls-separate-diggers-from-afghans-20121114-29cou.html

4 Masters, *Uncommon Soldier*, p.223.

5 John Cantwell, 'They Died in Vain', *The Monthly*, October 2012, p.30. Cantwell's reflections on the Australian aid commitment in Afghanistan are equally applicable to its military contribution: 'Our laudable national aid efforts are a miniscule drop in the ocean of misery and disadvantage in Uruzgan' (Cantwell, *Exit Wounds*, p.328).

around 4,900.[6] Uruzgan, where the majority of the ADF's force strength is committed, is 'one of the poorest provinces in one of the world's most impoverished countries' and 'an isolated backwater, even by Afghan standards.'[7] Whatever the ADF achieves on the ground in Uruzgan will have little impact on the outcome of a struggle whose critical centres of gravity are located further to the east on the border with Pakistan, or deeper to the south in the Taliban's heartland provinces, Kandahar and Helmand. For an Australian audience, the fate of the Afghans and their country is of little moment and the fighting there matters only in so far as it provides a platform for deeds of valour and sacrifice that showcase essential national qualities. Consequently the ADF is highly sensitive about how it is portrayed by the fourth estate and has, until recently, maintained an iron grip over who among the media gets to travel to Afghanistan, where they go, what they see and whom they can talk to when they get there.

In the 12 months to April 2009, 28 journalists from seven agencies were hosted by the ADF in Afghanistan, only three of whom were able to accompany troops on patrols 'beyond the wire.'[8] Between February 2009 and the end of 2010 around 25 more journalists accompanied Australian forces to report on operations beyond the wire in Uruzgan.[9] This sudden increase in the numbers of reporters moving beyond the confines of base resulted from the ADF's introduction of a formal embedding program in early 2010, after it conducted an embedding trial in August 2009 – nine years after the first arrival of Australian troops in Afghanistan and three years since they had returned to the country in force.[10] Yet even then, Australian reporters continued to work at a disadvantage to their colleagues from the US, the UK, Canada and the Netherlands. As a number of Australian journalists pointed out, the ADF version of embedding was 'more constraining than it needs to be.'[11] Indeed, given the way the embedding trial ran and the media's

---

6 Comprehensive information on troop commitments can be found at www.isaf.nato.int/troop-numbers-and-contributions/index.php

7 Cantwell, *Exit Wounds*, p.251.

8 A further 12 accompanied visiting politicians and other VIPs. See Zöe Hibbert, 'Managing the "battlefield effect" of media in Afghanistan', *What are we doing in Afghanistan?* p.47.

9 Author correspondence with Linden, 2010. The Department of Defence seems to have a different interpretation of 'embedding' from the more general understanding of the term, in that it regards journalists accompanying VIPs who visit Afghanistan as 'embeds'.

10 After an August 2009 trial of the embedding program, the first reporters under the new program, Nick Butterly and Lee Griffith of the *West Australian*, were embedded in February/March 2010.

11 Karen Middleton, 'Who's Telling the Story?', p.155. This, she noted, was the 'sense among a number of my colleagues'.

responses to it, it is a surprise that a formal program ever eventuated. In an open letter to then Defence Minister, Senator John Faulkner, one of the guinea pigs in the trial, News Limited's Ian McPhedran, offered a scathing assessment of its conduct and premises:

> From the outset it should be noted that the word 'embedding' is not the correct term to describe what the Australian Defence Force is offering to the Australian media in Afghanistan.
>
> True embedding, as practiced by US and British forces, involves journalists agreeing to a set of well-defined and binding ground rules and then being attached to a military unit without an escort officer. The level of access granted to the journalist becomes a matter between the commanding officer and the journalist.
>
> The ADF model should be called 'media hosting.'[12]

McPhedran noted that not only did he and his fellow reporters on the trial, Sally Sara of the ABC and News Limited photographer, Gary Ramage, have to struggle to get to Afghanistan, and then fight harder to get out on patrol with the troops, but once there they were subjected to a relentless hard sell from the ADF, who, seeing the captive media contingent as a handy conduit for PR, hawked feel-good stories about the successes of their mission:

> Having military personnel trying to sell stories about schools or bridges or hospitals, when the real story is out in the 'green zone' with the infantry patrols, simply wastes valuable time and generates major frustrations. The best stories from the visit came from the three foot patrols that we were permitted to accompany ...The 'soft' PR stories about diggers doing good works have a place and that place is the Army News newspaper or on the defence website, it is not in the pages of major metropolitan newspapers. We would never dare suggest where the CO should place his troops, so we shouldn't be told how to do our job or what is a good story.[13]

When one sets McPhedran's allegations about the aggressive promotion of a PR agenda alongside the limited scope of the ADF embedding program

---

12 Ian McPhedran, '"Embedding" trial report', p.1. www.abc.net.au/mediawatch/transcripts/s2705312.htm. For a parallel report of this information see Ian McPhedran, 'Defence coy on embedding media', *The Australian*, 14 September 2009, np.

13 McPhedran, '"Embedding" trial report', p.2.

– the Dutch and Canadian militaries embedded, respectively, 20 and 40 times as many media per unit rotation as the ADF – one might reasonably infer that that the aim of the program was less to ensure that the media could keep the public reliably informed about the war than it was to counter criticism that it was not informing them at all. As a consequence, what the ADF was actually doing in Afghanistan remained a mystery. The military's continued stranglehold over the reporters' access to and freedom of movement among the troops ensured that for the Australian public and the reporters tasked with informing them, 'the story' of the Afghan War, 'like the barren wastes of Uruzgan province, was a mostly empty canvas.'[14] In the light of this, Jason Logue's review of the ADF's embedding program in Afghanistan should make interesting reading for his superiors. His analysis of the coverage for 2011 not only revealed that 'the overall trend of Australian media reporting concerning operations in Afghanistan was favourable' but that 'the coverage sourced from media embed participants, a relatively small percentage of overall coverage, was of considerably higher favourability than reporting from afar.' Not only was the embeds' reporting favourable, it 'showed a strong correlation with the identified favourable messages', the positive narrative about the war that the ADF was so keen to promote, namely 'the ADF supporting its personnel, the military/personal conduct of ADF personnel as "beyond reproach" and that ADF operations were making progress towards strategic goals.'[15] Given these outcomes, commanders in the ADF may not only look to sanction the timely introduction of embedding in future conflicts, but also kick themselves for not having done so earlier in Afghanistan.

The ADF's refusal to afford reporters a freer rein meant that many 'Australian journalists ... took to working with soldiers of other nations, notably Americans, because of a range of barriers to the Australian story.'[16] Fairfax's Chief Correspondent, Paul McGeough, has been a prominent commentator on the war in the Australian media but, until his trip to Uruzgan in early 2013, described in the previous chapter, he was notable for his absence from the ADF area of operations. His earlier experiences with the ADF help explain why he kept away. When McGeough accompanied former Defence Minister Robert Hill during a visit to Afghanistan in 2006, the ADF

14 Masters, *Uncommon Soldier*, p.83.

15 Logue, *Herding Cats*, pp.26, 27. For more detail on the methods and findings of Logue's study see *Herding Cats*, pp.22–29.

16 Masters, *Uncommon Soldier*, p.xviii.

PA officers ensured that neither he nor any of the media contingent were 'permitted to eat with or speak to the troops,' restrictions that McGeough described as 'appalling' and 'shameless.'[17] Ian McPhedran notes that by 2009 the ADF's restrictions on media reporting had grown so obstructive that 'there is more value in Australian reporters seeking help from British or American or Dutch or Romanian forces on operations than there is from the Australians.'[18]

A June 2009 symposium at the National Library in Canberra demonstrated that the media also have to accept their portion of responsibility for the failure to provide the Australian public with an accurate record of what its troops are doing in Afghanistan. For all his indignation about ADF obstruction, McGeough, his high profile colleagues Peter Cave of the ABC, Lindsay Murdoch of Fairfax, and many of their more illustrious forebears, have had little inclination to deal with Australian forces who they regard – not without merit – as minor players in this and most other conflicts.[19] Their professional reputations, and their egos, demand that they follow the main game and to do this they need to be in the thick of the action. Accordingly in Afghanistan they sought accreditation with US or British forces. Their indignation about ADF incompetence, whatever its truth, lent an impasto of principle to what was, at heart, a coldly calculating professionalism. The 'feel free to fuck off' principle evidently worked in both directions.

All Aboard

Prior to the introduction of a formal embedding program in 2010, the only way for Australian reporters to access their own troops in Afghanistan, other than through accidental encounters when embedded with other ISAF forces, was via the sponsored visits or 'bus tours' that the ADF used to bring the Australian media to Camp Holland, the joint Dutch-Australian base outside Tarin Kot.[20] These tours ran intermittently from 2002, and then more regularly from 2008, using spare capacity on ADF re-supply flights to save on costs. The program was closely managed by ADF PA who 'fixed'

17 Anderson and Trembath, *Witnesses to War*, p.335.

18 McPhedran, 'War! What War?' p.71.

19 McPhedran is not highly regarded by many of his colleagues who think him a little too gung-ho. However, he is always passionate about covering the ADF in combat and would much rather embed with his own troops than those of a foreign military.

20 Middleton, 'Who's Telling the Story?' 148. McPhedran describes them as 'bus trips', 'War! What War?' p.71.

the reporters' itineraries 'well in advance.'[21] Once the journalists were on base the PA officers 'chaperoned' them 'every step of the way.'[22] The standard schedule took them past a selection of prestige training and reconstruction projects – most notably the Trade Training School and the Tarin Kot Provincial Hospital – exposed them to selected personnel, primed to respond to the reporters' questions, and incorporated routine visits to nearby villages. Photojournalist Sean Hobbs recalled how, 'steered through itineraries designed to demonstrate the important work being done by the Australian Army,' he found the whole 'brief, glossy experience more akin to a battlefield Contiki Tour' than a real taste of war.[23] To maintain the 'Contiki Tour' effect the ADF ensured that reporters were kept away from Australian troops out on patrol. Little was left to chance. As SBS's Karen Middleton notes, the ADF's determination to minimise the scope for surprises or negative publicity ensured that as a journalist with the ADF in Afghanistan, while 'You can't be sure what will happen during your allotted time in country or what kind of stories you will be able to do … You can be absolutely certain you will be subject to considerable restriction.'[24]

On occasions these restrictions reached farcical proportions. During her first visit to Afghanistan in March 2007, having spent around ten days 'behind the wire' in Tarin Kot and Kandahar 'talking to carefully selected Australian troops and being shown what they were doing,' Middleton and her colleagues found themselves temporarily stranded waiting for a flight out of Kandahar Air Field.[25] 'Nobody was sure how or when we would be going home and we were … put on a short leash.'[26] The escort officer called Middleton and her colleagues together to pass on a message from Canberra that 'as our official program had ended, Defence did not believe it had any obligation to facilitate our work any further. In other words, we would not only get no more help in securing interviews or briefings (help we had received upon our arrival), we would be prevented from seeking them. Unless we were going to the toilet or being escorted to get food or coffee, we were to be confined to barracks until somebody figured out how to get us out.'[27]

---

21 Sean Hobbs, 'How to build a pergola: With the ADF in Afghanistan', *What are we doing in Afghanistan?* ed. Kevin Foster, Melbourne: Australian Scholarly Publishing, 2009, p.92.
22 Hobbs, 'How to build a pergola', p. 92.
23 Hobbs, 'How to build a pergola', p.92.
24 Middleton, 'Who's Telling the Story?' p.152.
25 Karen Middleton, *An Unwinnable War: Australia in Afghanistan*, Melbourne: Melbourne University Press, 2011, p.195.
26 Middleton, 'Who's Telling the Story?' p.151.
27 Middleton, 'Who's Telling the Story?' p.152.

The ADF considered the bus trips a vital means of promoting the successes of its mission in Uruzgan, but later conceded that they had persisted with them longer than they should have done, and that in the long run they damaged the military's credibility: 'The decision to operate this way made sense during the initial phases of the conflicts [in Iraq and Afghanistan] with their heavy Special Forces presence, but once large bodies of conventional troops were on the ground, Defence's ongoing justification became untenable. The negative comparison between the coalition approaches became the subject of increasing political pressure.'[28] For the media, the bus tours were a source of profound irritation: 'ferried to and escorted around operational zones by a cadre of Public Affairs personnel', unable to undertake even routine questioning of soldiers without the presence of a PA officer, Ian McPhedran felt that the relentless emphasis on promotion ensured that 'the message becomes repetitive and the frustrations immense.'[29] Though the bus tours may have been 'of very limited value' to the media, they were highly revealing of the military's practices and priorities.[30] *The Australian*'s Mark Dodd noted that a key focus of any media visit to Camp Holland was the Tarin Kot Provincial Hospital, recently refurbished by the Australians. Yet the renovation of the hospital, and the addition of a maternity wing, was not the good-news story it seemed. While the ADF was 'rightfully proud' of this achievement and visitors were 'inevitably ... briefed about the showcase project' few saw it in operation, as 'no foreign aid organisation has been willing to staff the hospital or provide the sort of support envisaged.'[31] This was no isolated example. At a Senate Committee hearing in March 2013 the DoD 'admitted it has no idea whether nearly two-thirds of projects built under a $34 million development fund in Afghanistan – including schools and hospitals – are actually working.' Deputy Secretary for Strategy, Brendan Sargeant, confirmed that 'once the bricks and mortar were in place

---

28 Logue, *Herding Cats*, pp.13–14.

29 McPhedran, 'War! What War?' p.71. Ironically, for all the derision they inspired, Sean Hobbs noted that it was 'notoriously difficult' to secure a spot on one of these visits: numbers of 'respected Australian journalists and photojournalists have tried repeatedly and without success to join one'. Sean Hobbs, 'How to build a pergola', p.92.

30 McPhedran, 'War! What War?', p.71.

31 Mark Dodd, 'Battle for progress', *The Australian*, 9 October 2008, p.11. As at 1 June 2011, AusAid's briefing on its projects in Afghanistan indicated that it had 'provided equipment for the Trade Training School in Tarin Kowt and the Tarin Kowt Hospital'. There was no indication that the hospital was staffed or operational. See www.ausaid.gov.au/country/country.cfm?CountryID=27886219&Region=AfricaMiddleEast.

on projects such as schools, hospitals, compounds and storage facilities, they were handed over to local authorities. "We have no information, so we're unable to report … The projects may or may not be viable. Once the ADF has done their job, it leaves."'[32] Clearly, the hospital and these other projects were of greater benefit to ADF PR than they were to the people they ostensibly served. They offer a compelling emblem of the ADF's reluctance to admit its failures in Afghanistan, and its continued determination to promote its successes, regardless of actual setbacks. They stand as concrete testament to the primacy of public affairs in the ADF's operations in Afghanistan.

If the public affairs agenda had a stranglehold over the reporting and perception of day-to-day events in Afghanistan, it also looks set to play a key role in historical assessments of the Australians' engagement there. Despite his appointment as an Official War Artist with a commission from the Australian War Memorial to photograph Australian troops in the Middle East for the Memorial's collection, Sean Hobbs discovered that when he arrived in Afghanistan he 'could not get beyond the public affairs screen and the carefully constructed narrative it promoted.'[33] Refused permission to go out and capture his own photographs of the nation's men and women at war, he was expected to stick to the party line and courier the good news generated by the ADF back to Australia. Arriving at Camp Holland, Hobbs recalled, the Commanding Officer treated him to

> a standard media spiel … detailing the excellent work being performed by the Australian Army provincial Reconstruction Task Force (RTF) who, I was told, were building schools, hospitals and renovating mosques. However, I would not be permitted to travel outside the wire to see any of these philanthropic activities. No explanation was forthcoming as to why this was the case, but I was assured that a Defence Public Affairs photographer had extensively documented the Army's activities beyond the perimeter and that this material was available should I wish to take it back to the War Memorial instead … I was to be told nothing and taken nowhere – with one notable exception. At the first opportunity I was escorted to see the Afghan 'Trade Training School' on base, where Australian Army Engineers taught a select bunch of Afghan youths to use a hand plane, wire a light switch and build a pergola. It was perfectly clear that I was only

32 David Wroe, 'Defence in the Dark', *The Saturday Age*, 23 March 2013, p.2.
33 Hobbs, 'How to build a pergola', p.96.

> meant to see and record this 'hearts and minds' operation, the feel-good experience, and none of the grit. Not only was I being presented with a one-sided, unremittingly positive view of the Australian Army's military objectives in this part of Afghanistan, it was assumed this was the version I would document for posterity via the collections of the Australian War Memorial.[34]

Ian McPhedran feared that the ADF's overzealous promotion of 'feel-good' stories would bequeath generations to come a misleading vision of what Australian forces were doing in Afghanistan: 'The first draft of history is written by journalists. If the ADF continues to block the media's access to the troops … the only true reporting and recording of Australians in action will be accidental, when an Australian media crew embedded with foreign forces happens upon some Aussies on exchange or during a joint operation.'[35] At the Chief of Army's Military History Conference in 2008, then Chief of Army, Lieutenant General Ken Gillespie, worried that 'the history of the Australian Army of the late 20th - early 21st century is going to be a work of fiction.'[36] His fears arose from the military's embrace of modern electronic communication and his belief that this was depriving the chroniclers of 'the essential building blocks of the historian's trade … written records.'[37] While Gillespie may be half-right about the effects of rapid technological change on the writing of the nation's military history, he wholly overlooks the role of his own organisation's communications strategies in contributing to this looming crisis and the scripting of the fictive responses to it. Speaking as the only press representative at the same conference, Karen Middleton pointed out that: 'How much of history we are able to record depends on how much we are allowed to record.'[38] If we want a truly Australian chronicle of what Australian forces are doing in Afghanistan, Middleton reflected, then the ADF has to grant its national media sufficient access to gather its raw materials: 'During my Afghanistan visit, the most telling descriptions of the level of preparedness and resourcing and state of mind of soldiers in the field came from a British officer, obtained in casual conversations while our escort officer slept … Now, Defence may congratulate itself that no such

34 Hobbs, 'How to build a pergola', pp.95–6.
35 McPhedran, 'War! What War?' p.72.
36 Lieutenant General Ken Gillespie, 'Introduction', *The Military, the Media and Information Warfare*, eds Peter Dennis and Jeffrey Grey, Canberra: Australian Military History Publications, 2009, p.2.
37 Gillespie, 'Introduction', p.2.
38 Middleton, 'Who's Telling the Story?' p.157.

musings emerged, through us, from its own forces. But why? It means we end up with a British perspective, not an Australian one.'[39] Likewise, Ian McPhedran feared that as a result of military censorship, 'future generations of Australians will view these modern wars through a British or an American prism, and what a tragedy that would be.'[40]

Operation Radio Storm

If Hobbs, McPhedran, Middleton and others like them advocated uncomfortable truth telling and were not prepared to act as uncritical conduits for ADF PR, others were less punctilious. Defence correspondents were in the minority among those making the trip to Tarin Kot – Middleton herself is SBS Television's Chief Political Correspondent and a member of the Parliamentary press gallery with, by her own admission, 'only a smattering of operational and conflict experience' before she first went to Afghanistan in March 2007.[41] As a result, while her focus on the domestic political ramifications of the war was richly nuanced and her observations on the impediments to reporting were pertinent and well-made, her coverage of the conflict lacked specialist insight and was mostly pedestrian.[42] Sean Hobbs noted that 'representatives of less-inquisitive media,' commercial radio DJs, breakfast talk-show hosts, 'lads' magazines' and reporters from news outlets linked to the soldiers' home bases, were regulars on the bus tours.[43] Comedian broadcasters, Hamish Blake and Andy Lee, were foremost among the 'less-inquisitive media.' Framing the war within their customary context of banter and spoof – they played with night vision goggles, mounted guard over the camp and mistook heavy weapons fire for a thunderstorm – their Fox FM broadcasts from Afghanistan in April 2008, 'Operation Radio Storm', were fabulous PR for the ADF.[44] Hamish and Andy reinforced the links between

39 Middleton, 'Who's Telling the Story?' p.156.

40 McPhedran, 'War! What War?' p.73.

41 Middleton, 'Who's Telling the Story?' p.148.

42 This link to Middleton's reports from Afghanistan provides a good cross-section of her work with everything from reports on the preparedness of the ANA, ADF fears of further 'green on blue' attacks, to items on ballistic underwear and explosive detection dogs: www.sbs.com.au/news/article/1703023/On-assignment-in-Afghanistan-Karen-Middleton-repor Indeed there were plenty of dogs in the coverage of the war in Afghanistan, but no ponies.

43 Hobbs, 'How to build a pergola', p.92.

44 Selections from the broadcasts can be accessed here: www.2dayfm.com.au/shows/hamishandandy/australian-troops/the-giggle-bunker For ADF coverage of the visit see www.defence.gov.au/opEx/global/opslipper/images/gallery/2008/0418/index.htm.

Figure 1. Hamish and Andy in 'The Giggle Bunker'
Reproduced courtesy of Department of Defence

the public and the military, emphasising the fact that the men and women of the ADF, amused by the same things as their civilian listeners, were ordinary Australians performing extraordinary feats of courage in one of the world's most dangerous places: 'We've been blown away by the good work being done by these soldiers to help the Afghans get back on their feet.'[45]

Like Hamish and Andy, a significant number of the journalists – when they were journalists – who reported from Afghanistan, had little or no experience of defence or overseas postings. As a consequence they were easy, and often enthusiastic, vehicles for uncritical puffery dressed up as 'colour', opinion or news. Glen Williams of *Woman's Day* reported on a number of servicewomen and aid workers serving with the Australians for his April 2010 profile of 'Aussie women on the front line in Afghanistan.'[46] The encomiastic nature of the resulting coverage was shaped not only by the nature of the invitation extended to *Woman's Day* 'by the Australian Government's overseas aid agency, AusAID, to see first-hand how the Australian military is bringing new light to this all-too-dark, long-running conflict in

45 www.defence.gov.au/opEx/global/opslipper/images/gallery/2008/0418/index.htm.
46 Glen Williams, 'Aussie women on the front line in Afghanistan', *Woman's Day*, 19 April 2010.

Afghanistan,' but also by the restrictions within which he worked, confined to reporting on 'life behind the wire in Kamp Holland.'[47]

A few months earlier, in January 2010, Jo Chandler of *The Age* also reported on gender in the war zone, focusing on those women whose roles exposed them to the hazards outside the wire. By embracing the sort of danger formerly reserved for their male colleagues, her subjects, an ADF photographer, an Army nurse, an Inspector in the Australian Federal Police (AFP) and an AusAid development adviser, occupied the 'murky extremities of the gender front line, where commentators debate whether female participation [in war] signals feminist victory or defeat.'[48] While the article celebrated the women's professionalism and tenacity and the equal opportunity access to deadly peril that this had afforded them, its apparent interest in substantial matters of gender politics was contradicted by a more considered focus on softer gender issues – the shortage of ablution facilities, looking after your skin in such a hostile environment, maintaining long-distance relationships, etcetera. More importantly, while celebrating the down-to-earth daring of the women in the story, Chandler failed to mention at any point in the article that, unlike her subjects, she had been forbidden to travel beyond the wire and report on them in the field and that she was denied this opportunity not because she was a woman but because she was a journalist. If Chandler's article implied that the ADF was reforming its attitudes about women on the front lines, her experiences demonstrated that its views about reporters had undergone no such renewal and were still shaped by enduring prejudices – prejudices that she refused to name or confront in her piece. Why did she fail to disclose that she was confined to the base? Protected from harm by men (and women) whose disdain for her profession kept her behind the wire, Chandler's dilemma was a common one for reporters in the field: how to manage the tension between her personal gratitude towards the military and her professional responsibility to offer an objective account of their actions and behaviour. Chandler, a senior reporter for *The Age* at the time, with no experience of defence reporting, seemed to assume that she could not do both. As a consequence, in this case, the personal trumped the professional and the public were left in the dark about the ADF's continuing hostility towards the fourth estate.

While ABC Queensland's Kathy McLeish was an experienced reporter who had 'won awards for rural, business, investigative, disability, mental

47 Williams, 'Aussie women on the front line in Afghanistan'.
48 Jo Chandler, 'Women at War', *The Age: Good Weekend*, 23 January 2010, p.14.

health and current affairs reporting', she had no experience of the defence round before she embedded with the ADF in Afghanistan in mid-2012.[49] With Queensland-based troops comprising the main body of the Australian force commitment at that time, the ADF recognised the promotional value in sending a Queensland journalist with no defence experience to cover a Queensland battalion at war. At the mercy of her PA escorts her reporting was notable for its readiness to proffer ADF PR standards as 'news'. In an interview with Chris O'Brien on ABC Queensland's *7.30 Report* on 6 July 2012, her description of the ADF's insistence on control and surveillance, the restrictions she worked within as an embedded reporter and the freedoms she enjoyed, not only echoed the official mantra on information management but was represented by McLeish as a form of personal and professional enhancement. To be embedded, McLeish reported, was to be 'embraced by the ADF,' to be 'within the effort that's happening in Afghanistan.' While 'there are a lot of operational security issues ... things that shouldn't be shown, or things that you might see that you shouldn't mention that could put people at risk ... so there are limitations on that, at the same time you're very free to wander round and speak to people and have conversations with anybody ... you're just a part of the system.'[50] Surely one of her principal responsibilities as a reporter was to separate herself from 'the system', not least the information management system, and to subject it to rational and objective analysis. Her celebration of the troops' camaraderie – 'there's an extraordinary bond and a sense of mateship ... you get swept up in it, whoever is there is part of that, everybody's in the same situation in that area of conflict' – not only reflected her inability to maintain a vital level of professional detachment from her subjects, it offered a compelling demonstration of why the ADF has been so happy to embed non-defence specialists.[51]

When Townsville journalist and radio personality, Steve Price, visited Australian forces in Afghanistan in October 2009, his brief dispatches rarely got beyond breathless admiration for the nation's service personnel to say anything about what they were actually doing there. When he interviewed 'chief of staff, Aussies middle east', Commodore Trevor Jones, he gave no indication of any of the questions he had put to the Commodore,

---

49 www.ruralpressclub.com.au/item.cfm?page_id=10

50 www.abc.net.au/news/2012-07-06/730s-kathy-mcleish-joins-qld-troops-in-afghanistan/4115848

51 www.abc.net.au/news/2012-07-06/730s-kathy-mcleish-joins-qld-troops-in-afghanistan/4115848

or the latter's responses to them.[52] This interview was symptomatic of his broader 'reporting' from Afghanistan, which amounted to little more than sycophantic drool: 'What a fantastic man. His thoughts on this conflict and Aussies in general is [*sic*] extraordinary. I have indeed met some amazing people, and I am very, very honoured.'[53]

A more accomplished journalist, Trent Dalton of the *Courier-Mail*, travelled to Afghanistan in October 2008 to cover the unveiling of a memorial to Trooper David Pearce of the Gold Coast, killed by a roadside bomb in October 2007. The resulting article, 'Brave Digger "Poppy" Pearce gets Afghan Memorial', paid due respect to the dead man but served principally as a vehicle for a more general endorsement of the ADF mission in Afghanistan – explicitly articulated by another Queenslander interviewed by Dalton: '"It's dangerous, but I want to do it," he said. "I was here with RTF 1 ... We've done a hell of a lot since then. I hope we can see it through to the end." It was a sentiment shared by all the Diggers on our convoy. They want to be here. They want to serve.'[54] The day after the piece was published in the *Courier-Mail*, the Department of Defence web site featured a story on the 'Trooper David "Poppy" Pearce Memorial Service' held on the preceding day at Lavarack Barracks in Townsville: 'A devoted family man,' the report observes, 'Trooper Pearce died serving the country he loved, while deployed with the Reconstruction Task Force in Afghanistan. His heroic sacrifice will always be remembered by those who attended the morning Memorial Service.'[55] Setting these stories side by side, it is clear that journalism and promotion have been deployed in a carefully coordinated pincer movement designed to corral and command public sympathy. One can be forgiven for wondering where the official work of intra-governmental communication ends and the public relations offensive on the broader population begins.

McLeish, Price, Dalton and their many compatriots are the type of reporters the ADF has preferred to take to Afghanistan in place of experienced Defence correspondents.[56] Unlikely to ask curly questions, they can be relied

---

52 Steve Price, 'Homeward bound', *The Townsville Bulletin*, 9 October 2009, np. www.townsvillebulletin.com.au/article/2009/10/09/85131_rightprice.html. He is not to be confused with the Melbourne broadcaster of the same name.

53 Price, 'Homeward bound,' np. Commodore Jones was the Chief of Staff and Deputy Commander of Joint Task Force 633.

54 Trent Dalton, 'Brave Digger "Poppy" Pearce gets Afghan Memorial', *Courier-Mail*, 8 October 2008.

55 Department of Defence, 'Trooper David "Poppy" Pearce Memorial Service', www.defence.gov.au/media/download/2008/oct/20081009/index.htm

56 Williams and Chandler travelled to Afghanistan at the invitation of AusAid.

on to provide an objective channel for the ADF's public affairs message and assist the military in communicating with and recruiting from its target demographic. British journalists complained of a similar phenomenon in the MoD's information management of the war. When the *Guardian*'s James Meek was embedded in Helmand in 2006 in a relatively quiet zone, his requests to visit bases where soldiers were fighting were refused: 'I was told quite candidly that the priority was the tabloids and television because it was important for recruitment.'[57] In September 2008, *The Times*' Defence correspondent, Christina Lamb, was shunted off to a quiet zone in Helmand so that Tom Newton Dunn of the *Sun* could travel with the troops, see a bit of action and write appropriately stirring material for a 'red-top' consumed by hundreds of thousands of young male Cs and Ds – the bull's eye in the Army's target demographic.

If the British military went out of their way to engineer media opportunities for the popular press, up until 2011 the ADF seemed dedicated to keeping a healthy distance between Australian defence reporters and its combat personnel. Why? Despite regular protestations about 'operational security' this was not because some of these men were Special Forces and so off limits to the media, but because until its media embedding program began in earnest, the ADF had most need of the independent media not to report the war but to provide objective validation for the military's version of its key narrative features. In promoting this narrative, ADF public affairs regarded the media not merely as superfluous but as a threat to the effective communication of its core message. In response, along the lines first envisaged during Operation Warden in East Timor, basic reporting tasks that had once been monopolised by the media – the nomination, gathering and editing of news from the front lines – were brought in-house and taken over by uniformed 'reporters' organised into small field units known as Military Camera Teams (MCTs) from the 1st Joint Public Affairs Unit.[58] Tasked to promote the ADF, to ensure that when the nation's forces do good they are 'seen to be doing good,' the MCT members are trained to operate cameras, take photographs, conduct interviews, and then edit the material for press or broadcast.[59] The independent media are brought into the process only at the point of dissemination when the material gathered for them by the military is made available to newspapers and television

57 Gray, Stephen (2009) 'A lack of cover'. *Guardian*, 15 June 2009, np.
58 MCTs were formerly known as Deployable Field Teams (DFTs).
59 Phil Smith, 'The Story of Aceh', *The Defence Reserves Yearbook 2004–2005*, ed. Bill Rowling, Melbourne: Executive Media, p.6.

networks. As a consequence, as Tom Hyland noted in 2008, up to that point 'almost every picture and video of Australian troops, every audio "grab" and almost every quote from a digger comes from ADF "public affairs and imagery specialists."'[60]

The military have often expressed surprise and disappointment at the media's scant use of the material its public affairs personnel gather and make available.[61] Yet the material gathered by MCTs, journalists point out, is unfailingly promotional, focused on the winning of hearts and minds or the celebration of military successes, infrastructural improvements and the attainment of training milestones. The MCTs are engaged in a process of marketing and endorsement, not one of newsgathering or assembling a factual record of events. As Tom Hyland observes, the ADF's public affairs personnel 'call it "newsgathering", but it is not. Some members of these Defence media teams say they are following in the footsteps of famous war correspondents like Osmar White and Damien Parer, but they are not.'[62] Their practices are inductive rather than deductive. They begin from certain established premises – that the ADF is a moral, professional, force for good, moving steadily towards the successful completion of its mission in Afghanistan – and produce evidence to support these assumptions, rather than observing what is around them and drawing their conclusions from the evidence they gather. As a consequence, as Hyland points out, the public is proffered an unrealistically positive portrait of the men and their mission in Afghanistan: 'From these stories, Australian soldiers are an exceptional breed – they are all happy in the service, they think their kit is great, their leaders exceptional, their training first class, and their mission successful. Funny sort of soldiers: they never complain. Funny sort of army: everything works. Funny old war: everything goes according to plan.'[63]

Not only are the military zealous in their promotion of this narrative, they are aggressive in their defence of it. When Sally Neighbour suggested to an Australian commander that his account of how a 12-year old would-be suicide bomber had been recruited by the Taliban 'sounded like

---

60 Tom Hyland, 'Stifling soldiers of spin', *The Sunday Age*, 20 July 2008, p.21.

61 Brigadier Alison Creagh, former Director General Strategic Communication, at the 'Information Warfare: Shaping the Stories of Australians at War' conference, November 2010, University of New South Wales at the Australian Defence Force Academy.

62 Tom Hyland, 'Funny Old War: The News from the ADF', *What are we doing in Afghanistan?* p.115.

63 Tom Hyland, 'Funny Old War', p.116.

an apocryphal story' she received 'a curt response' from the officer: 'If you think I'm telling apocryphal stories, we will terminate the interview right now.'[64] If the military are adept at bullying reporters in defence of the party line, they are more practised still at keeping their own personnel on message. In Iraq when the media complained (again) about lack of access to Australian forces 'the ADF offered up an RAAF [Royal Australian Air Force] Hornet pilot for a brief, stage-managed news conference. He was not allowed to say if he had been shot at. Pressed if he had been afraid during bombing missions, as one reporter later wrote, "he looked nervously at a Defence Force public relations officer monitoring the conversation and said: 'I'm going to stop there'". The encounter was revealing: we did not learn if the pilot was afraid of Iraqi fire, but he was certainly afraid of Defence Public Affairs.'[65]

Sticking to the Script

Yet it was not only the media who stood between the ADF and a seamless public relations exercise in Afghanistan. In the second half of 2009, as the political situation in the country plumbed new lows, the coalition suffered a rising casualty toll at the hands of the Taliban and the western media openly questioned the value of further loss of life, Defence and the government sought to put a positive spin on whatever news they had to hand. At first, the Presidential election of 20 August 2009 looked like a good-news story as the indomitable Afghan public, protected by their coalition allies, turned out in the face of Taliban intimidation to affirm their faith in the power of the ballot box.[66] The day after the elections, before the facts about vote-rigging and wholesale ballot stuffing by the Karzai camp fully came to light, then Defence Minister John Faulkner issued a media release in which he claimed that 'the conduct of yesterday's Presidential and Provincial elections in Afghanistan strengthened democracy in that country.'[67] In Uruzgan, he

---

64 Sally Neighbour, 'Taliban conflict "cannot be won" in Afghanistan', *The Australian*, 10 July 2008, p.5.

65 Tom Hyland, 'Funny Old War', p.105.

66 The same day saw the election of 420 men and women to the Provincial Council. After a long period of vote counting, and the investigation of allegations of vote rigging, intimidation and interference, a run-off vote between the two leading candidates, President Hamid Karzai and Dr Abdullah Abdullah, was scheduled for 7 November. However, after Dr Abdullah withdrew from the contest on 1 November, claiming that it was impossible to conduct a transparent election, Karzai was declared the winner.

67 Department of Defence, Media Release 021/2009, www.defence.gov.au/DefenceBlog/2009/0817_0823.htm.

observed, 'voters proved their resilience and determination by turning up and casting their votes.'[68] The following days' revelations made a mockery of this claim. As Carlotta Gall of the *New York Times* noted: 'In the southern provinces like Kandahar, Helmand, Uruzgan and Zabul, turnout was as low as 5 to 10 per cent.'[69] The Liaison Office, an independent Afghan NGO, observed that 'Compared to the 2004 presidential elections, voter turnout for the August 2009 presidential and Provincial Council elections dropped precipitously throughout the south and east' of the country.[70] In Uruzgan, Afghan election observer, Abdul Raziq, confirmed what was well known to the ADF and its commanders on the day, that voter turn out was negligible and the election a farce. He spent three hours outside one polling station in Tarin Kot trying to persuade so-called election officials to let him in so that he could do his job and observe the election. During that time, he recalled, no more than 60 or 80 Afghans turned up to cast their votes. 'No one was voting because there were rockets ... Finally, when they let me in, I saw all the ballot boxes were full.'[71]

As the election story turned into political and PR poison, the ADF shifted the focus of its media offensive from civilian to military matters. Its media releases promoted the increasingly close and productive relationships between Australian and Afghan forces, emphasising in particular the more central role undertaken by ANSF personnel in joint operations and their growing professionalism. A Department of Defence Media Release of 13 October 2009 alerted the media to 'Three news stories' that it had ready 'for broadcast/publication ... 1. SPECIAL FORCES MENTORING IN ORUZGAN BEARS FRUIT ... 2. OPERATIONAL SUCCESS IN SOUTHERN AFGHANISTAN' and '3. SPECIAL FORCES GROUNDWORK SETS CONDITIONS FOR STABILITY.'[72] What unites these items is their common focus on – and here I am quoting from the three separate texts introducing the stories – 'The partnership between ... Afghan and Australian forces,' how this is 'creating stronger relationships between Afghan locals and the Afghan and coalition forces'

---

68 Department of Defence, Media Release 021/2009.

69 Carlotta Gall, 'Two Claim to Lead Afghan Race for President', *New York Times*, 21 August 2009. www.nytimes.com/2009/08/22/world/asia/22afghan.html.

70 The Liaison Office, *The Dutch Engagement in Uruzgan, 2006–2010: a TLO socio-political assessment* (Kabul: The Liaison Office), 2010, p.32. For an online version of the report see www.humansecuritygateway.com/documents/TLO_Dutch_Engagement_In_Uruzgan-2006-2010.pdf .

71 Jerome Starkey and Jon Swain, 'President Hamid Karzai takes 100 per cent of votes in opposition stronghold', *The Sunday Times*, 6 September 2009, p.3.

72 See www.defence.gov.au/media/AlertTpl.cfm?CurrentId=9580.

and how, when put to work as it was in Operation Baz Panje, these new relationships put 'pressure on insurgent sanctuary areas' and 'pave the way for a permanent coalition and ANSF presence in [Uruzgan] provinces [*sic*] Mirabad region.'[73] The ADF has been pushing this line about enhanced cooperation with an increasingly competent Afghan military, with ever decreasing subtlety, for many years. As the ADF's departure from Afghanistan draws nigh, this focus on the ANA's improved capacity and growing independence constitutes a central thread in Defence Media releases from Afghanistan and the core element in the political justification for the timing and circumstances of Australia's withdrawal.[74]

In its promotion of the ANA's performance and competence the ADF is employing a media strategy first made familiar in Vietnam during the 'Vietnamisation' period of the war as the US prepared to disengage and Vietnamese forces assumed the greater burden of the fighting. More recently, this same process was on display in Iraq as the US prepared to hand over security responsibility to local forces and withdraw. In *The Forever War* (2008), Dexter Filkins furnished an exemplary case when he described a US military assault on the Saddam Hussein Hospital in Ramadi where, it was believed, Iraqi insurgents were based and significant quantities of materiel were being stored. Preparing to leave for the operation, Filkins recalled: 'One of the officers mentioned that some Iraqi army soldiers would be coming along, twenty-seven of them, but I didn't see them at the briefing.' Well before dawn, with the area secured, 'the marines swarmed into the hospital ... They broke the locks on all the doors, to the supply rooms, the operating rooms, the patient wards ... They set up machine-gun posts at each end of each floor to isolate the violence in case things got out of control.' They found little in the way of arms or explosives and the expected battle with the 'insurgents' came to nothing. But that, as it turned out, was not the point of the exercise: 'About an hour later, after they'd let the reporters in and the hospital was mostly secure, I saw the Iraqi soldiers. I was on the first floor when they came sauntering in ... They looked good: nice uniforms, well trained. The Iraqi soldiers fanned out and began searching the rooms the Americans had left for them ...

73 See www.defence.gov.au/media/AlertTpl.cfm?CurrentId=9580.

74 See, for example, MECC 317/11 (26/07/2011) 'Special Forces support Afghan National Security Forces in dismantling insurgent drug network'; MECC 327/11 (01/08/2011) 'New Afghan National Army unit conducts successful security operation in Uruzgan'; MECC 331/11 (04/08/11) 'Afghan led security operation in Uruzgan completes first phase'. All accessible at www.defence.gov.au/op/afghanistan/media.cfm.

With the Americans looking on, the Iraqi soldiers kicked open each ward door with great precision and swung their rifles inside and stormed in, to find only emptiness.' Their job done, the Iraqis found an empty ward where they made themselves comfortable and 'had a good nap.' While they were sleeping, the US military issued a press release describing the events: '"Early this morning Iraqi Security Forces, with support from Coalition forces, began searching a hospital in northern Ramadi, which was being used as a center for insurgent activity" the release said. "This Iraqi Army-led operation will deny the insurgents use of the Saddam Hospital."'[75] The operation that Filkins describes here makes it clear that when the ADF issues media releases claiming that 'Afghan National Security Forces (ANSF), with support from Australian Special Forces and other coalition troops, have uncovered significant munitions caches,' Afghan leadership of this exercise was as much a political and public affairs necessity as it was ever a tactical reality.[76]

Though politicians from ISAF contributing nations still claimed that the mission was about ensuring Afghanistan never again became a safe-haven for terrorists, on the ground, as the US, Britain and Australia prepared to draw down their forces and exit the country, 'The war had morphed into something else. The battle now was to protect a hard-fought investment, to ensure a departure with as much honour intact as possible, to shape something of benefit from the mire, and to leave the area having done more harm than good.'[77] Central to that narrative was the development in Afghanistan of a national security apparatus that the coalition could credibly claim was ready to shoulder the burden of protecting its borders and deal with insurgent forces within them after it withdrew. Yet despite plans to train and equip a combined army and police force in excess of 350,000, quarterly reports from the office of the Special Inspector General for Afghanistan Reconstruction (SIGAR) record a recurring pattern of wasted money, missed deadlines and performance failures.[78] In January 2013, for example, it reports that a US$7.3 million Border Police Headquarters in Kunduz province still sits largely unused.[79] In evidence to the House Armed Services Committee, Vanda Felbab-Brown of the Brookings Institution noted that 'The ANA

---

75 Dexter Filkins, *The Forever War*, New York: Vintage, 2008, pp.312, 313, 314.

76 MECC 349/09 (19/10/2009) 'Weapons and Munitions Caches Seized', www.defence.gov.au/media/DepartmentalTpl.cfm?CurrentId=9596.

77 Masters, *Uncommon Soldier*, p.277.

78 The SIGAR website can be accessed at www.sigar.mil accessed 23 February 2013.

79 See www.sigar.mil/pdf/inspections/2013-01-29-inspection-13-05.pdf accessed 23 February, 2013.

appears to be increasingly weakened by corruption' and that while this was not a new problem, 'it may be intensifying.' This manifests itself in the form of patronage and prejudice. The 'ethnic fissures and patronage networks' running through the military threaten to fatally undermine operational efficiency, as 'excellent soldiers are not being promoted because they do not have influential friends', while 'Conversely, many extra positions, at the level of colonel, for example, are being created so that commanders can give pay-offs to their loyal supporters.'[80] Little wonder then that Australian special forces felt that their relationships with the personnel they were mentoring were not moving, as per the script, towards the production of a more independent, more lethal capability, but had discernibly 'gone backwards.'[81]

Dogs and Donkeys

In the face of the recalcitrant realities on the ground – limited military progress, stubborn Taliban resistance, political inertia, growing Afghan hostility to the foreign 'crusaders' and the increasing unpopularity of the war on the domestic front – in late 2009 Defence Public Affairs and the ADF drew to the public's attention a stirring tale of survival against the odds as a model of the personal and collective qualities evinced by Australian forces in Afghanistan. The protagonist of this narrative was not a serviceman or woman but an Explosives Detection Dog, a black Labrador bitch called Sarbi.[82] The dog had been 'declared MIA [Missing in Action] in September 2008' after she became separated from her handler 'during the same battle with the Taliban in which SAS Trooper Mark Donaldson won his Victoria Cross.'[83] For twelve months there was no trace of the dog and it was presumed dead until miraculously, in September 2009, US troops stumbled across her and returned her to the care of the ADF. Donaldson was delighted to hear of the dog's unexpected reappearance, claiming that it 'gives some closure for the handler and the rest of us that served with her in 2008. It's a fantastic morale booster for the guys.'[84]

---

80 www.brookings.edu/research/testimony/2012/08/02-afghanistan-security-felbabbrown accessed 23 February, 2013.

81 Masters, *Uncommon Soldier*, p.273.

82 Sarbi was spelt incorrectly as 'Sabi' in early press releases. I will correct the spelling where appropriate. For more on Sarbi see Sandra Lee, *Saving Private Sarbi: The True Story of Australia's Canine War Hero*, Sydney: Allen and Unwin, 2011.

83 MSPA 386/09 'Australian Dog Returns Home After a Year in the Afghan Wilderness'.

84 MSPA 386/09 'Australian Dog Returns Home After a Year in the Afghan Wilderness'.

Australian Government
Department of Defence

Minister | Navy | Army | Air Force | Department

Search

Media Room | Reports and Publications | Careers and Recruiting | Industry and Contracts | Other Defence Links

Sarbi

Sarbi
Sarbi home
Latest Images
File Images
Video Gallery
Sarbi Stories

Multimedia
Images
Video
Audio
File Images

Media
Defence News
On the Record
Social Media
Subscribe to Media Room

Community
Leaders
Our People
Information for Families
Messages for the Troops

Operations & Exercises
Global Operations
Exercises

Inquiries
Inquiry Reports
Inquiry FAQ

Sarbi

Home > Sarbi

Sarbi's story is one of survival...

For nearly 14 months, Sarbi an Australian Special Forces Explosive Detection dog, was separated from her handler in Afghanistan.

The black Labrador-cross had been declared missing in action following a battle with the Taliban that left nine soldiers wounded, including her handler. A rocket-propelled grenade (RPG) had exploded close to Sarbi, breaking the clip that attached her lead to her handler's body armour. It was the same battle where Trooper Mark Donaldson earned his Victoria Cross.

A US soldier knew his Australian mates were missing Sarbi, and spotted her wandering with an Afghan man near an isolated patrol base in north-eastern Oruzgan Province. Sarbi was flown to Tarin Kowt to be reunited with her Australian Special Forces trainer.

The Australian trainer knew instantly it was Sarbi.
"I nudged a tennis ball to her with my foot and she took it straight away. It's a game we used to play over and over during her training," the trainer said.

At the time of her disappearance Sarbi was coming to the end of her second tour of duty in Afghanistan, having previously deployed to Oruzgan in 2007.

Sarbi had also deployed with the Incident Response Regiment during the Melbourne Commonwealth Games in 2006.

We will never know what Sarbi saw during her time alone in the desert, but what we do know is that if she could talk, that would be one great story.

A recent check of Sarbi's regimental record, revealed that Sarbi's name has been previously incorrectly spelt in Defence public reporting and the record is now corrected to show the spelling as Sarbi, not 'Sabi'.

Figure 2. Sarbi's Webpage: http://www.defence.gov.au/sarbi/
Reproduced courtesy of Department of Defence

Yet the Department of Defence's aggressive promotion of the story – they issued nine press-releases on Sarbi between November 2009 and April 2011 and she still has a dedicated webpage on the Defence website – positioned her as something more than a mere 'morale booster.'[85]

85 Nine press releases on Sarbi between 12 November 2009 and 5 April 2011 marked the stages of her journey from the 'wilderness' back to full military honours and the garlands of war. See MSPA 386/09 'Australian Dog Returns Home After a Year in the Afghan Wilderness', MSPA 388/09 'Media Doorstop for Return of Explosive Detection Dog Sabi', MSPA 425/09 'Sabi the Special Forces Dog Laps it Up', MSPA 130/10 'Sabi spends Anzac Day in Afghanistan', 02/06/2010 'Sarbi takes next steps on her journey home', MSPA 582/10 'Explosives detection dog Sarbi returns to Australia', MSPA 588/10 'Sarbi the dog in quarantine', MSPA 7/11 'Meet Sarbi the Explosive Detection Dog', 5 April 2011 'RSPCA awards Sarbi the Purple Cross'. Sarbi's webpage can be found at www.defence.gov.au/sarbi/index.htm.

While Sarbi provided a welcome distraction from a campaign whose political aims were increasingly suspect and whose strategy seemed to be failing, the dog and the tale of her apparent death and resurrection served less to distract the public's attention from the war than to return it to what should have been its rightful focus all along – the men and women of the ADF, the sacrifices they were making and the values of heroism and mateship that they were upholding. Sarbi's quasi-biblical journey from exile and suffering in the wilderness to the warm embrace of home and family, the public recognition she enjoyed and the formal honours bestowed upon her, mirrored the ADF's deepest fears and most cherished hopes for its personnel serving in Afghanistan. They reflected the military's trepidation that the people had abandoned their armed forces and that the losses they had suffered in Afghanistan had been in vain, while also echoing their longing for public approval and official recognition of their work. In recording her attendance at the Dawn Service, her connection with Mark Donaldson VC and her warm reception from the Governor-General, the press releases ensured that Sarbi, a two-tour veteran of Afghanistan, was closely aligned with the key markers of Australian military exceptionalism – Anzac Day, the Victoria Cross, the Commonwealth and the Crown.[86] As he farewelled her from JTF 633's HQ in Kuwait before she began her journey back to Australia, Major General John Cantwell drew attention to Sarbi's representative status, noting that while she would be 'remembered for her actions,' it was 'important to note that there are a lot of other dogs doing the same dangerous work as her in Afghanistan and we need to continue to support and recognise them as we have Sarbi.'[87]

On her return to Australia Sarbi lived the soldier's dream. Accorded a hero's welcome, she was greeted by the press, feted by the nation's highest-ranking officers and publicly honoured with the award of the Purple Cross,

---

The Head of News at ninemsn, Hal Crawford, told Gideon Haigh in 2012 that dog stories are exceptionally popular on Facebook, generate significant traffic and often find their way into the mainstream media via social media sharing. As a consequence, as Crawford notes, 'we're now trying to get our guys to write stories that will be shared. To choose a mundane example, dogs do really well. If you've got a choice to write a dog story or a food story, do the dog. People love the anthropomorphic. If the dog is acting like a person you have sharing gold'. Gideon Haigh, *The Deserted Newsroom*, Melbourne: Penguin, 2012, p.54. Perhaps ADF PA were ahead of their time in their use of Sarbi.

86 Sarbi attended the Anzac Day dawn service, was feted by the Governor-General and counted Mark Donaldson VC among her friends and admirers.

87 Defence Mediaops Press Release, 2 June 2010, 'Sarbi takes next steps on her journey home'.

Figure 3. One Man and his Dog: Major General John Cantwell and Sarbi

Reproduced courtesy of Department of Defence

the 'RSPCA's most prestigious animal bravery award', bestowed upon 'animals that have shown outstanding service to humans, particularly if they've shown exceptional courage.'[88] Acknowledging this award, the Chief of Army, Lieutenant General Ken Gillespie, drew explicit parallels between Sarbi's service, and recognition, and the unacknowledged valour of the men and women risking their lives for their country in Afghanistan: 'I am very

88 Defence Mediaops Press Release, 5 April 2011, 'RSPCA awards Sarbi the Purple Cross'.

proud of the professional and dedicated work of our combat engineers and dog handlers, and the vital role they play in keeping our soldiers safe on deployment … I am thrilled that the RSPCA has chosen to honour Sarbi, and by extension, all of Army's working dogs and their handlers with this award.'[89] As such, while at one level the story of Sarbi provided welcome relief for a public disillusioned by a campaign that had lost its way, it actually served to remind Australians about what their men and women were fighting for and who they really were.

While the dog and pony show played out in Defence's media releases, in September 2007 the ADF went online to hammer home its core message of fruitful cooperation with an ever-improving ANSF, establishing a media channel on YouTube to help disseminate the message to Generation Y. In doing this the ADF was following in the footsteps of the US Department of Defense who, in May 2007, in an effort to stem rising negative publicity about its intervention in Iraq, launched its own YouTube channel, MNFIRAQ (Multi-National Force – Iraq), whose stated goal was to give 'viewers around the world a "boots on the ground" perspective of Operation Iraqi Freedom from those who are fighting it.'[90] In fact, as Susan Carruthers notes, the channel was established specifically to counter such images. The DOD had grown increasingly concerned by soldiers posting graphic material depicting 'the aftermath of IED attacks, the (mis)treatment of prisoners, and other images falling into the category known as "body horror"' to YouTube, MySpace and bulletin boards including NowThat'sFuckedUp.com.[91] In response, the US military limited their soldiers' contributions to these sites by restricting access to them and imposing explicit prohibitions on the nature of material that could be uploaded. It was in this context that it launched MNFIRAQ which 'hosted a series of short clips shot by US forces.'[92] In contrast to the graphic material posted by individual personnel, the clips on MNFIRAQ offered a more sanitised image of the war, editing out audible profanity while avoiding 'overly graphic, disturbing or offensive content.'[93]

Likewise in Australia, the ADF's bold advance into the world of Web 2.0 and the exclusion of the independent media from all stages of the news

89 Defence Mediaops Press Release, 5 April 2011, 'RSPCA awards Sarbi the Purple Cross'.

90 Carruthers, *War and the Media*, p.247.

91 Carruthers, *War and the Media*, p.246.

92 Carruthers, *War and the Media*, p.247.

93 Christian Christensen, 'Uploading dissonance: YouTube and the US occupation of Iraq'. *Media, War and Conflict*, Vol. 1, No. 2, (August 2008), pp.163.

production process that this enabled furnished the military with a platform for the unfiltered articulation of its preferred narrative of the war. However, the freedom to launch a seamless public affairs offensive laid bare certain contradictions between the official account of events in Afghanistan and the views and experiences of those best placed to endorse or challenge the official line – ADF personnel on the ground. For example, the voiceover on the ADF YouTube video 'Afghan and Australian forces offer no let-up against Taliban insurgents in Operation Zamarai Lor', claimed that 'The Australians say that the Afghan forces are showing real promise as a fighting force and have grown in confidence and capacity to plan and conduct operations.'[94] But this is not what the soldiers mentoring and working with the Afghan forces said about them. When the question of ANA capability came up during Tom Hyland's embed with the ADF in March 2009 some of the soldiers 'were scathing, particularly towards the Afghan commander, who they complained was obstructive, lazy, reluctant to fight and unwilling to conduct the detailed planning that is normal for Australian troops.'[95] Transcripts of interviews conducted by the Centre for Military and Veterans Health with former and serving troops that were leaked to *The Weekend Australian* record a similar disdain. One soldier described his experience of working with the ANA as 'Shithouse, dodgy, dodgy as hell, no trust.'[96] Military photographer, Rachel Ingram, described the ANA troops she worked with as 'like an under six soccer team with weapons.' She told Chris Masters that on 'one patrol she saw an Afghan soldier hiding under a bush the RPGs [Rocket Propelled Grenades] he was supposed to be carrying. He looked at her and said: "too heavy."'[97]

In combat situations the ANA's passivity posed a direct threat to the security of their mentors. In early January 2009 when an OMLT patrol, comprising 18 ANA soldiers and two Australians, led by Lieutenant Ben Gooley, came under heavy RPG and machine-gun fire near Kakarak, the ANA soldiers 'inert as sandbags, offered little to no resistance.'[98] Anxious to support his sergeant, who was pinned down by fire, Gooley 'grabbed the collar of an ANA soldier with a PKM [machine-gun] and tried to drag him forward. But he "curled into a foetal position" and could not be moved.

94 See www.youtube.com/watch?v=wIG3OqWQVFQ&feature=channel.
95 Tom Hyland, 'Death inquiry reveals Afghan troop failings', *The Sunday Age*, 26 July 2009, p.4.
96 Sean Parnell and Rory Callinan, 'Soldiers' despair confronts Defence', *The Weekend Australian* 10–11 July 2010, p.4.
97 Masters, *Uncommon Soldier*, p.203.
98 *Masters, Uncommon Soldier*, p.186.

"Others"', Gooley recalled, '"were digging in with their eyelids."'[99] Scorn for the ANA's loyalty, confidence and capacity stretched from the lively vernacular of the front lines to the bland bureaucratese of officialdom. The Inquiry Officer's report into the death of Corporal Matthew Hopkins, killed in a fire fight near Kakarak on 16 March 2009, notes that: 'Throughout the main part of the contact', which lasted for around 50 minutes, 'there appears to have been limited involvement by the ANA patrol personnel.'[100]

Fears about the capacity of the ANA have been augmented by concerns about their loyalty after a series of so-called 'green on blue' incidents, where Afghan soldiers have shot and killed a number of ISAF servicemen and civilian contractors, among them seven Australians.[101] As a consequence of these attacks, as of November 2012, 'Australian Army bases in Afghanistan have been physically separated from the Afghan National Army to protect the soldiers from their allies' and 'No armed ANA soldiers are allowed on the Australian side.'[102] Despite this obvious, and understandable expression of distrust in the ANA, Lieutenant Colonel Trent Scott, the commanding officer of Forward Operating Base Mirwais, where ADF and Afghan forces were separated by a barbed-wire fence and a locked door, continued to claim

---

99 *Masters, Uncommon Soldier,* p.185.

100 Colonel W.R Hanlon, *Inquiry Officer's Report into the Death of Corporal M.R.A. Hopkins in Afghanistan on 16 March 2009*, Canberra: Department of Defence, 2009, para. 30. A redacted version of the report can be accessed at www.defence.gov.au/coi/index.htm The report notes systemic problems with joint ADF/ANA patrols, that 'planning for operations in support of the ANA lacks certainty due to the disparate nature of the level of ANA BLANK and the BLANK supported commander', Hanlon, 2009: para. 15. It should be noted that though outranked and considerably outnumbered by their Afghan allies, it was the Australian soldiers who took charge of the situation when Corporal Hopkins was fatally wounded. It was the ADF who re-organised the ANA, mounted a fighting defence and called in a medevac chopper for their colleague.

101 The Australian victims of the 'green on blue' attacks are: Andrew Jones (30 May 2011), Bryce Duffy, Ashley Birt, Luke Gavin (29 October 2011), Stjepan Milosevic, Robert Poate, James Martin (30 August 2012). See Brendan Nicholson and Jeremy Kelly, 'Slain Digger Andrew Jones "shot at random"', *The Australian*, 3 June 2011 www.theaustralian.com.au/national-affairs/defence/slain-digger-shot-at-random/story-e6frg8yo-1226068247947.

102 Colin Crosier, 'Walls separate diggers from Afghans', *The Age*, 14 November 2012, www.theage.com.au/national/walls-separate-diggers-from-afghans-20121114-29cou.html In Kandahar US Forces had separated their troops from their allies a little earlier: 'The U.S. military now is employing "guardian angels," armed troops who keep watch whenever American personnel are in the vicinity of Afghan allies. It is erecting higher blast walls and razor wire. U.S. forces are limiting joint operations and constructing separate, armed compounds at bases where they once lived side by side with the Afghan army and police'. David S. Cloud, 'As "insider attacks" grow so does U.S.-Afghanistan divide', *Los Angeles Times*, 7 November 2012, articles.latimes.com/2012/nov/07/world/la-fg-afghan-insider-attacks-20121107.

that 'our troops will carry on with the ANA and our relationship is still good.'[103] Free from the imperative to promote the mission that some ADF officers evidently felt they operated under, a truer picture of the effects on relations between the two militaries was offered by Lieutenant Colonel Patrick Michaelis, a US battalion commander in Kandahar, who observed: 'As we decide whether to do an operation now,' we have to consider, 'is the main risk from the enemy? Or from our own partners?'[104]

An Army of Victims

Back in Australia the ADF's determination to retain a stranglehold over how its personnel are portrayed stretches beyond death, as the case of the repatriation and funeral of Private Benjamin Ranaudo, reveals.[105] In the last days of July 2009 when Private Ranaudo's body was returned to his family at Avalon Airport near Melbourne, a media release from the Department of Defence advised that 'At the request of the family the media will not be invited to attend this solemn event.'[106] Defence media releases, like this one, are notable for their moral and emotional prescription: was there any suggestion from anybody that the return of this man's body would be anything other than 'solemn'? Was the decision to exclude the media related to the 'solemn' nature of the ceremony – was it feared that they could not sustain the designated tone? The next day, in a further media release describing the 'solemn repatriation ceremony', Defence passed on the family's 'request that the media respects their privacy as they grieve their loss and lay Benjamin to rest.'[107] One can hardly complain about this. Intrusive media scrutiny of the family at such a time would have been callous, and the commercial media duly kept their distance. But if the Ranaudos were hoping that the military would safeguard their privacy they were sadly disappointed as Defence and the ADF engineered detailed scrutiny of the body's repatriation and funeral. The Prime Minister, the Minister of Defence, the Minister of Defence Personnel, Materiel and Science, the Chief of the Defence Force, the Deputy Chief of the Army, their entourages and attendants were all at

103 Crosier, 'Walls separate diggers from Afghans', www.theage.com.au/national/walls-separate-diggers-from-afghans-20121114-29cou.html.
104 Cloud, 'As "insider attacks" grow', articles.latimes.com/2012/nov/07/world/la-fg-afghan-insider-attacks-20121107.
105 Though subtle, media releases are still subject to foolish errors. The original Defence Media Release (MSPA 223/09) on 19 July 2009 announcing Private Ranaudo's death spelt his surname incorrectly ('Renaudo').
106 MSPA 233/09.
107 MSPA 234/09.

the funeral, almost outnumbering the dead man's family and friends, and Defence and the ADF ensured that the whole country knew they were there.

To make certain that the public were exposed to and appropriately affected by the 'solemnity' of the repatriation and the funeral, contrary to the express wishes of the family, the military did not exclude the media from either ceremony, they simply invited their own. Both of the press releases I have alluded to above offer details about where and when the moving and still images of the ceremonies captured by the ADF's in-house or approved media would be made available to the media at large. Defence and the military were not opposed to media coverage of the ceremonies *per se*, they simply wanted to ensure that they organised, directed and controlled it so that an appropriately reverent tone was maintained and their version of what the ADF was doing in Afghanistan, and how the men who served and died there should be remembered, would remain unchallenged.

Ironically, the ADF's determination to retain strict control over how it was portrayed had far-reaching and inadvertently negative effects on the broader representation of the war, and thereby on public support for it. Just as Canadian journalists pulled back from reporting on their soldiers in the field to observe the 'death watch' at Kandahar Airfield, so the Australian media, largely excluded from the front lines for the greater portion of the ADF's commitment in Afghanistan have, as a result, tended to focus on the war only when members of the ADF have been killed or seriously wounded. This has narrowed public discussion about the war and distorted the nation's understanding of and responses to it. The focus on Australian casualties has arisen, in part, from the reluctance of the ADF and Defence to say more about what the troops *are* doing – especially when they are engaged in dangerous or controversial operations. This problem has been compounded by the fact that those members of the ADF who were doing the most exciting work, the Special Forces soldiers, notorious for their 'dread of ink over blood,' were inaccessible to the media.[108] Those who were accessible, the members of the various Mentoring and Reconstruction Task Forces, were mostly carrying out the well intentioned work of nation building, mentoring members of the ANSF, sinking wells, building schools, training Afghans in basic trades and drinking lots of tea with community elders. While this is worthy work it is also earnest and dull, and in the nature of most counter-

108 Masters, *Uncommon Soldier*, p.91. Chris Masters did manage a first when he persuaded the CDF to allow him to accompany and report on the actions of Special Forces. See *Uncommon Soldier*, pp.254–6, 287–332.

insurgency activities produces little to excite the editor or stimulate the public interest.[109]

For the greater part of a decade 'at least half of Australia's Afghanistan story ... the other story, of the fight being taken to the Taliban ... had gone untold' and, as a consequence, the public had little idea of just how aggressive the ADF campaign had been .[110] Chris Masters notes that 'In 2007 alone, Australian Special Forces killed and identified more than 400 Taliban.'[111] Four years later, in May 2011, the *West Australian* reported that 'Australian forces have killed about 1500 insurgents in the past 12 months, during some of the most vicious fighting seen by the military since the Vietnam War.'[112] Perhaps surprisingly the ADF 'drew no attention' to these numbers, while the men responsible for them were 'determinedly off limits' to the media.[113] The resulting focus on the casualties suffered by the ADF rather than those they had inflicted ensured that the only body count the public became familiar with was our own. In parliament, where there is bipartisan support for the deployment, the conflict has most often attracted broader public attention when the Prime Minister rises to lead a condolence motion. Over the succeeding days, in a now familiar choreography of collective grief, the media reveal more about the age, marital status, dependents, affiliations and personal qualities of the casualty ('the fallen'), before focusing on the formal farewelling of the body from Afghanistan ('sombre procession'), its repatriation to Australia ('solemn ramp ceremony'), and the funeral, with full military honours ('flag-draped coffin ... an awaiting gun carriage'), attended by the nation's most senior political and military officials ('supreme sacrifice'). In the light of this focus on the ADF's losses, and the archaic and discredited vocabulary used to commemorate them, 'It is not hard to understand why a sense of Australians as more victim than victor had formed', and why, as a result, so many Australians opposed the war.[114]

Underpinning this narrative of victimhood, politicians and service chiefs routinely describe the death of Australia's soldiers in Afghanistan as 'tragic.'

---

109 As Thomas Rid and Mark Hecker have observed: 'effective counterinsurgency is a game much less attention-grabbing and much more resource-consuming than effective insurgency'. Thomas Rid and Mark Hecker, *War 2.0: Irregular Warfare in the Information Age*, Westport CT: Praeger Security International, 2009, p.3.

110 *Masters, Uncommon Soldier*, p.255.

111 *Masters, Uncommon Soldier*, p.14

112 Andrew Probyn and Nick Butterly, 'Enemy toll as high as 1500', *The West Australian*, 25 May 2011, http://au.news.yahoo.com/thewest/a/-/national/9509508/enemy-toll-as-high-as-1500/ accessed 20 February 2013.

113 Masters, *Uncommon Soldier*, pp.14, 255.

114 Masters, *Uncommon Soldier*, p.14.

Nobody doubts that the deaths of these men are a dreadful blow to their families, friends and colleagues – but 'tragic' for the nation as a whole? A little under half of Australia's casualties in Afghanistan have been Special Forces personnel who spend their days getting into rip-snorting fire fights with the enemy and their nights ambushing Taliban commanders and bomb-makers. Every one of them knows and embraces the risks of serving in Afghanistan. Death, for these men, is not an unforeseen or unexpected visitation, it is an occupational hazard – no more a tragedy than are broken bones for a jockey or damaged knees for a professional footballer. The limited access to the area of operations that the Australian media endured for so long has ensured that the deployment in Afghanistan is framed and understood principally within the context of death and its ceremonial acknowledgement. The attendant lexicon of religious sanctification, with its solemn absolutes and moral certainties, makes any discussion of the war – let alone questioning or dissent – however respectful, seem discourteous, if not sacrilegious. When Tom Hyland published an article in June 2011 questioning the coverage of military funerals and the language employed by the media in doing so, he was at great pains to make it clear that he intended no disrespect: 'I'm trying to tread carefully here.'[115] As a consequence, the dominant narrative context within which Australians have experienced and understood the war in Afghanistan has ensured that there can be no considered, rational, mature discussion about its aims, viability, conduct or results.

Self-Censorship

Throughout the course of the war in Afghanistan, at the very time that reporters and editors should have been leading – or at least prompting – a national conversation about the ADF's role and purposes there, they were distracted by the greatest crisis confronting the mainstream media in its modern history – the demise of its traditional funding model. As Gideon Haigh has noted: 'The effect of the internet [on the mainstream media] has been as profound as it would have been on any oligopoly suddenly confronted by overpowering quantities of high-quality, real-time content priced at zero. It has shivered markets to fragments, atomized and energized audiences, and gnawed business models away at each end, impacting newspapers' abilities both to attract advertising and to charge for news, winnowing television

115 Tom Hyland, 'Media squabbles miss the real question about war', *The Sunday Age*, 5 June 2011, p.19.

audiences away and eroding vulnerable network balance sheets.' [116] This assault on the media industry's conventional sources of funding threw it into turmoil and led to massive job losses among editorial staff.[117] Figures from the Australian Bureau of Statistics indicate that in the five years between 2006 and 2011 the newspaper industry shed almost 13 per cent of its workforce.[118] The Media Entertainment and Arts Alliance, the main trade union for media employees, estimated that over the winter of 2012, 1 in 7 journalism jobs disappeared.[119] Foreign bureaux were closed down or mothballed, specialist reporters with foreign and defence experience took redundancy packages and their expertise was lost to the industry.[120] As a consequence, the mainstream media in Australia today employs only a handful of dedicated defence correspondents.[121]

These broader economic circumstances clearly impacted the media's capacity to report on the war in Afghanistan. Already 'one of the toughest assignments on the media horizon', Chris Masters notes that under the more straitened circumstances of the current funding crisis, the truth about what was happening in Afghanistan was 'harder than usual to come by.'[122] While Government and Defence routinely spun the news to 'shape and misshape the truth' for their own ends and the ADF maintained its stranglehold over access to and freedom of movement within the area of operations, it became increasingly apparent to journalists that the 'lack of evidence based coverage' of what Australian forces were doing in Afghanistan was 'not only down to the ADF being obstructive.'[123] Journalists

---

116 Haigh, *The Deserted Newsroom*, p.2.

117 In June 2012, Fairfax Media, owners of the *Sydney Morning Herald* and *The Age* announced 1900 job losses, including 380 journalists. News Limited cut 500 editorial positions in 2012. Peter Trute, 'News Limited announces redundancies', *Sydney Morning Herald*, 6 December 2012.

118 Australian Bureau of Statistics, 'Graphic Designer – the most popular cultural occupation', *Employment in Culture*, Australia 2011, Media Release, 20 December 2012.

119 See www.alliance.org.au/news-limited-redundancies-should-be-the-last.

120 Early in 2013 *Crikey* reported that *The Australian* was soon to close its London, Washington and Tokyo bureaux, while Fairfax was also looking to close its London bureau having mothballed its Kabul office. See Matthew Knott, 'Foreign bureau get the chop as News, Fairfax cut costs', *Crikey*, 9 January, 2013. media.crikey.com.au/dm/newsletter/dailymail_e034edb700ec5d29edf45c4d76b17320.html article_22103 Accessed 9 January 2013.

121 They include Max Blenkin at AAP, Ian McPhedran at News Limited, Brendan Nicholson at *The Australian*, Dylan Welch and David Wroe at Fairfax, Nick Butterly at WA News, Hugh Riminton at Channel Ten, and a few others.

122 Masters, *Uncommon Soldier*, p.207.

123 Masters, *Uncommon Soldier*, p.207; Masters, 'The Media's Left and Right of Arc,' p.37. Hot issues briefs are 'two or three-page reports provided to senior Defence staff and Defence Minister, Stephen Smith, about issues considered politically sensitive

recognised that among the newspapers and broadcasters they served, 'editorial commitment' to reporting the war was 'weak' and there was 'no appetite for sustained and detailed coverage except when there was an extraordinary event.'[124] This was evidenced in both incidental and more substantial demonstrations of the media's reluctance to vigorously pursue the story. In some cases media organisations were disinclined to meet the full costs of transporting or insuring reporters who went to cover the war.[125] In others they baulked at the bonuses and allowances to which their employees were entitled. Chris Masters recalled that while the ADF applied a maximum threat level to Afghanistan, thereby entitling its personnel to an extra $141.36 per day, tax free, when he notified his superiors that he and his film crew would be travelling to Uruzgan to make a documentary 'the ABC asked that we take a reduced travel allowance, advancing the rationale that we would have no use for it.'[126] More damningly, over the course of the conflict the media were loath to invest in the requisite personnel or resources to ensure that the public had access to sustained and comprehensive coverage. For more than nine years no Australian media outlet stationed a permanent correspondent in Afghanistan. This situation was finally rectified in January 2011 when the ABC opened a Kabul bureau headed by Sally Sara. Yet when her posting ended twelve months later the national broadcaster promptly mothballed the office.[127] In the absence of a permanent cadre of well-informed specialists, coverage of the war was left to a shifting band of differently qualified reporters who, in the main, dropped in on brief embeds before leaving the country, and their readers, little wiser about the conflict than they were before. As a consequence of these arrangements the greater portion of the reporting from Afghanistan struggled to illuminate the war's complex origins, geography and alliances, falling back on the reliable staples of death, injury and the occasional scandal.

In the domestic reporting context Tom Hyland recalled that there was a subtle but determined resistance among his editors to stories about the

---

or potentially embarrassing' (Dylan Welch and Tom Hyland, 'Defence releases over 100 documents on "hot issues."' *The Age*, 21 January 2012, http://www.theage.com.au/national/defence-releases-over-100-documents-on-hot-issues-20120120-1qacl.html accessed 9 March, 2013).

124 Masters, 'The Media's Left and Right of Arc', p.37; author telephone interview with Tom Hyland, 19 December 2012.

125 Nick Butterly notes that 'insurance is a killer for newspapers going to Afghanistan', Logue, *Herding Cats*, p.47.

126 Masters, *Uncommon Soldier*, p.219.

127 Masters regarded this situation as 'a scandal'. Masters, 'The Media's Left and Right of Arc', p.37.

war that went beyond the conventional narratives of death and commemoration: 'I was never told, "I'm not going to run that story." But I was told that I'd struggle to get onto page one.'[128] When one of his Afghan stories made it to the front page his editor pointed out that casual sales of that day's edition were down on figures from previous weeks. The message was clear: as far as the paper's editors were concerned, the public was not interested in the war in Afghanistan. Hyland's editor was not expressing a purely personal prejudice here. Fairfax had undertaken a considerable amount of market research and focus group work in an effort to better understand the mood, psychology and motivations of the Sunday newspaper buyer. One of the principal findings of this research was that 'Sunday newspaper readers didn't want to be troubled.'[129] It was the editor's responsibility to ensure that these readers were free to wander the enchanted glades of fashion, food and celebrity gossip untroubled by revenants from the world of realpolitik, to keep the war out of the paper, or where it unavoidably featured, to steer it off the front page. As such, it is clear that if the public was ill-informed about the basic facts of the war in Afghanistan this ignorance was consciously engineered and that it owed as much to the Australian media's hindrance of its own reporters as it did to the ADF's efforts to censor them.

But just how ill-informed about the origins, progress and purposes of the war was the Australian public? Is there a necessary correlation between limited access to straitened sources of information about the war and the public's understanding of why the ADF was in Afghanistan and what it was doing there? The following chapter will consider how media coverage of the war shaped and was itself informed by public opinion. It will examine the public opinion polling that has been carried out and consider who measured it, how often they did so, how widely their polls were disseminated and with what – if any – measurable effects. It will examine how public opinion was informed by the media's obsessive focus on casualties, and what its responses to these deaths and injuries reveal about the public's grasp of why Australian forces were in Afghanistan. It will consider how political bipartisanship on the war shaped media coverage of it, how this stifled broader public debate about the conflict, deafening politicians, the military and the media to the voices of the rank and file servicemen and women who bore the burden of the fighting, and of the people in whose name they did so.

128 Author interview with Hyland, 19 December 2012.
129 Author interview with Hyland, 19 December 2012.

Chapter 5

PUBLIC OPINION AND POLITICAL DEBATE

Casualty Tolerance

In Australia, major media and polling organisations ordinarily conduct large scale, scientifically credible public opinion polls on a weekly, bi-weekly and monthly basis. The weekly polls are conducted by Essential Media and Communications (EMC), bi-weekly polling is conducted by Newspoll for News Corp media outlets, and Nielsen conducts a monthly poll for 10 months of the year in association with Fairfax. These are supplemented by less-scientific internet, SMS and phone-in polls run on an almost daily basis by broadcasters, the metropolitan press and online media outlets. Daily polls can be found in, among others, the *Herald Sun*, and on the ABC's 24-hour radio news service, *News Radio*. The more scientific polls focus, almost exclusively, on the performance of the major political parties and their leaders as refracted through topical issues. Political parties and the media follow the ebb and flow of the numbers with intense interest, as the stakes could not be higher. Bad polling results can, and have, brought down Prime Ministers.[1] Contemporary scientific polling advertises the reliability of its numbers, ensuring representative participation by gender, age group, and state. Yet for all its claims to demographic validity and the authority this purportedly brings its data, the opinion poll, as Murray Goot and Rodney Tiffen note:

---

1 This was evidenced most recently in the fall of then Prime Minister Julia Gillard in June 2013, who had herself engineered the toppling of her predecessor, Kevin Rudd. The move against Rudd was stimulated, in part, by a dramatic fall in the ALP's popularity as reflected in a number of opinion polls taken at the time, most notably, a *Sydney Morning Herald*/Nielsen poll published on 7 June 2010 which showed that 'The Rudd government would be wiped out if an election were held today', Philip Coorey, 'Labor faces wipeout', *Sydney Morning Herald*, 7 June 2010 www.smh.com.au/national/labor-faces-wipeout-20100606-xn7v.html accessed 22 February 2013.

> is a peculiarly dependent, fragile and at the same time artificial and limited form of social knowledge. Nothing else gives such an authoritative map of the sentiments, values and attitudes of the nation. But its only reality is limited to a set of responses ... usually designed to provide short, simple stories for the press. Typically, it does not distinguish between those with an interest in the question and those without; between intense and casual opinion, or informed opinion and the ignorant. Nor does it probe the qualifications and contingencies which may attend answers to seemingly straightforward questions. The picture of opinion can vary markedly with apparently minor changes in the wording of questions, with the ways in which responses are channelled into pre-determined categories and in response to changes in events. No set of data ever represents a comprehensive or 'pure' view of public opinion, and in interpreting poll results close attention must be paid to the timing of polls and the nature of the questions asked.[2]

Nowhere in contemporary Australia is the contingent nature of the social knowledge afforded by opinion polls clearer than in the measurement and reception of public opinion about the war in Afghanistan. Relative to many of its coalition partners in Afghanistan, Australian polling on the war has been 'scarce and scattered', and its results 'frustratingly contradictory.'[3] Academics, pollsters and the media have rarely investigated the sample to distinguish between intense and casual opinion, between informed views and ignorant prejudice, to explore the contingencies and qualifications implicit in apparently straightforward responses – indeed the data the polls have yielded has scarcely been examined at all. Despite – if not because of – the absence of such scholarly analysis, the polling has been used mostly to furnish a blunt measurement of public approval for the war.

Despite the shallow and intermittent nature of the polling and the limited uses to which it has been put, a closer analysis of the data it has produced suggests that public responses to the conflict are more nuanced and subtle than politicians, the military and the media have been prepared to acknowledge. The data, examined longitudinally and in fine detail,

---

2 Murray Goot and Rodney Tiffen, 'Public opinion and the politics of the polls', *Australia's Vietnam: Australia in the Second Indo-China War*, ed. Peter King, Sydney: Allen and Unwin. 1983, p.129.

3 Charles A. Miller, *Endgame for the West in Afghanistan? Explaining the Decline in Support for the War in Afghanistan in the United States, Great Britain, Canada, Australia, France and Germany*, Carlisle, PA: Strategic Studies Institute, 2010, p.36. Miller complained about the paucity of Australian data.

reveals that while Australians are inclined to back the men and women on the ground almost unconditionally, their grasp of why the ADF is in Afghanistan and what it is likely to achieve there is surprisingly sophisticated. However, as this reading of the polls contradicts the 'short, simple stories' of the war promulgated in parliament and the media, it has been largely ignored.

On 4 June 2012, the Lowy Institute for Public Policy, Australia's premier independent international policy think tank, released its eighth annual *Australia and the World* poll examining Australians' opinions about *Public Opinion and Foreign Policy*.[4] The poll, undertaken between 26 March and 10 April 2011 by Field Works Market Research, was based on 1005 interviews conducted by telephone. With quotas in place for age, gender, state and territory the 'sample was designed to be nationally representative of all Australians 18 years and older.'[5] Alongside data on public attitudes towards foreign investment in Australian farms, selling uranium to India, relations with Fiji, the tenth anniversary of the Bali bombings and the prospect of US troops being based in the Northern Territory, the poll offered – as it has since 2007 – a measurement of public opinion on the nation's military engagement in Afghanistan. Since 2007, the first year that questions about the war in Afghanistan were included in the survey, one question has consistently featured in the poll:

Q. Should Australia continue to be involved militarily in Afghanistan?[6]

	2012	2011	2010	2009	2008	2007
Yes	33%	40%	43%	46%	42%	46%
No	65%	59%	54%	51%	56%	46%
Don't Know	2%	2%	4%	3%	2%	8%
Refused	N/A	N/A	N/A	N/A	N/A	1%

4 The 2012 poll, for the first time, included data from and about New Zealand. From 2006 to 2011 the poll data was sourced and focused on responses solely from Australia.

5 Fergus Hanson, *The Lowy Institute Poll 2012: Australia and New Zealand in the World: Public Opinion and Foreign Policy*, Sydney: Lowy Institute for International Policy, 2012, p.31.

6 Hanson, *Australia in the World*, 2012, p.19. Reflecting Australia's imminent withdrawal from Afghanistan, the 2013 Poll replaced this longstanding query with a new question: 'All in all, considering the costs to Australia versus the benefits to Australia, do you personally think the war in Afghanistan has been worth fighting, or not worth fighting?' Alex Oliver, *The Lowy Institute Poll 2013: Australia and the World: Public Opinion and Foreign Policy*, Sydney: Lowy Institute for International Policy, 2013, p.21.

The 2012 results reveal that public support for the deployment had fallen to a new low of 33 per cent, down 7 per cent on 2011, and a full 10 per cent on the 2010 figure, with an increasing majority opposed to the troop commitment. In 2012, 65 per cent of Australians disagreed with the proposition that the nation's armed forces should 'continue to be involved militarily in Afghanistan', an increase of 6 per cent from 2011, 11 per cent from 2010 and 14 per cent from 2009.[7]

At first glance these numbers look quite straightforward, confirming a solid, sustained and, since 2008, steadily increasing majority opposed to Australia's engagement in Afghanistan. When they are put in the context of ADF casualties over this period the numbers tell a more nuanced story, laying bare the complex nature of Australian public opinion about the war. In his study of the correlation between casualties and popular support for the Korean and Vietnam Wars, John E. Mueller noted that while Americans were 'sensitive to relatively small losses in the early stages' of the wars, by the later stages 'only large losses' registered.[8] He identified an algorithmic relationship between casualties and public support, noting that 'every time American casualties increased by a factor of 10 (i.e., from 100 to 1,000 or from 10,000 to 100,000) support for the war dropped by about 15 percentage points.'[9] Needless to say, no such research has so far been undertaken in relation to Australian public support for the war in Afghanistan, or for any war in which Australia has been involved.

A closer analysis of public responses to ADF casualties as measured through opinion polls not only suggests that Mueller's formulations do not carry across to Australia, but that they might be reversed – that the public has been more sensitive to smaller losses later in the war. In the thirteen months that elapsed between the interviews for the 2007 and 2008 polls, when the ADF lost five men in Afghanistan, support for the nation's commitment of troops fell from 46 per cent to 42 per cent, while opposition to continued deployment rose 10 per cent from 46 per cent to 56 per cent.[10] Confoundingly, in the twelve months between the 2008 and 2009 polls, when the ADF suffered a further five fatalities in Afghanistan, support for the nation's military engagement grew from

---

7 Hanson, *Australia in the World*, 2012, p.19.

8 John E. Mueller, 'Trends in Popular Support for the Wars in Korea and Vietnam', *The American Political Science Review*, Vol. 65, No. 2 (June 1971), p.367.

9 Mueller, 'Trends in Popular Support', p.366.

10 The five fatalities between the 2007 and 2008 polls were: David Pearce (9 October 2007), Matthew Lock (25 October 2007), Luke Worsley (23 November 2007), Jason Marks (28 April 2008), and Sean McCarthy (11 July 2008).

42 per cent to 46 per cent and opposition to the deployment fell from 56 per cent to 51 per cent.[11] This figure is more remarkable when one considers that one of the fatalities, that of Private Benjamin Ranaudo, occurred on 19 July 2009, during the period between 13 and 25 July 2009 when polling was taking place.[12] There were no deaths between the release of the 2009 and 2010 polls when support for the war fell 3 per cent from 46 per cent to 43 per cent and opposition to Australia's continued engagement grew by a corresponding amount from 51 per cent to 54 per cent. Between 31 May 2010 and 28 June 2011, when the 2010 and 2011 polls were released, the ADF lost 16 men, five more than the total number of casualties it had suffered over the course of its decade long commitment in Afghanistan, with 12 of these occurring before the polling was completed between 30 March and 14 April 2011.[13] In the succeeding twelve month period, between 29 June 2011 and 4 June 2012, when the 2012 poll was released, the ADF suffered a further 12 casualties.[14] Despite the sharp rise in combat deaths between 2010 and 2011, support for the commitment contracted by a modest 3 per cent, as it had between 2009 and 2010, while opposition to the ADF deployment grew at a moderate but increasing pace, growing by 3 per cent between 2009 and 2010, and 5 per cent from 2010 to 2011. Overall, between 2007 and 2011, opposition to ADF participation in the war increased by a total of 13 per cent, from 46 per cent to 59 per cent, while support for the presence of Australian forces declined at a steady, though slower, rate, falling only 6 per cent in the five years since 2007, from 46 per cent to 40 per cent.

---

11 The five fatalities between the 2008 and 2009 polls were: Michael Fussell (27 November 2008), Gregory Sher (4 January 2009), Matthew Hopkins (16 March 2009), Brett Till (19 March 2009), and Benjamin Ranaudo (19 July 2009).

12 Fergus Hanson, *The Lowy Institute Poll 2009: Australia and the World: Public Opinion and Foreign Policy*, Sydney: Lowy Institute for International Policy, 2009, p.29.

13 The sixteen fatalities between 31 May 2010 and 28 June 2011 were: Jacob Moerland (7 June 2010), Darren Smith (7 June 2010). Tim Aplin (21 June 2010), Ben Chuck (21 June 2010), Scott Palmer (21 June 2010), Nathan Bewes (9 July 2010), Jason Brown (13 August 2010), Grant Kirby (20 August 2010), Thomas Dale (20 August 2010), Jared MacKinney (24 August 2010), Richard Atkinson (2 February 2011), Jamie Larcombe (19 February 2011), Brett Wood (23 May 2011), Andrew Jones (30 May 2011), Marcus Case (30 May 2011), Rowan Robinson (6 June 2011).

14 The twelve casualties between 29 June 2011 and 4 June 2012 were: Todd Langley (4 July 2011), Matthew Lambert (22 August 2011), Bryce Duffy, Ashley Birt, Luke Gavin (29 October 2011), Blaine Diddams (2 July 2012), Nathaniel Gallagher, Mervyn McDonald, Stjepan Milosevic, Robert Poate, James Martin (30 August 2012), Scott Smith (21 October 2012). The victims of the green on blue attacks were Duffy, Birt, Gavin, Milosevic, Poate and Martin.

Though there were fewer fatalities between 2011 and 2012 than there had been in the preceding year, support for continued involvement in the war fell by 7 per cent, more than double the number in each of the preceding years, while opposition to the war grew by 6 per cent, double the increase from 2009 to 2010. What made the fatalities between 2011 and 2012 different was that half of them were inflicted in 'green on blue' attacks by the ADF's putative allies in the ANSF. This would seem to suggest that casualties deliberately inflicted by the ADF's allies produce a more direct effect on public measures of support and opposition to the war than those inflicted by the Taliban in the normal course of patrolling or battle, not least because they seemed to challenge the fundamental rationale for the Australian presence in Afghanistan – to help the local people reclaim their country from terrorism and put it on the road to security self-sufficiency. Yet as we will see below, this conclusion is not borne out by the data from other opinion polls. Accordingly, the most that one can reasonably deduce from these figures is that while public tolerance of casualties may be a factor in broader measures of approval and disapproval of the conflict, there seems to be no straightforward correlation between the numbers or the causes of ADF losses and overall public support for or opposition to the war.

Opinion polls taken in the immediate wake of Australian fatalities often register an extreme response to losses, though these aberrant indicators soon moderate. For example, between 7 June and 9 July 2010, within a week of the release of the 2010 Lowy Poll, the ADF suffered six fatalities in Afghanistan, with a further four deaths between 14 and 24 August, almost doubling the nation's total losses to that point from 11 to 21. Responses to the first of these casualties were measured in an opinion poll released on 21 June by Essential Media Communications in its weekly 'Essential Report', where it repeated the questions it had last posed in a March 2009 poll regarding the nation's engagement in Afghanistan.[15]

15 There was a minor amendment to one of the questions. The 2009 poll had asked: 'do you think Australia should – Increase the number of troops in Afghanistan *if asked by the US*' (Essential Research, *Essential Report*, 30 March 2009, p.5) (my italics).

Q. Thinking about the Australian troops in Afghanistan, do you think Australia should –[16]

	Total	Vote Labor	Vote Lib/Nat	March 09
Increase the number of troops in Afghanistan	7%	7%	7%	14%
Keep the same number of troops in Afghanistan	24%	25%	32%	24%
Withdraw our troops from Afghanistan	61%	61%	55%	50%
Don't know	8%	7%	6%	12%

The striking increase in those committed to the withdrawal of troops, from 50 per cent in March 2009 to 61 per cent fifteen months later, attracted considerable media attention, featuring in a number of editorials and opinion pieces by lead political writers.[17] At the end of a fortnight when five Australian servicemen lost their lives – the poll was released on the same day that three Special Forces soldiers were killed in a helicopter accident – the results suggested a significant deepening of opposition to the war.[18] When EMC next polled its respondents on their reactions to the war in Afghanistan five months later, on 11 October, 2010, a steep fall in the numbers calling for the withdrawal of the ADF, from 61 per cent to 49 per cent, suggested that the June figure was a knee-jerk response to a sudden spate of losses and an aberration in the overall trend – an interpretation backed up in subsequent polls conducted later in October 2010, in March 2011 and May 2011.

Between 9 May and 29 August, 2011, when EMC released its next poll results on Afghanistan, the ADF lost six men.[19] The results of this are

---

16 Essential Research, *Essential Report*, 21 June 2010, p.9.

17 See Editorial, *The Age* 23 June 2010, p.16; Daniel Flitton, 'Divided We Stand', *The Age* 23 June 2010, p.15; Michelle Grattan, 'Poll shows most want our troops withdrawn', *The Age* 22 June 2010, p.6.

18 The main difference between the results of the June 2010 and the March 2009 Essential Media polls is a fall of 7 per cent in those keen to increase numbers in Afghanistan, and a 4 per cent fall in the 'Don't knows'. In the 2010 figures these 11 per cent combine to add their weight to the numbers calling for withdrawal – those committed to maintaining the same number of troops has remained steady at 24 per cent. What this means is that 50 per cent of those formerly committed to the more aggressive prosecution of the war now favour complete withdrawal. It would seem that those looking for an immediate improvement in conditions in Afghanistan as a result of the ISAF intervention have lost faith in the coalition's chances of achieving victory and now seek that visible effect through withdrawal.

19 The six ADF casualties between 9 May and 29 August were Brett Wood (23 May 2011), Andrew Jones (30 May 2011), Marcus Case (30 May 2011), Rowan Robinson (6 June 2011), Todd Langley (4 July 2011), Matthew Lambert (22 August 2011).

reflected, predictably, in a sharp increase in those committed to the withdrawal of Australian forces from Afghanistan, from 48 per cent to 64 per cent and a commensurate fall in those supporting the maintenance of existing numbers from 36 per cent to 26 per cent.

Q. Thinking about the Australian troops in Afghanistan, do you think Australia should –[20]

	29 Aug 2011	9 May 2011	21 Mar 2011	25 Oct 2010	11 Oct 2010	21 June 2010	March 2009
Increase the number of troops in Afghanistan	4%	6%	5%	10%	13%	7%	14%
Keep the same number of troops in Afghanistan	26%	36%	30%	30%	24%	24%	24%
Withdraw our troops from Afghanistan	64%	48%	56%	47%	49%	61%	50%
Don't know	7%	11%	9%	14%	14%	8%	12%

Of the six men killed between 9 May and 29 August 2011, two were the victims of IED blasts, two were shot in fire fights with the Taliban, one was the victim of a helicopter accident and one, Andrew Jones, was shot, or 'murdered', by a 'rogue' member of the ANA.[21] On 29 October 2011 a further three ADF personnel were killed by another 'rogue' ANA soldier in another green on blue attack.[22] Little more than a week later, on 8 November 2011, three more ADF troops were wounded at their base in the Charmestan Valley by yet another 'rogue' Afghan soldier. The death of Australian servicemen was one thing: the killing of them by their putative allies, the very people they were there to assist, was another. The measurable effects of this view in the data are mirrored in broader media and public responses. As one letter to the *Herald Sun* noted: 'If our soldiers are not treated with respect by the Afghan military and government, they should not be putting their lives on the line.'[23]

20 Essential Research, *Essential Report*, 9 May 2011, p.11.
21 Ian McPhedran, 'Cook Lance Corporal Andrew Jones killed by a coward in Afghanistan', *Daily Telegraph* (Sydney), 18 June 2011.
22 The three men killed on 29 October 2011 were Ashley Birt, Bryce Duffy and Luke Gavin.
23 Letters, *Herald Sun*, 2 June 2011.

The then Prime Minister, Julia Gillard, conceded that the attacks 'corroded' trust between Australian and Afghan forces.[24] Editors, correspondents and experts queued up to express their disdain for the mentoring and liaison strategy that seemed to have comprehensively failed. Two days after the killing of Andrew Jones, the headline of the nation's largest selling daily paper, Melbourne's *Herald Sun,* identified the ANA as the 'ENEMY WITHIN', while in an opinion piece in *The Age*, headlined 'RATS IN THE RANKS', Rafael Epstein and the paper's then Defence correspondent, Dan Oakes, acknowledged that 'After the killing of Lance-Corporal Andrew Jones, some are asking if Australian soldiers working with Afghan forces are training tomorrow's terrorists.'[25] Phone-in polling echoed these opinions, revealing a dramatic spike in opposition to Australia's continued engagement in the war. When, on 1 June 2011, the *Herald Sun* asked its readers, 'Should Australia withdraw its troops from Afghanistan?' 81.5 per cent of those who responded by telephone did so with a 'Yes'.[26] However, it is notable that more scientific opinion polls undertaken by EMC over this period and published on 21 November 2011 and 19 March 2012 show little evidence of any dramatic increase in opposition to the war – indeed the number committed to the withdrawal of Australian troops remained at 64 per cent in all three polls, with only a 4 per cent decrease in support for maintaining troop numbers at their current levels, from 26 per cent in August 2011 to 22 per cent in November 2011 and March 2012.

Q. Thinking about the Australian troops in Afghanistan, do you think Australia should –[27]

	19 March 2012	21 Nov 2011	29 Aug 2011
Increase the number of troops in Afghanistan	4%	3%	4%
Keep the same number of troops in Afghanistan	22%	22%	26%
Withdraw our troops from Afghanistan	64%	64%	64%
Don't know	10%	11%	7%

24 Julian Drape, 'Attacks on diggers "corrodes" trust: PM', *Sydney Morning Herald*, 9 November 2011.

25 *Herald Sun*, 1 June 2011; Rafael Epstein and Dan Oakes, 'RATS IN THE RANKS', *The Age* 2 June 2011.

26 'Voteline', *Herald Sun*, 2 June 2011.

27 Essential Research, *Essential Report*, 21 November 2011, 4; 19 March 2012, p.4.

Most striking, though, were the results of the polls in the wake of the events of 30 August 2012, when the Australian army suffered its 'darkest day since Vietnam', losing two men in a helicopter accident and three more 'murdered by [an] Afghan traitor' in another green on blue attack.[28] In a rare show of unity, the national media registered a common sense of shock and outrage. *The Age* described a 'DAY OF TRAGEDY', noting in its front page headline that the 'Death of five Diggers stuns the nation.'[29] On the front page of the *Herald Sun* an Australian Army badge sat amid headlines reflecting anger, disbelief and despair at the day's losses: 'TRAGEDY IN AFGHANISTAN,' '5 LOST HEROES – OUR DARKEST DAY,' 'DIGGERS BETRAYED AGAIN.'[30] As a measure of the gravity of the situation the Prime Minister immediately flew back from the Pacific Islands Forum in the Cook Islands to be briefed by Defence chiefs. However, polling data reveals that the public were less prone to such emotional outpourings. When, on 31 August 2012, the *Herald Sun* repeated the poll question it had last asked fifteen months earlier in the wake of the first green on blue fatality, 'Should Australia withdraw its troops from Afghanistan?' despite having just suffered its 'darkest day on the battlefield since the Vietnam War,' only 836 people bothered to phone in, of whom 614, or 74 per cent, answered in the affirmative – a notable decrease from the 81.5 per cent who had voted 'Yes' to the same question in June 2011.[31] Further, of the four people stopped for a 'vox pop' on the question 'Is it time to pull our troops out of Afghanistan', one thought 'No', one 'Yes', while two were 'Not sure'. The subjects of the interviews were two men and two women aged between 39 and 69, and their longer responses fill out the ambivalence behind simple 'Yes', 'No', 'Not sure' measures of opinion: 'I still think they are doing some good so I think they should maybe stay, but I am unsure as to how long.'[32] This equivocal response was borne out in the Essential Poll of 10 September 2012. Though the data for the poll was collected less than a week after 'Australia's darkest 24 hours of military horror in almost 50 years', neither the casualties, nor the media's outrage at the insider attacks seem to have influenced the public's responses.[33] In fact support for keeping the same number of troops in Afghanistan rose

28 Brendan Nicholson and Amanda Hodge, 'Five fall in darkest day for army since Vietnam', *The Australian*, 31 August 2012, p.1.

29 *The Age*, 31 August 2012, p.1.

30 *Herald Sun*, 31 August 2012, p.1.

31 Dylan Welch, 'Defiant PM vows to stay the course', *The Age*, 31 August 2012, p.1; *Herald Sun*, 3 September 2012, p.22.

32 *Herald Sun*, 3 September 2012, p.23.

33 Patrick Lion, 'Death in the night for Diggers', *Herald Sun*, 31 August 2012, p.4.

by 1 per cent, while those committed to the withdrawal of the troops fell by 2 per cent. The data thus suggests that though the media were up in arms about the latest casualties the public was less perturbed than it had been by earlier losses.[34]

Q. Thinking about the Australian troops in Afghanistan, do you think Australia should –[35]

	10 Sept 2012	19 Mar 2012	21 Nov 2011	29 Aug 2011	9 May 2011	21 June 2010
Increase the number of troops in Afghanistan	4%	4%	3%	4%	6%	7%
Keep the same number of troops in Afghanistan	23%	22%	22%	26%	36%	24%
Withdraw our troops from Afghanistan	62%	64%	64%	64%	48%	61%
Don't know	11%	10%	11%	7%	11%	8%

These poll numbers raise the question that if the Australian public's gradually growing disenchantment with the war was not driven by rising casualty figures or treacherous Afghans, then what was fuelling it? Charles A. Miller notes that the first Australian polls showing majority opposition to the war appeared in 2008 after the ADF had suffered only 5 casualties. He compares this with the figures from the Canadians, one of our closest comparator militaries in terms of troop commitment, mission and location in Afghanistan: 'By the time Canada had passed the same threshold as a percentage of their total military forces, Canadian support was at the same level it had been in the immediate aftermath of 9/11.'[36] Miller offers two explanations for the apparent timorousness of Australian public opinion in the face of casualties: 'Either Australia has a lower preexisting casualty tolerance than Canada, which is unlikely, or Australian casualties had a heavier effect on public opinion because they came at a later stage of the operation, when the prospects for the war had worsened. In either event, casualties alone cannot account for the difference.'[37]

34 Prominent among those advocating swift withdrawal from Afghanistan was the Foreign Editor of *The Australian*, Greg Sheridan; see 'Over-exposed, over-sacrificed … and over it', *The Australian*, 31 August 2012, p.4.

35 Essential Research, *Essential Report* 10 September 2012, p.7.

36 Miller, *Endgame for the West in Afghanistan?* p.36.

37 Miller, *Endgame for the West in Afghanistan?* p.37.

Miller may be correct in arguing that falling support coincides with and stimulates the growing conviction that the war is un-winnable and that every casualty magnifies this view. The fact that the greater number of ADF losses (11 from 2002–2009, 29 from 2010–2013) have come over the last four years, after almost a decade of ISAF engagement in Afghanistan with little tangible progress to show for it, would tend to support this assertion, thereby reversing Mueller's thesis that in the latter stages of a conflict only larger losses register. I would propose a further, allied explanation for the Australian public's earlier arrival at majority opposition to the conflict, which, drawing on a comparison between Australian, Dutch and Canadian media coverage of the war, suggests a direct relationship between public opinion and public information about the conflict. As noted in Chapter 3, the greater portion of the news that Australians have received from Afghanistan has been gathered not by independent reporters but the military's own uniformed public affairs personnel. The Australian media's access to, freedom of movement within, and liberty to report from the battle space has been strictly circumscribed. By comparison, between January 2006 and mid-April 2007, 230 journalists embedded with Canadian Forces in Afghanistan, an average of 80–90 embeds per six month rotation, while in the first ten weeks of 2007 the Dutch facilitated 370 external visitors to Afghanistan, a significant proportion of whom were reporters. They routinely embedded around 40 journalists per six-month rotation.[38] It is not difficult to see a connection between these disparities in access, the reporting of the actual conditions on the ground in Afghanistan and the differing responses to the conflict in the three countries. The Dutch sustained an extended and often heated debate on their Afghan engagement, with a clear understanding that the public needed to be apprised of the risks it entailed. Discussions about the nature and scope of the mission continued in parliament and the media until a dispute over the further extension of the deployment brought down the coalition government in February 2010, resulting in the withdrawal of its military from Uruzgan in August of the same year.[39] Likewise, between 2005 and 2007, politicians, the press and the military in Canada engaged in a wide-ranging, drawn-out and very public discussion about the deployment to Afghanistan, the preparedness of Canadian forces, the adequacy of their equipment and the very high number of casualties that they suffered – 158

---

38 See Hobson, *The Information Gap*, p.12; Mans et al, *Eyes Wide Shut?* pp.25–6.

39 See David Batty, 'Dutch government collapses after Labour withdrawal from coalition', *Guardian*, 20 February 2010.

to that point.[40] In both of these countries the likelihood of casualties was a matter for public debate from the earliest days of the conflict, and the public were prepared for the worst. In Canada, as the nation's forces prepared to redeploy to Kandahar in early 2006, 'numerous stories in the media about the dangers inherent in the new area of operations and the increased possibility of Canadian military casualties … prompted the Minister [of Defence, Bill Graham], Lieutenant-General Hillier [the Chief of the Defence Staff] and his senior officers to dispense with the reassuring vocabulary of peacekeeping … and start speaking plainly about what the Canadians would be expected to do in Kandahar.'[41]

By contrast, in Australia, limited media access resulted in scant coverage of the war, little sense of the true conditions in the ADF's area of operations and virtually no discussion of it in parliament or the public at large. John Martinkus notes that when, in a report for SBS's *Dateline* in mid-2006, he warned that the Afghanistan deployment 'would be the one where the ADF, which had had such luck in avoiding casualties in Iraq, would be likely to suffer a number of casualties,' he was 'criticised for the prediction as somehow supporting the other side or wishing harm upon the troops.'[42] Up until early 2009 when Australian casualties were still in single figures, politicians and the media continued to regard death in action not as a routine hazard of the deployment but as a tragic industrial accident, an unexpected misfortune that was doubly distressing when it did occur. This view of casualties owed a good deal to the ADF's provision of a relentlessly optimistic account of its actions and progress in Afghanistan and its rigorous exclusion of independent reporters who might contest it. In this context, with little or no discussion of or preparation for the likelihood of combat deaths, it is scarcely surprising that when Australian servicemen began to lose their lives, regardless of the numbers or causes of their deaths, public support for a conflict whose potential costs had barely been considered hitherto, gradually turned to opposition.

---

40 See Hobson, *The Information Gap*, pp.9–11. For an explanation of why Afghanistan dropped out of political debate in Canada see Kim Richard Nossal, 'Making Sense of Afghanistan: The Domestic Politics of International Stabilization Missions in Australia and Canada', Paper presented at the Conference of the Association for Canadian Studies in Australia and New Zealand, University of New England, Armidale, New South Wales, 5 July 2010, http://post.queensu.ca/ percent7Enossalk/papers/Nossal_2010_Making_Sense.pdf.

41 Hobson, *The Information Gap*, p.11.

42 Martinkus, 'The Road to Tarin Kowt', *What are we doing in Afghanistan?* ed. Kevin Foster, Melbourne: Australian Scholarly Publishing, 2009, p.80.

For and Against

That Australian public opinion on the war and its casualties is more layered and more nuanced than current polling can capture, is further borne out in other polls taken in June 2010, albeit less reliable self-selecting telephone and web surveys. On 23 June 2010, forty-eight hours after the special forces helicopter accident referred to above, *The Age* published the results of two readers' polls conducted over the previous 24 hours, the first in print versions of *The Age*, the second a web poll in *The National Times*, an online supplement that publishes a range of opinion, commentary and analysis from Fairfax's print and online mastheads. In the print poll, 58 per cent of respondents answered 'Yes' to the question 'Should Australia bring forward its withdrawal date from Afghanistan?' with 42 per cent responding 'No'.[43] While *The Age*'s readers were keen to see the timely return of the troops from Afghanistan, a majority in *The National Times* – which presumably included a significant number of those who also read *The Age* – continued to back the nation's engagement there while it had a demonstrable purpose. Of the 3296 that responded to the question 'Do you support Australia's involvement in the war in Afghanistan?' 56 per cent were in favour of hanging on, 'Yes, it is tough but we have an important part to play in the battle', while 44 per cent opposed continued engagement: 'No, it's too distressing to see the death toll of Australian troops continue to rise'.[44] Though these polls do not claim to offer a representative portrait of public opinion – *The National Times* conceded that they are 'not scientific and reflect the opinion only of visitors who have chosen to participate' – they do drive home the point that the blunt instrument of simple 'for' or 'against' measures of support is insufficiently finetuned to register the complexity of public opinion about the conflict.[45] In this case, taken together, the polls suggest that at that time, while a majority of Australians were opposed to increasing troop numbers and eager to see the military come home, they also wanted to see the ADF finish the job, however painful.

That the Australian public's grasp of international current affairs was more sophisticated than the common round of 'Yes/No' polling implied or revealed was demonstrated in the 2010 Lowy Poll when respondents were asked to consider whether the greatest threat to Australia's security came from the war in Afghanistan, instability in Pakistan or Iran's nuclear

43 *The Age* 23 June 2010, p.16.

44 *The Age*, 23 June 2010, www.theage.com.au/polls/opinion/politics/australia-in-afghanistan/20100622-ytel.html.

45 *The Age*, 23 June 2010, www.theage.com.au/polls/opinion/politics/australia-in-afghanistan/20100622-ytel.html.

program. The war in Afghanistan was regarded as the least threatening of the trio, with 35 per cent nominating Iran's nuclear program, 31 per cent instability in Pakistan and only 26 per cent the war in Afghanistan.[46] The further implications of this view were hinted at in the 2011 Lowy Poll, in which respondents were asked to choose from a number of statements the one that they felt best explained why Australian forces should remain committed in Afghanistan:

> I am now going to read you a few different arguments that have been made as to why Australia should remain militarily involved in Afghanistan. For each one please tell me whether you personally agree or disagree it is a reason why Australia should remain militarily involved in Afghanistan.
>
> 'If Australia and its allies withdrew from Afghanistan Afghan women might have their rights seriously violated by an extremist government;' 'Australia participated in the invasion of Afghanistan, so we have an obligation to stay on until the job is done;' 'Australia is a US ally and we should stay in Afghanistan as long as the United States does, so the US will continue to regard us as a reliable ally;' 'If Australia's military withdraws from Afghanistan there is a higher risk that terrorists will be able to mount an attack against Australian civilians in Australia or elsewhere around the world.'[47]

Notably, the government's official position on why the nation's forces were in Afghanistan, the assertion that 'If Australia's military withdraws from Afghanistan there is a higher risk that terrorists will be able to mount an attack against Australian civilians in Australia or elsewhere around the world,' was afforded least credence by the public and scored lowest on the poll, with only 37 per cent agreeing with the proposition and 62 per cent disagreeing. From these figures it would seem that as memories of and public anxiety about the 9/11 attacks and the bombings in Bali and Jakarta faded, Australians were less inclined to accept the government's assertion that its forces were in Afghanistan to ensure the 'strategic denial of an operational base for international terrorist organisations.'[48] The public's

---

46 Fergus Hanson, *The Lowy Institute Poll 2010: Australia and the World: Public Opinion and Foreign Policy*, Sydney: Lowy Institute for International Policy, 2010, p.13.

47 Fergus Hanson, *The Lowy Institute Poll 2011: Australia and the World: Public Opinion and Foreign Policy*, Sydney: Lowy Institute for International Policy, 2011, p.27.

48 Australian Associated Press (AAP), 'Australian terror threat comes from Afghanistan says Labor', Sydney: AAP, 12 July 2005. For the reiterated articulation of this official

views on the real reason why the ADF were in Afghanistan had been made clear in the responses to a question that featured in the 2007 and 2008 Lowy polls but was subsequently withdrawn.[49]

Q. Thinking about Australia's military involvement in Afghanistan, please say which of the following statements most closely reflects your own view. Australia is involved militarily in Afghanistan[50]

	2008	2007
To help fight international terrorism	35 %	31 %
To support the United States under the US alliance	38 %	35 %
To promote Western strategic interests in the region	10 %	9 %
To support the democratic government	17 %	20 %
Don't Know	0 %	5 %

The responses reveal that for Australians, at this time, the war in Afghanistan was as much about reaffirming a partnership as it was about defeat ing an enemy, that while the men and women of the ADF were struggling *against* the Taliban and Al Qaida they were also, if not more immediately, fighting *for* the alliance with the US. With a significant commitment of forces to Afghanistan since 2006, *why* the ADF was in Afghanistan was evidently considered, after 2008, as a less important matter than whether or not it should remain there. When this open-ended question, requiring a complex comparison of motive, was removed from the questionnaire in 2009 it gave place to an invitation to express a straightforward preference, '*Should Australia continue to be involved militarily in Afghanistan?*' An

stance see: 'War on Terror will not end soon, PM says', Sydney: AAP, 25 February, 2006; 'Digging in for Taliban fight', Sydney: AAP, 20 April 2006: 'Afghanistan troops face long, difficult task: PM', Melbourne: AAP, 10 April 2007; 'PM, Nelson announce long-awaited Afghan deployment', Sydney: AAP, 10 April 2007; 'Howard warns of dangers for diggers' Sydney: AAP, 9 July 2007; 'SAS death won't change Govt resolve on terror, says PM', Sydney: AAP, 26 October 2007; 'Australia Committed to Afghanistan conflict: Rudd', Sydney: AAP, 15 October 2008. See also Patrick Walters, 'Out of our depth', *The Australian*, 3 May 2008.

49 Fergus Hanson of the Lowy Institute, who was responsible for the production of the *Australia and the World* polls from 2008 to 2012, indicated that this question was dropped because 'we are always very tight for space with the poll' (Email correspondence with author 17 September 2010).

50 Fergus Hanson, *The Lowy Institute Poll 2008: Australia and the World: Public Opinion and Foreign Policy*, Sydney: Lowy Institute for International Policy, 2008, p.21

invitation to analyse was trumped by the instigation to react. The loss of this question is regrettable in that it stripped the post-2008 data of some critical contextualisation. At the very point that the probity of the Karzai Government came under renewed scrutiny, the intensity of the Taliban insurgency increased and Australian and ISAF casualties began to climb, when concerns about why the ADF was in Afghanistan and what it was doing there were proliferating, the one question in the survey that might have given some insight into public opinion about the motives and purposes of Australia's commitment was dropped.

By 2011, the polls suggest, the public had definitively rejected both the explicit rationale for Australia's presence in Afghanistan and its widely recognised subtext, that though denying terrorists safe-haven in Afghanistan and support for the US alliance might have taken the ADF into Afghanistan these were no longer sufficient reasons to keep it there. The 2011 poll results indicate that the public believed the nation's principal obligation was no longer to the alliance with the US or the cause of combating terrorism, but to Afghanistan and its people – particularly its women:

I am now going to read you a few different arguments that have been made as to why Australia should remain militarily involved in Afghanistan. For each one please tell me whether you personally agree or disagree it is a reason why Australia should remain militarily involved in Afghanistan.[51]

	If Australia and its allies withdrew from Afghanistan Afghan women might have their rights seriously violated by an extremist government	Australia participated in the invasion of Afghanistan, so we have an obligation to stay on until the job is done	Australia is a US ally and we should stay in Afghanistan as long as the United States does, so the US will continue to regard us as a reliable ally	If Australia's military withdraws from Afghanistan there is a higher risk that terrorists will be able to mount an attack against Australian civilians in Australia or elsewhere around the world
Agree	72%	57%	38%	37%
Disagree	24%	42%	61%	62%
No view / Don't Know	4%	1%	1%	2%

51 Hanson, *Australia and the World*, 2011, p.27.

In the light of this poll one might reasonably infer that what is steadily eroding public support for the war in Australia is not so much diminishing faith in the mission as the ever-growing recognition that the ADF's contribution to it is too localised and limited, too feeble and isolated to have any bearing on its larger outcomes. As a consequence the loss of Australian life can no longer be justified. Australia has demonstrated its reliability as an ally to the Americans. It has repaid the debt incurred to Afghanistan when it assisted in the invasion of the country, by installing much-needed infrastructure and helping to train the security personnel whose job it will be to safeguard the nation after the departure of the last ISAF troops in 2014. Australians care about what happens to the Afghans (provided they don't turn up on boats seeking asylum in Australia) but recognise that this is increasingly an Afghan conflict that will require an Afghan political solution. In this context further loss of Australian life merely drives home the futility of the ADF's continued engagement in Afghanistan. As such, while the media lauds the dead as embodiments of the Anzac spirit, the data suggests that though the public is respectful of their sacrifice and sympathetic to their families' loss, it increasingly regards them as emblems of the war's pointlessness.

Bipartisanship and the Big Lie

While the Lowy, EMC and the few other polls conducted since 2007 enable a series of educated inferences about public opinion on the war and how media coverage shaped and was shaped by it, they demonstrate above all else that if we want a more comprehensive, more nuanced, more revealing picture of what the Australian people think about the aims and progress of the fighting, what its forces are and should be doing in Afghanistan, under what conditions and when they should be withdrawn, the pollsters and their media masters need to ask more of the public a greater number of more carefully considered questions more often. We need more sensitive poll data, finer tuned and more regular measures of where public opinion sits, what shifts it and why. But we seem unlikely to get it. The year 2008 saw the publication of only two polls soliciting public opinion on the war in Afghanistan; there were six in 2009; five in 2010; six in 2011; and two in 2012.[52] None of the 2009 polls focused exclusively on Afghanistan. The

52 The six polls in 2009 were: a Newspoll conducted 20–22 March 2009; a Nielsen poll conducted in late March (no date available); a poll conducted for the ANU by the Social Research Centre in Melbourne 17 March–1 April; a poll conducted by

conflict there featured as one among a range of contemporary political issues covered by the polls including, in the case of the first EMC poll, voting intentions, the performances of the then Prime Minister and then leader of the Opposition, and security at airports. Only two of the six polls, a Newspoll and a Nielsen Poll, both conducted in mid-late March, were undertaken on behalf of national media organisations, ensuring widespread distribution of and debate about their results. Not that they invited much debate. Both polls focused on a narrow range of concerns about the war, notably whether the then newly installed US President, Barack Obama, would ask Australia to commit more troops to Afghanistan. Three of the five in 2010 were conducted by EMC, with only one, an *Age*/Nielsen Poll of 25 October, conducted on behalf of a national media company. In 2011, only the Galaxy Poll of 4 June was carried out on behalf of a major news organisation, News Corp's Melbourne daily the *Herald-Sun*. In 2012 neither poll was conducted on behalf of a national, mainstream media organisation.

By contrast, at a rough count, in both 2010 and 2009, British and US media organisations and think tanks, conducted, respectively, four and nine times as many public opinion polls on the war in Afghanistan as were undertaken in Australia.[53] The frequency, scope and detail of this polling have elicited rich and revealing responses.[54] For example, the US polls offer a thorough, comprehensive and frank portrait of how the public thinks the war in Afghanistan is going, what its men and women are fighting for, how long they are likely to do so, and what effect the outcome will have on the domestic sphere. These results are presented longitudinally so that subtle shifts in public opinion can be registered and their causes examined.

Essential Research in Melbourne 17–29 March; a second Essential Research poll, 4–10 May; the Lowy poll, 13–25 July. In 2010 the five polls were: the Lowy Poll (31 May), three Essential Polls (21 June, 11 October 25 October), and one *The Age*/ Nielsen Poll (25 October). In 2011 the polls were the Essential Polls (21 March, 9 May, 29 August 21 November); the Lowy Poll (30 March–14 April), and a Galaxy Poll, (4 June). In 2012 both were Essential Polls, 19 March and 10 September. Essential Media produces a weekly poll on the standing of the two parties and the preferred Prime Minister. Nielsen polled the public on these issues seven times before the election was called in 2010, eight times in 2009 and seven in 2008. For the details see http://au.acnielsen.com/news/200512.shtml Newspoll conducts a fortnightly poll, see www.newspoll.com.au/cgi-bin/polling/display_poll_data.pl?url_caller=&mode=trend&page=show_polls&question_set_id=1.

53 These figures are taken from http://en.wikipedia.org/wiki/International_public_opinion_on_the_war_in_Afghanistan.

54 See www.pollingreport.com/afghan.htm for a number of excellent examples from the US.

Reading such polls, one wonders why Australians lack equivalent data. Clearly our pollsters have the capacity to gather it, so what might explain the comparative lack of frequency or detail in Australian opinion polling focused on the war in Afghanistan? It is my belief that disinterest in the public's views about the conflict, and the limited scope of debate about Afghanistan in parliament and the media, are a direct product of bipartisan political support for the war.

In the run up to the 2010 Federal election, Dan Oakes, then *The Age*'s Defence Correspondent, predicted that 'Bipartisan support for all overseas military deployments means that there is likely to be little heat and light around defence during the campaign.'[55] He was right: defence barely featured a mention in the campaign, let alone providing the focus for any substantive debate. Far from being embarrassed about their failure to canvas or represent the views of their constituents, Oakes noted, the nation's parliamentarians characterised 'the bipartisan approach to the Afghanistan deployment as a great success and the measure of a mature democracy.'[56] Yet the outcome of the August 2010 Federal election, when neither of the main parties gained an outright majority, suddenly saw politicians, and the media, sit up and take an interest in Afghanistan. When Andrew Wilkie, one of the independents holding the balance of power in the House of Representatives, joined the Australian Greens, who occupied the same position in the Senate, 'in calling for a debate on the nation's future involvement in the war,' Afghanistan finally arrived in the political and media mainstream.[57] Unfortunately, the parliamentary debate, which began in the House of Representatives on 19 October 2010 and concluded, after a parliamentary recess, on 16 November 2010, was a profound disappointment. Indeed this was less a debate than a mass, multivocal re-statement of the current strategy and its increasingly tenuous rationale, a prolonged affirmation of the need for 'forward defence' against potential terrorist threats and an extended love-in with the military.[58] The debate produced no substantive change in strategy, unearthed no new facts

55 Dan Oakes, 'Main parties will keep Afghanistan off radar', *The Age* 26 July 2010, p.6.
56 Oakes, 'Main parties', p.6.
57 Wilkie claimed 'We certainly do need a debate about why we're there', (*The Age*, 25 August 2010).
58 For the record of the debate in the House of Representatives see Hansard dailies for the following dates: 19 October, 692–706; 20 October, 872–915; 21 October, 1069–1108; 25 October, 1262–1282, 1315–1328; 26 October, 1677–1741; 27 October, 1927–1985; 28 October, 2123–2133; 15 November, 2366–2397; 16 November, 2453–2491, 2618–2630, all accessible via www.aph.gov.au/hansard/hansreps.htm.

about the Australian engagement, and more topically, had no effect on liberalising the nature or amount of information that the public was privy to about Afghanistan. Until there is clear air between the two major parties on Afghanistan, until the war there becomes a focus of domestic political contention, one of the issues on which a change of government may hinge, then it is unlikely that the conflict will assume a prominent place in the regular round of polling and so public opinion about it will continue to be ignored or misunderstood.

Currently, the most comprehensive source of information about what the ADF is doing in Afghanistan is not the independent media but the Department of Defence via its regular media releases and the Defence Minister's quarterly statements to parliament. Whatever their intended purpose, the length and detail of these statements serve to nullify rather than to stimulate broader discussion about the war in parliament or the community. In a statement on Afghanistan on 23 June 2010, former Defence Minister Senator John Faulkner offered a comprehensive overview of Australian strategy and operations. He surveyed the work of the Provincial Reconstruction Teams, the progress of training, the consequences of the impending Dutch withdrawal, recent casualties suffered by the ADF and the problems presented by Pakistan, and gave a sketch of current operations. He spoke for more than 14 minutes and the transcript covers eleven double-columned pages of Hansard. This speech elicited not a single question, attracting only a 78 word response from Eric Abetz, the then Leader of the Opposition in the Senate, who, brimming with the spirit of bipartisanship, commended the Government's steadfastness and the 'magnificent work' of the ADF, serving 'the cause of freedom both for us here in Australia and for the international community.'[59] Former Defence Minister Stephen Smith's statement to the House, on 12 May, 2011, covered why the ADF are in Afghanistan, what progress they are making, reconciliation with and reintegration of former Taliban fighters, detainee management and much more besides, and took 17 minutes to deliver. It was greeted by a counter-statement from the then Shadow Minister for Defence Science, Technology and Personnel, Stuart Robert, that endorsed the fundamentals of the Government's strategy, mirrored its key areas of coverage, raised minor points of difference and was almost identical in its duration.[60]

---

59 Hansard, 23 June 2010, 4194.

60 Hansard, 12 May 2011, 3787–3796 www.aph.gov.au/hansard/hanssen.htm For a comprehensive list of and links to further statements by the Minister see www.minister.defence.gov.au/category/smith/category/smith/statements-smith/?y=2012.

This sort of exchange, like the formal debate of late 2010, demonstrates that where the war in Afghanistan is concerned, parliament has functioned less as a forum for meaningful exchange than as an echo chamber where members of the legislature find comfort in the restatement and endorsement of their views. The nature and substance of their discussions indicate that if the pollsters are disinterested in Australian public opinion about the war, most of our elected representatives seem oblivious to it. Despite the polls showing a clear and growing majority of the population opposed to the continuing deployment of Australian forces in Afghanistan and eager to see the troops brought home, neither of the major parties recognises this constituency and neither speaks for it. Only the Greens have raised the issue of public opposition to the war in any consistent fashion. On 18 March 2010, the then leader of the Greens, Senator Bob Brown, called for the withdrawal of Australian forces from Afghanistan 'consistent with the majority opinion of the Australian populace at large.'[61] More recently, as the timetable for troop withdrawal has become a matter of public knowledge, individual MPs from both sides of parliament have been emboldened to speak out against the continued deployment, though more as a matter of conscience than in an effort to influence policy. In the wake of the five casualties suffered by the ADF on 30 August 2012, the former Speaker of the House of Representatives, Anna Burke, claimed that 'We should never have gone there in the first place.' The ALP Deputy Whip, Jill Hall asserted 'I've always said I would support early withdrawal,' while on the Opposition benches, Liberal MP Mal Washer argued that 'The only way of stopping more loss of life is to get out of Afghanistan'.[62] Noble sentiments, no doubt, but many years too late to be of any real interest to the media or the public.

Clearly, until the wash-up from the 2010 Federal election, the Government's long-standing policy on the war went largely unquestioned by the media despite growing evidence of its rejection by individual MPs and other contributors to the military coalition. Andrew Wilkie argued that 'One of the big lies of this federal election campaign ... is that we have to be there to fight terrorists for ... national security ... We're not there because of terrorists. The terrorists morphed years ago into a global network, making Afghanistan irrelevant.'[63] This was much the same conclusion that Canada's

61 Hansard, 18 March 2010, 2262. www.aph.gov.au/hansard/hanssen.htm

62 Samantha Maiden, 'Deaths fuel withdraw push', *Sunday Herald Sun*, 2 September 2012, p.4.

63 Dan Oakes and Tom Hyland, 'Toll adds to exit pressure', *The Age*, 26 August 2010, p.1.

Prime Minister, Stephen Harper had arrived at when, on a farewell visit to his nation's forces in Kandahar ahead of the cessation of their combat role in July 2011 and the withdrawal of most of the troops soon after, he noted that Afghanistan 'does not represent a geostrategic risk to the world. It is no longer a source of global terrorism.'[64] That the Australian Government continues to promote the 'forward defence' argument, the Opposition to endorse it and the media to faithfully report it suggests that the first casualty of bipartisanship is not necessarily truth but the sort of vigorous, open debate that might reveal it.

This stifling of broader debate about the aims and conduct of the campaign has not only put the nation's politicians out of step with the public, it has also drawn fire from within the Defence community. Peter Leahy observes that the 'suppression of a wide-ranging and informed professional debate on the changing nature of war and conflict within the services' impedes the professional development process and the lessons learned from previous conflicts and that this could have dire consequences for future military operations:

> The service chiefs and their in-house military studies centres and professional journals are hampered in developing this debate by the realisation that ministers and minders are ready to pounce at the first expressions of genuine debate or dissent that may be seen to be politically damaging ... This is an unwarranted politicisation of a necessary development process within the services. The ministers and minders do not seem to understand that this is a necessary and healthy debate that seeks to engage academics and the interested public in important questions about the future of our national security.[65]

Much of the anger within the ADF, particularly the Army, has focused on the fact that as a result of the Government's micromanagement of the gathering and flow of news from Afghanistan and their costive approach to its release, Defence and the ADF are missing out on a raft of 'opportunities to provide information to the Australian public that promotes their causes, the men and women who carry them out, and the institutions themselves.'[66] Overzealous information management by politicians, their minders and Defence bureaucrats is obstructing the development of closer ties and greater

---

64 Canadian Broadcasting Corporation (2011), 'Afghanistan is no longer a risk: Harper', www.cbc.ca/news/politics/story/2011/05/30/pol-harper-afghanistan.html.

65 Leahy, 'The Government, the Military and the Media', p.8.

66 Humphreys, 'The Australian Defence Force's Media Strategy', p.33–4.

affection between the military and the public. As a result, in Peter Leahy's phrase, 'the nation is being denied its heroes, and its heroes are being denied their heroism.'[67] During his time as Commander of JTF 633, Major General John Cantwell knew exactly who was responsible for choking off the supply of positive news stories from Afghanistan:

> I approve scores of media updates, make or release dozens of newsy videos, provide commentary on our challenges and progress, and look for every opportunity to tell the Australian people what our troops are doing, and how well they're doing it. Most of these messages sink without a trace in the Defence and parliamentary precincts of Canberra. I get more mileage from the story of sending home a long-lost and rediscovered explosive-detection dog, Sarbie, than from all of my other media engagements combined. In general, the work of our service men and women seems to be invisible in the Australian media. It's partly the fault of the press, but largely due to the draconian control of information by the Department of Defence Public Affairs Office and the Defence Minister's office.[68]

According to James Brown, a former member of the special forces and now a Military Fellow at the Lowy Institute, the soldiers who have served or are serving in Afghanistan 'suspect much of what they do is either misunderstood or ignored at home' and, as a consequence, 'Many are starting to ask why there isn't more public debate on Australia's Afghan strategy.'[69] The evidence suggests that there isn't more public debate on the nation's strategy in Afghanistan because neither the politicians nor the top ranks in the ADF will tolerate it and the editors of the mainstream media do not want it. The resulting conspiracy of silence suits all of the major players. Only those in the ADF who are fighting the war, and the public, in whose name they are waging it, are left feeling ignored and misled. But those are casualties our political and military leaders are evidently prepared to tolerate.

---

67 Leahy, 'The Government, the Military and the Media', p.10.

68 Cantwell, *Exit Wounds*, p.326.

69 James Brown, 'And then there's their battle back home', *Sydney Morning Herald*, 28 July 2010, p.11. In his encounters with soldiers in Afghanistan Chris Masters recalls 'I was surprised by the trace of anger I heard when soldiers spoke of a failure to understand what they are doing back at home' (Masters, *Uncommon Soldier*, p.xviii).

Chapter 6

REPUTATION MANAGEMENT AND REDEMPTION

Disarmed Forces

In the years prior to their deployment of troops to Afghanistan in, respectively, 2002 and 2006, neither the Canadian military nor the Dutch armed forces enjoyed the esteem of their politicians or the affection of their people. Though this coolness towards the military had its immediate origins in the misadventures that befell both militaries in the mid-1990s, both Canada and the Netherlands have historically evinced a deep ambivalence about the role and place of the armed forces in their societies.

With its unionised personnel and its rights-driven culture, the Dutch armed forces are regarded as one of the world's first truly post-modern militaries, where civilian standards and values have superseded conventional military forms.[1] As Jan van der Meulen notes, the 'policy of integrating the armed forces more fully and more quickly into society' is encapsulated in a popular vision of their ethos and purpose: 'As civilian as possible, as military as necessary.'[2] In keeping with this approach, the Dutch military share the burden of their principal responsibility – to defend the Netherlands from attack – with better-equipped forces that have strategic interests in the area. According to Olivier and Teitler, the Dutch have lived for centuries under the protection of first the British and later the US, neither of whom were prepared to see control of the low countries pass to an opposing great

1 For more on the development of the post-modern military see Charles C. Moskos, John Allen Williams and David R. Segal, eds, *The Postmodern Military: Armed Forces after the Cold War*, New York: Oxford University Press, 1999. Jan van der Meulen notes that in 1999, '80 percent of Dutch defense personnel are union members' (Jan S. van der Meulen, 'The Netherlands: The Final Professionalization of the Military', *The Postmodern Military*, eds Moskos et al, p.108).

2 van der Meulen, 'The Netherlands', p.117.

power.[3] In this light, if, as Charles Moskos' asserts, the probability of war is one of the key factors that define a society's relationship with its armed forces, the Dutch military's partial outsourcing of its national security interests helps explain why, despite its imperial history, the Netherlands might be thought of as the quintessential 'warless society.'[4]

Safe under the aegis of superpower protection, free from the anxiety of invasion or conquest and thus relieved of the necessity to equip and maintain a cutting-edge combat force, the Dutch Government could direct its resources to social and economic development, and the military were consigned to a more marginal place in the national imaginary.[5] Compounding this phenomenon, after the collapse of the Soviet Union and the fall of the Eastern Bloc states, 'Western nations no longer deployed their armed forces to deter a known adversary but rather to maintain or reinforce peace in regions where their interests were in jeopardy or where human rights were being abused.'[6] The Dutch military, along with the Canadians, have been among the foremost supporters of such a role for their forces and have dedicated a significant portion of their defence resources to overseas peacekeeping missions for many years. These have enjoyed broad support in the Netherlands where, as Koch notes, the population has become notable for its pacifist attitudes and limited trust in the military.[7] As a consequence, not only Dutch society but the armed forces too have come to think of themselves as 'non-martial', and their role at home and abroad as essentially 'unheroic.'[8] In the light of this, as Liora Sion notes, it is hardly surprising that 'the status of the Dutch military and the level of [the] Dutch public's trust in the armed forces are

---

3 See Fritz Olivier and Ger Teitler, 'Democracy and the Armed Forces: The Dutch Experiment', *Armed Forces and the Welfare Societies, Challenges in the 1980s: Britain, the Netherlands, Germany, Sweden and the United States*, ed. G. Harries-Jenkins, New York: St Martin's Press, 1983, pp.90–91.

4 See Charles C. Moskos, 'Armed Forces in the Warless Society'. *Armed Forces After the Cold War*, eds Jürgen Kuhlmann and C. Dandier, Munich: German Armed Forces Institute for Social Research, 1992, pp.3–10.

5 Between 1990 and 2000 the Defence budget was reduced by 20 per cent.

6 Liora Sion, '"Too Sweet and Innocent for War"? Dutch Peacekeepers and the Use of Violence', *Armed Forces and Society*, Vol. 23, No, 1 (2005), p.3.

7 K. Koch, 'Civilian Defence: An Alternative to Military Defence?' *The Netherlands Journal of Sociology*, Vol. 20, No. 1, (1984), pp.1–12. In the Netherlands, van der Meulen notes, 'Participation in new peacekeeping missions is generally welcomed' (van der Meulen, 'The Netherlands', p.113).

8 Stefan Dudink, 'The Unheroic Men of a Moral Nation: Masculinity and Nation in Modern Dutch History'. *The Postwar Moment: Militaries, Masculinities and International Peacekeeping*, eds Cynthia Cockburn and Dubravka Zarkov, London: Lawrence and Wishart 2002, pp.146–61.

definitely lower than they are in the United Kingdom, in France, or in the United States.'[9]

This low opinion was reinforced and amplified by the parlous state of relations between the military and the media that long prevailed in the Netherlands: 'The terms *defensive* on the part of the military and *offensive* on the part of the press suggest the lack of congruency that became typical.'[10] Ulrich Mans notes that as the Dutch had little 'involvement in conflict zones during the Cold War, there was no need for the Ministry of Defence to develop a proactive policy towards the national media.'[11] In turn, reflecting the values of an increasingly 'warless society', the Dutch media directed its attention to more pressing domestic and global matters and when the spotlight turned back to the military, found that it had 'no significant track record in covering conflict areas ... as compared to its international counterparts.' As a consequence, when its reporters left to cover the nation's peacekeepers in the Balkans in the early 1990s, 'Dutch journalism did not possess a reputation for in-depth coverage [of defence issues] in complex, fragile surroundings.'[12]

The situation is not dissimilar in Canada where 'the military is becoming more interdependent with institutions and organizations of civilian society.'[13] Not that this has had much effect on public perceptions of the armed forces: 'in the absence of a visible enemy, national security and defense barely enter most Canadians' consciousness.'[14] The media have traditionally shared the broader populace's indifference to the nation's armed services. Sharon Hobson notes that until their attention was absorbed by the deployment of Canadian Forces to Kandahar in early 2002, the media had spent years 'ignoring defence issues that were not scandal related' – though there were plenty of those to keep them busy.[15] Media and public disinterest in the military has a long history in Canada. Kim Richard Nossal has shown that a deeply entrenched ambivalence about Canadian

---

9 Sion, '"Too Sweet and Innocent for War"?' p.4. Just how low is a matter of dispute. Jan van der Meulen plumped for 'pragmatic, with an undercurrent of idealism', insisting that 'apathetic and indifferent' were 'not the right terms to describe the country's post-Cold War mood towards the armed forces' (van der Meulen, 'The Netherlands', p.114).

10 van der Meulen, 'The Netherlands', p.115.

11 Mans, *Eyes Wide Shut?* p.12.

12 Mans, *Eyes Wide Shut?* p.12.

13 Franklin C. Pinch, 'Canada: Managing Change With Shrinking Resources', *The Postmodern Military*, eds Moskos et al, p.157.

14 Pinch, 'Canada', p.163.

15 Hobson, *The Information Gap*, p.5.

participation in imperial conflicts, how the dead might be commemorated, and a determination during the inter-war years not to celebrate Canada's military 'as an institution that helped forge the nation ... had long-term consequences, affecting attitudes and practices towards the armed forces.' These were most clearly reflected in 'a progressive depreciation' of the military's 'war-fighting abilities ... under the Liberal governments of both Lester Pearson [1963–68] and Pierre Elliott Trudeau [1968–1979 and 1980–84] – a trend continued under the Progressive Conservative government of Brian Mulroney [1984–1993]. The dominant view was reflected most clearly in the name of the forces themselves, which allowed politicians and other elites to neatly strip the "Armed" from the name.'[16] Deep cuts in the Mulroney government's 1989 Federal Budget resulted in the closure of bases, the shrinking of personnel numbers and the cancellation of a range of equipment purchases. This not only demoralised an already disheartened military, it also deepened the armed forces' estrangement from their political masters and the general public:

> Canadians are not very knowledgeable about their military – particularly in the urban areas ... Direct experience and appreciation of military affairs has declined markedly over the past 20 years, both in the political elite as well as in broader sections of the population. Most people's experience of the military is gained second-hand from the media. This is a result of the long-term decline in the size of the military establishment, which leads to a corresponding diminution in the number of military and ex-military personnel in society. In addition, Base closures mean that the 'footprint' made by the military on society has diminished ... Lower numbers, less visibility and a high number of overseas deployments mean less interaction with Canadian civilians.[17]

Profound changes in Canadian society over the past half-century have further estranged the military from the community it serves. As Michael Adams noted in his study of Canadian social values, the military ethos and the virtues it prizes, duty, integrity, discipline and honour, are increasingly identified as 'the values of the older generations in Canada', putting them out

---

16 Kim Richard Nossal, 'The Unavoidable Shadow of Past Wars: Obsequies for Casualties of the Afghanistan Mission in Australia and Canada', *Australasian Canadian Studies*, Vol. 26, No. 1, 2008, p.92.

17 Donna Winslow, 'Canadian Society and its Army', *Canadian Military Journal*, Winter 2003–2004, pp.18–19.

of step with the younger, numerically superior baby boomers, Generations X and Y, for whom 'Instant gratification, desire for independence, and hedonism all seem to take priority.'[18] In the face of overwhelming evidence of the younger generations' rejection of the military virtues, their refusal to subordinate themselves to the group, their unpreparedness to sacrifice their lives for the common good, Donna Winslow concludes that 'Canada is not a militaristic society, nor is it likely to become one in the future.'[19]

Srebrenica Syndrome

In the mid-1990s, demographic and cultural changes furnished the context rather than the stimulus for a deepening *froideur* between the media, the public and the armed forces in Canada and the Netherlands. The specific catalyst for the breakdown in military-civil relations lay in widely publicised and traumatic operational failures that brought political outrage and public scorn on the heads of both militaries.

For the Dutch armed forces, the watershed event that so signally shaped its contemporary relations with the media, the public, the political establishment and the international community was the fall of Srebrenica in North-Eastern Bosnia-Herzegovina in July 1995 during the Yugoslav civil war.[20] Bosnian Serb forces had lost the town in heavy fighting against Bosnian Government troops in 1993 and despite a UN directive declaring it a 'safe area,' they were determined to recapture and ethnically cleanse it. In June and July 1995 as thousands of Bosnian Serbs troops and irregulars surrounded the town with tanks and artillery, cutting off its supply lines and escape routes, the only protection for Srebrenica's terrified civilian population came from the United Nations Protection Force (UNPROFOR), represented on the ground by 400 lightly armed Dutch troops. When the encircling forces made their final assault on Srebrenica, from the 6th to the 11th of July, the Dutch repeatedly called on NATO to provide air support as their defensive lines were pushed back or overrun. Two Dutch Air Force

---

18 Winslow, 'Canadian Society and its Army', p.21. For more detail see Michael Adams, *Sex in the Snow: Canadian Social Values at the End of the Millennium*, Toronto: Penguin Books, 1997.

19 Winslow, 'Canadian Society and its Army', p.21.

20 For more on the massacre that succeeded the fall of Srebrenica see David Rohde, *Endgame: The Betrayal and Fall of Srebrenica. Europe's Worst Massacre Since World War 2*, New York: Farrar, Straus and Giroux, 1997; Jan Willem Honig and Norbert Both, *Srebrenica: Record of a War Crime*, New York: Penguin, 1997; Mark Danner, 'Bosnia: The Great Betrayal', *The New York Review of Books*, 26 March 1998.

F16s were finally cleared for a sortie on the morning of 11 July, dropping their bombs on Bosnian Serb tanks. But when the commander of the invading forces, General Ratko Mladic, threatened to execute Dutch and French hostages that his men held should the raids be repeated, no further air assets were made available to the troops on the ground. When, later the same day, the Bosnian Serb forces completed their conquest of the town, the Dutch surrendered with barely a shot fired.[21]

The *Dutchbat* contingent's failure to protect Srebrenica or prevent Bosnian Serb forces from carrying off and then massacring around 8000 Bosnian men and boys was a traumatic failure for the military and Dutch society more broadly. According to Liora Sion, news of the surrender and the succeeding massacre

> provoked an eruption of public anger in the Netherlands. Both the press and members of parliament began to ask embarrassing questions and attacked what they perceived to be the 'passivity' or even 'cowardliness' of the Dutch UN soldiers. On August 4, 1995, the headline of the weekly newspaper *HP De Tijd* declared that Dutch soldiers were 'too sweet and innocent for war.' In numerous articles, the fall of the Srebrenica enclave was listed among a string of Dutch military defeats ranging from the German invasion of May 1940, to the colonial wars in the former Dutch East Indies and Dutch New Guinea, up to and including peace missions such as those in the Balkans. From the perspective of the media, the Dutch armed forces were nothing but losers.[22]

If the Dutch armed forces already suffered from 'low status' at home, the events at Srebrenica 'diminished the status of the military even further' to the point where it became 'a threatened organization.'[23]

In the years that followed, Srebrenica remained an open wound in Dutch society and a focus for agonised introspection within the military. As the mass graves in the Balkans were mapped and the victims exhumed, the perpetrators of the genocide identified, apprehended and sent for trial at the International Criminal Tribunal for the Former Yugoslavia, those directly involved in the protection and fall of Srebrenica, the United Nations, the French and the Dutch, undertook a series of investigations

---

21 Though it is important to note that the Dutch force was hopelessly outnumbered and outgunned so, in practical terms, beyond forcing a military confrontation and embracing certain annihilation, there was little they could have done.

22 Sion, 'Too Sweet and Innocent for War?' p.4.

23 Sion, 'Too Sweet and Innocent for War?' pp.2, 4, 2.

into and published a succession of reports on the massacre.[24] The most comprehensive of these investigations, not surprisingly, was undertaken on behalf of the Dutch Government who, in 1996, assigned the Netherlands Institute for War Documentation (NIOD) to research the events 'prior to, during and after the fall of Srebrenica.' When NIOD published its 6000 page final report on 10 April 2002, it concluded that little blame could be apportioned to the troops on the ground who had done the best they could in appalling circumstances with inadequate direction and insufficient support.[25] The failure of the *Dutchbat* mission lay in its muddled strategy and poor planning. Six days later the Dutch government accepted partial political responsibility for the Srebrenica massacre and resigned.

Caught up in what must have seemed like an endless round of accusation, recrimination and apology, the invitation to contribute troops first to Iraq, from 2003 to 2005, and then to Afghanistan in 2006 as part of a renewed security and reconstruction effort in the south of the country, presented the Dutch military with the opportunity to move on from Srebrenica, to win back the confidence of the politicians and the respect of the public – it offered them a chance at redemption. In order to affect any of this the military had to demonstrate their professional prowess and their moral bona fides to the widest possible audience at home, and they could only do that by forging an entirely new relationship with the media. As Robin Middel noted, for the first time the Dutch armed forces had to 'open up for the public and make sure that they know what you are doing.'[26]

Prior to the events in Srebrenica, the media had had little opportunity, and less inclination, to work closely with the military. The MvD was regarded as 'a closed and impenetrable stronghold, unwilling to cooperate with the nation's media.'[27] Arnold Karskens, a freelance defence correspondent, recalled that during the conflict in the Balkans, though more than 'a hundred Dutch journalists, photographers and cameramen went to the battlefront', making it 'the best visited war ever' from a Dutch standpoint, there were 'recurring complaints' from the media about the 'inflexibility

---

24 In 1999 then UN Secretary General, Kofi Annan, presented his report on the fall of Srebrenica. In 2001 a Committee of the French Parliament published its report into the tragedy.

25 The NIOD Report can be accessed at www.srebrenica-project.com/index.php?option=com_content&view=article&id=140:niod Accessed 10 March 2013.

26 Author interview with Middel, 23 September 2010.

27 J. Wieten, *Background and Influence of Media Reporting of the Conflict in the Former Yugoslavia During the Period 1991–1995: A Study of Views and Methods of Dutch Journalists*, Amsterdam: Netherlands Institute for War Documentation, 2002: np.

and lack of improvisational ability on the Dutch side.'[28] The most notable consequence of the military's inflexibility was the failure of any Dutch journalists to access Srebrenica or witness the Serb takeover of the town. This failure also had its origins, in part, in the media's own inflexibility and lack of improvisational ability: 'None of the journalists took the risk to go to [Srebrenica] without military protection and therefore no Dutch journalists were present to witness one of the darkest pages in Dutch military history'. [29]

Among its other political and policy reverberations, the catastrophe in Bosnia fed a fear in the Netherlands of committing troops to overseas peace-keeping missions and the development of what Dutch commentators came to call the 'Srebrenica syndrome.'[30] One central means of countering this, the MvD recognised, was 'to ensure broad support for operations.'[31] To make certain that this was achieved, 'military engagements outside the Netherlands had to be better communicated to the home front.'[32] The 'closed and impenetrable stronghold' of old had to give place to the one-stop information shop, access all areas, open all hours. The brave new world of communication got off to a shaky start in Iraq. In August 2003 a little fewer than 1,350 Dutch troops deployed to As Samawah, near Basra, as part of Multi-National Force Iraq. To ensure that the public was kept informed about the troops' mission the Dutch instituted a limited form of embedding. The media were allowed to visit the troops at their base, Camp Smitty, to go on pre-arranged tours of the area, to accompany the men on patrol and witness the work they were doing in Al Muthanna Province. However, they were not permitted to stay with the troops overnight and were accommodated instead at a nearby hotel. This half-embedding suited neither party. The reporters complained that though 'it was possible for us to cover the story … because we are visitors we are not able to get completely into the story we would like to have.'[33] Likewise, the military felt that under the current arrangements their key narrative was not being communicated, that though the media could inform the public about

28 Quoted in Mans, *Eyes Wide Shut?* p.12; Wieten, *Background and Influence*, np.

29 Mans, *Eyes Wide Shut?* p.12.

30 A phrase clearly modelled on 'the Vietnam Syndrome' notionally identified by Ronald Reagan in a speech to the Veterans of Foreign Wars Convention, 18 August 1980, in Chicago. George H. Bush, Reagan's successor as US President, was convinced that the 1991 defeat of Iraq had 'finally kicked the Vietnam Syndrome' (Carruthers, *The Media at War*, p.140). For more on the Vietnam Syndrome see Bruce Cumings, '"No More Vietnams": The Gulf War', *War and Television*, London: Verso, 1992, pp.103–128.

31 Mans, *Eyes Wide Shut?* p.12.

32 Mans, *Eyes Wide Shut?* p.12.

33 Author interview with Middel, 23 September 2010.

what their troops were doing in Iraq they could tell them little about who they were. The military wanted coverage that projected the character of their people, not reporting that listed their duties.

When the Dutch assumed the lead role in Uruzgan in 2006 the MvD and the military seized their opportunity to facilitate such coverage. As noted in Chapter Three, they set in place a communications policy purposed to persuade the politicians that the military had an important role to play in the international projection of Dutch values and that it needed to be adequately equipped to perform that task.[34] At the same time the policy was intended to convince the public that the military was not only a force for good but a force to be reckoned with – a force ready to fight and die in defence of Dutch values and thus a force that the Dutch people could be proud to own. Joop Veen, Director of Communications at the MvD, noted that the policy he helped institute was specifically tailored to garner public support for the mission and the troops conducting it: 'We thought that by making visible that mission, automatically as it were, there would be support not only for the military over there – " We are standing behind you" – but also for the purpose of the mission. That the average Dutch citizen will say that mission is very useful because it has results. It has effects.'[35] While Veen conceded that the strategy failed to translate into popular support for the mission it certainly helped rehabilitate the armed forces in the eyes of the people. Peter ter Velde argued that as a result of the MvD's open and cooperative media operations policy and the reporting it enabled, the Dutch public's perceptions of the military have 'much improved ... Afghanistan ... showed that they could fight, that they could win battles ... So that ... the view in general of the public about [the] military has changed ... in a positive way and they became more like part of society, more than they were before Afghanistan.'[36]

Decade of Darkness

Like the Dutch, Canadians have long had an ambivalent view of their military and its place in the nation's history and identity, arising in part from the fact that 'English-speaking and French-speaking Canadians had fundamentally different views of the proper role of their country in global affairs.'[37]

---

34 Though this was done under the guise of pursuing a 'reconstruction' mission in Afghanistan for which the troops were providing security.
35 Author interview with Dr Joop Veen, 21 June 2012.
36 Author interview with ter Velde, 23 September 2010.
37 Nossal, 'The Unavoidable Shadow of Past Wars', p.90.

While English-speaking Canadians in the nineteenth and twentieth centuries regarded fighting in the defence of the British Empire as a filial duty, their French-speaking fellow citizens, who had had no formal connection to France since 1763, had a different perspective on what constituted the national interest. These divisions were brought to the surface by Conservative Prime Minister Sir Robert Borden's 1917 proposal to introduce conscription to top up the dwindling numbers of volunteers for the Great War. Borden's scheme split the country along linguistic lines, and the nation's subsequent losses on the Western Front entrenched among Canadians a deep-seated hostility to the pursuit of imperialist adventures. The Liberal Party harnessed this sentiment to maintain the support of Quebecois voters and so lock in a stranglehold on power that they held for the greater part of the twentieth century.[38] The prime minister in the inter-war years, Mackenzie King, 'framed his foreign policy with an eye to the avoidance of committing Canada to any conflict that might reopen the cleavages of the Great War.'[39] A key element in this political posture was the cultivation of what Nossal has called 'an attitude of indifference towards the Canadian military as an institution important for the building of the nation.'[40] In the decades after the Second World War this perception was little changed as 'more and more Canadians came to the view that the primary mission of the armed forces was peacekeeping, that Canadians were an "unmilitary people" and that Canada was a "peaceable kingdom."'[41] As a consequence, with the public disconnected from an understandably defensive military, little effort was dedicated to the cultivation of productive and mutually beneficial relations between the armed forces and the media.

By the late 1980s, years of political and financial neglect had left the Canadian Forces a depleted and disillusioned organisation. Soldiers on peacekeeping operations were forced to work with 'equipment that was old, shoddy and ill-suited for the environment.'[42] At least they had equipment. In the wake of the Mulroney Government's 1989 budget cuts, General Rick Hillier, later CDS, noted: 'we wound up parking whole fleets of vehicles

---

38 I am indebted to Nossal, 'The Unavoidable Shadow of Past Wars', pp.90–1, for this information. The Liberal Party ruled Canada for 69 years in the twentieth century, making it the developed world's most successful democratic party.

39 Nossal, 'The Unavoidable Shadow of Past Wars', p.91. William Lyon Mackenzie King enjoyed three periods as Canada's Prime Minister, 1921–26, 1926–30, and 1935–48.

40 Nossal, 'The Unavoidable Shadow of Past Wars', p.91.

41 Nossal, 'The Unavoidable Shadow of Past Wars', p.92.

42 General Rick Hillier, *A Soldier First: Bullets, Bureaucrats and the Politics of War*, Toronto: HarperCollins, 2009, p.114

and mothballing aircraft. All the Army's planning for the next two decades went out the window. Whatever vision there had been was gone, and there was nothing to replace it except further budget cuts and an ongoing struggle for survival.'[43] The public were indifferent to the military and its travails: 'the public's attitude seemed to be that we had all volunteered, so if we didn't like it, we could leave.' The effects on morale were catastrophic. Posted to command the Royal Canadian Dragoons in mid-1990, then Lieutenant Colonel Hillier was struck by the forces' lack of identity or purpose: 'Again and again I found that we were not really the Canadian Forces: we were just an army and not even a unified one at that.'[44] In this context it is not surprising that there were failures of command and leadership within Canadian Forces units, though nobody could have foreseen their immediate or long-term consequences.

In mid-1993 public and political indifference to Canada's armed forces was transformed into open hostility and revulsion. This violent response had its origins in the actions of Canadian troops who were part of the UN mission to Somalia in 1993. On 16 March, when soldiers found a Somali teenager, Shidane Arone, hiding in a portable latrine on an abandoned US facility adjacent to the Canadian camp at Belet Huen, he was handed over to members of the Canadian Airborne Regiment. Incensed by constant thefts from the camp and convinced that Arone had been bent on such a purpose, two soldiers, Clayton Matchee and Kyle Brown, led a small group who, over the course of the evening, tortured and beat the youth to death. One of the perpetrators thoughtfully photographed the events.

The arrest and prosecution of the men involved appalled the public. When Defence and the military sought to cover-up the failures of leadership that had led to this episode, and to shift blame for it, the scandal deepened and any residual respect politicians or the public might have harboured for the armed forces was replaced by 'scorn.'[45] The Liberal Government, returned to power in November 1993, launched a Commission of Inquiry that resulted in the disbanding of the Airborne Regiment and cost one Defence Minister and two Chiefs of the Defence Staff their jobs. Indeed, in the four years from 1993 to 1997 the Canadian Forces went through five Chiefs of the Defence Staff.[46] The Commission's final report

---

43 Hillier, *A Soldier First*, pp.110–11.

44 Hillier, *A Soldier First*, p.109.

45 Hillier, *A Soldier First*, p.115. For detailed coverage of the events in Somalia and their lengthy political ramifications see the Canadian Broadcasting Corporation's *The Somalia Affair* at http://archives.cbc.ca/war_conflict/peacekeeping/topics/723/.

46 See Hillier, *A Soldier First*, p.130.

offered a damning indictment of the civilian leadership in Defence, noting that 'the testimony of witnesses was characterised by inconsistency, improbability, implausibility, evasiveness, selective recollection, half-truths, and plain lies.'[47] The criticism of the military's failures was even tougher: 'the response of the chain of command to the administrative, operational, and disciplinary problems ... was weak, untimely, inadequate, self-serving, unjustifiable, and unbecoming the military leadership that our soldiers deserve and the Canadian public expects. Integrity and courage were subordinated to personal and institutional self-interest.'[48] In the wake of the report the military 'had no standing in Canadian society.'[49]

The episode at Belet Huen was, in Rick Hillier's view, 'one of the most traumatic events in our military's history,' and it marked the commencement of what he called 'the Canadian military's decade of darkness.'[50] As Dominique Price notes, its tarnished reputation rendered the DND especially 'vulnerable to budget cuts being made across the board by the Canadian government.'[51] Between 1993 and 2003 its already shrunken allocation of resources was cut by more than a third, while its personnel numbers fell by more than half between 1962 and 1999. At one point, in the wake of the Somali scandal, amid revelations about violent hazing rituals and allegations that repeated claims of sexual assaults had not been adequately investigated by the armed forces, the CDS directed CF personnel not to wear their uniforms off base for fear of provoking the public.[52]

When the US invaded Afghanistan in October 2001, 'the stench of Somalia' was still thick in the air in Canada and the nation's forces 'were in disrepute and despair.'[53] Public trust in the military had sunk as low as morale within it: 'Canadians did not recognize us as their armed forces and apparently couldn't have cared less about us.'[54] For Canada's politicians, keen to avoid a politically unpopular commitment in Iraq, the invitation to deploy forces to Afghanistan provided a convenient solution to a tricky political

---

47 Commission of Inquiry into the Deployment of Canadian Forces to Somalia, *Dishonoured Legacy: The Lessons of the Somalia Affair*, Ottawa: Minister of Public Works and Government Services, 1997, Executive Summary: www.dnd.ca/somalia/somaliae.htm.

48 *Dishonoured Legacy*, np www.dnd.ca/somalia/vol0/v0s20e.htm.

49 Hillier, *A Soldier First*, p.125.

50 Hillier, *A Soldier First*, pp.114, 123. See Nossal, 'The Unavoidable Shadow Past Wars', p.105 for a history of the use of the term.

51 Price, *Inside the Wire*, p.38.

52 Christian Lemay referred to this as 'a decision made to try to not impose our presence'. Author interview with Lemay, 19 October 2010.

53 Gross Stein and Lang, *The Unexpected War*, pp.12, 57.

54 Hillier, *A Soldier First*, pp.123, 125.

problem.[55] For the military, the nation's largest military commitment since Korea was heaven sent. It provided the Canadian Forces with the opportunity to demonstrate their relevance to their political masters, to leverage some much needed equipment, and above all else to show the Canadian public that it was a disciplined and moral fighting force.[56] Rick Hillier realised that the key task for the CF in Afghanistan was to reconnect with their public: 'the problem was that we had lost contact with Canadians, and if we were going to survive, the Canadian Forces had to win back their respect. We needed to recruit the entire nation and get the Canadian people back on our side.'[57] Their principal allies in this task would prove to be the media. Though it took the military time to adjust to the pervasive presence of a media contingent, if CF wanted to 'recruit' the Canadian people they had to give them a full and frank view of what they were doing – maximum publicity was the order of the day, hence the eventual liberality of the CFMEP.

The imperative to be seen to be doing good explains Hillier's rejection of an early offer from ISAF to serve under Italian leadership in Chaghcharan, Herat Province. Chaghcharan was rejected not because it presented particular operational difficulties for the CF but because there was insufficient opportunity for publicity there. As Hillier recalled: 'I didn't like the option of a deployment to Chaghcharan at all. There was no upside, no profile because Chaghcharan was so isolated. No one would have noticed that we were there.'[58] Instead, after early stints in Kandahar (2002) and Kabul (2003–5), the Canadians returned to Kandahar in 2006, among the most dangerous provinces in the country, where they assumed the lead role in Regional Command South.[59] The public would see plenty of their armed forces, and so would the enemy. In order to maximise coverage of its deployment to Kandahar the military set about organising a media policy through which it could press its case for material resupply and moral rehabilitation directly with the Canadian public.

The tide of public feeling towards the Canadian military had begun to turn before an effective media embedding policy was in place. This was

55 Canadian politicians referred to this as 'the Afghanistan solution'. For more on this see Gross Stein and Lang, *The Unexpected War*, pp.65, 67–8.

56 As Gross Lang and Stein put it: 'The mission would allow the Canadian Forces to show the public that they were a well-trained fighting force, and not just blue beret-wearing peacekeepers' (Gross Stein and Lang, *The Unexpected War*, p.19).

57 Hillier, *A Soldier First*, p.126. 'Recruit the Nation' became an official strategy: see Hillier, *A Soldier First*, pp.363–386.

58 Gross Stein and Lang, *The Unexpected War*, p.136.

59 For a detailed account of the Canadian deployment in Afghanistan see Piggot.

evidenced by the 'spontaneous outpouring of affection and grief' occasioned by the nation's first casualties in Afghanistan suffered in a friendly fire incident at Tarnak Farms near Kandahar in April 2002. So great was the public interest in these deaths that the Edmonton memorial service for the four victims was televised live on Canada's major television networks. 'For so many years,' Rick Hillier noted, 'we in the military had been ignored or at times even scorned by the Canadian public.' Suddenly, 'People were stopping soldiers in uniform in the streets and talking to them' in a spontaneous show of interest and affection that 'was almost completely overwhelming to everyone in uniform.'[60] Building on this renewed sympathy and in tandem with the more detailed coverage of the fighting in Afghanistan as it came on stream, in 2005 the Canadian Forces launched their 'Recruit the Nation' strategy to showcase the work being done by the nation's forces. Celebrities from the worlds of sport, entertainment, music, business and the media travelled to Afghanistan to meet and spend time with the men and women of the armed forces, thus providing a wealth of publicity opportunities. The strategy was to use the celebrities to reach a general audience and broker a new, better relationship between the public and the armed forces: 'NHL [National Hockey League] players like Guy Lafleur, "Tiger" Williams and Bob Probert reached audiences that we couldn't even begin to get to ourselves, and they reached them with powerful stories about our sons and daughters serving so far away.'[61]

Despite attempts by the Prime Minister's Office, from 2006 onwards, to downplay Canadian casualties in Afghanistan by banning the media from the repatriation of the dead at Canadian Forces Base (CFB) Trenton, the community response to the return of the bodies remained a focus for public displays of affection for and connectedness with the military. Hillier recalls that when the planes and their coffins returned, 'Crowds of ordinary men, women and children ... lined up along the chain fence that separated the air base from the main road in Trenton. It didn't matter what the weather was, there would be quite literally hundreds out by that fence, waving Canadian flags, showing their support for the families and grieving with them.'[62] The grieving went on for quite some distance: 'When the hearse carrying the coffin would start west down Highway 401 toward Toronto, it wouldn't get far before seeing the first incredible displays of public support. All along that 150 kilometre stretch of highway, on all fifty of the overpasses, thousands

60 Hillier, *A Soldier First*, p.254.
61 Hillier, *A Soldier First*, pp.374–5.
62 Hillier, *A Soldier First*, p.454.

of Canadians would wave flags, salute or just take off their caps and stand silently as the convoy with the hearse passed below.'[63] This public outpouring 'prompted the Ontario government to designate that portion of the highway as the "Highway of Heroes" to honour the fallen troops.'[64]

One day, flying to Toronto by helicopter having received a body at Trenton, Hillier looked down at the people 'stretched out below me: little children, older folks, younger people, paramedics, firemen and policemen with their vehicles, many with Canadian flags, saluting, waving or just standing there.'[65] The spectacle of large numbers of 'ordinary Canadians' going out of their way 'to show their respect and appreciation' for Canada's forces led him to reflect on how far the military's relationship with the public had come from the dark days of a decade earlier.[66] The people had moved from being enemies of the armed forces and had become their friends and ardent supporters, those who had so recently 'disowned' and 'scorned' the military now inspired the men and women in uniform to stick to their task: 'The actions of ordinary Canadians allowed us to continue in our service with confidence that the country was behind us.'[67] When *Globe and Mail* columnist Christie Blatchford's account of her time embedded with the Canadian Forces, *Fifteen Days: Stories of Bravery, Friendship, Life and Death from Inside the New Canadian Army* (2008), was published in 2008 it soon became a national bestseller and carried off the Governor General's Literary Award, one of the nation's most prestigious writing prizes. The popularity of the book demonstrated that the military's public affairs campaign had been a resounding success. The people liked the look of the *New* Canadian Army and they welcomed them back to the bosom of the nation. Mission accomplished.

What's Wrong With Anzac?

In Australia, both popular and political perceptions of the ADF leading up to the war in Afghanistan could hardly have been more distinct from the Dutch and Canadian views of their armed forces. When in July 2011 Greg Sheridan, Foreign Editor of *The Australian*, proposed that 'no

---

63 Hillier, *A Soldier First*, pp.454–5.

64 Nossal, 'The Unavoidable Shadow of Past Wars', p.82. For more on the Harper government's endeavours to downplay casualties and the public's response to them see pp.79–81.

65 Hillier, *A Soldier First*, p.455.

66 Hillier, *A Soldier First*, p.455.

67 Hillier, *A Soldier First*, p.455.

single Australian institution is as well known, or as well respected, internationally and within Australia, as the Australian Army', few of his countrymen would have questioned this assertion.[68] The military in Australia occupy a position of respect bordering on reverence. Indeed, an EMC Poll of 6 February 2012 reported that the ADF was the nation's most trusted institution with 78 per cent of respondents having 'a lot of' or 'some trust' in the military.[69]

The ADF cultivates this favourable opinion by carefully managing its links with its key stakeholders in the public and private sectors. For business owners and senior managers in the public sector whose employees include many thousands of reservists, the ADF runs a suite of Employer Engagement Programs. The most prominent of these is 'Exercise Boss Lift', which offers employers the opportunity to learn 'first-hand what the Australian Defence Force does on exercises and operations.'[70] The program transports a select band of employers to an exercise or an area of operations where their employees are serving with the reserves. Here, while they 'experience some of the more diverse aspects of military life, such as eating from ration packs and visiting the firing range', they also get to 'see their staff use both their civilian and military skills.'[71] Witnessing the 'Teamwork, leadership, and resilience' of their employees, 'all attributes that are clearly needed for success on operations as well as in the workplace', the program is intended to both entertain and to edify, to give employers the chance to dress up and play soldiers for a few days and, while they are enjoying themselves, to provide them with 'a better understanding of the benefits employing a Reservist will bring to your organisation.'[72]

Within government, the Australian Defence Force Parliamentary Program (ADFPP) offers parliamentarians a range of 'attachment options ... to engage with elements of the Australian Defence Force in the many areas of

---

68 Greg Sheridan, 'Too much for too few in the Defence con job', *The Weekend Australian*, 9–10 July 2011, p.24.

69 Essential Media Communications (2012), *Essential Report*, 6 February 2012, Melbourne: EMC, p.11. The *Reader's Digest*'s annual survey of the nation's most trusted professions regularly puts the Armed Forces in or close to the top-ten. In the 2011 survey the ADF posted 11th. By comparison, Religious Ministers came in at 30, Lawyers at 33, Journalists at 40 and Politicians at 44. For more information see www.readersdigest.com.au/australias-most-trusted-professions-2011.

70 www.defencereservessupport.gov.au/for-employers/get-the-reservist-experience/exercise-boss-lift.aspx.

71 Defence Media Centre Press Release, 'Employers to visit reserve employees in East Timor', 20 August 2012.

72 Defence Media Centre Press Release, 20 August 2012; www.defencereservessupport.gov.au/for-employers/get-the-reservist-experience/exercise-boss-lift.aspx.

operations around the globe' and with that, 'wonderful opportunities to see first hand some of the new capabilities coming on line.'[73] These opportunities to 'embed' with the military play 'an invaluable role in building mutual understanding between the Australian Defence Force and Senators and Members of Parliament.'[74] This is further cemented by the program's 'exchange element, whereby up to 15 Australian Defence Force personnel are hosted by a Senator or a Member of Parliament during a sitting week.'[75] The participants, carefully selected 'from across the ranks of the three services as being representative of the ADF's future leaders', not only 'gain a unique insight into the machinations of the federal parliament', they also ensure that the next generation of defence chiefs know how parliament works, can meet current and emerging political heavyweights and, through personal as well as formal relations, ensure that defence matters retain a high priority in Canberra.[76] Donna Winslow noted that this was exactly the sort of relationship that was missing in Canada where 'there is little direct Member of Parliament experience of the military.'[77] The resulting estrangement between politicians and the military ensured that when successive Canadian governments decided to 'pillage and burn' the defence budget their determinations were largely unencumbered by questions of personal or professional loyalty to the armed forces.[78] The ADF has no intention of suffering a similar fate.

The national esteem enjoyed by the ADF has its origins in the landings at Gallipoli on 25 April, 1915, the eight months of fighting that ensued there, the three subsequent years that the Australian Imperial Force [AIF] spent on the Western Front and the myth of Anzac their exploits spawned. After many years of declining public interest in Anzac, most markedly in the years immediately after the First and Second World Wars, the period of the Howard Government, 1996–2007, saw the wholesale resurgence of the myth.[79] Among other manifestations this was reflected in a renewed

73 www.defence.gov.au/adfpp/index.htm

74 Australian Defence Force Parliamentary Program Brochure 2012, np. For more information on the program see www.defence.gov.au/adfpp/index.htm.

75 www.defence.gov.au/adfpp/index.htm

76 www.defence.gov.au/adfpp/index.htm

77 Winslow, 'Canadian Society and its Army', p.19.

78 Hillier, *A Soldier First*, p.123.

79 For more on the decline see Robin Gerster, *Big Noting: The Heroic Theme in Australian War Writing*, Melbourne: Melbourne University Press, 1987. For an analysis of the myth's resurgence see Mark McKenna, 'Anzac Day: How did it become Australia's national day?' *What's Wrong With Anzac? The Militarisation of Australian History*, eds Marilyn Lake and Henry Reynolds with Mark McKenna and Joy Damousi, Sydney: New South Press, 2010, pp.110–134.

effort on the part of Federal and State governments to ensure that its key components were communicated to the next generation through the generous funding of curriculum development and materials for primary and secondary schools.[80] Despite occasional setbacks in the civil-military relationship, the tensions generated by Vietnam, episodes of bastardisation and more recent evidence of systemic sexism within the forces, the military brand remains untarnished.[81] As the Anzac Day Commemoration Committee noted in 2009: 'the spirit of ANZAC is a cornerstone which underpins our Australian image, way of life, and indeed is an integral part of our heritage.'[82] Accordingly, if 'In the story of Anzac lies the emotional locus of Australian narratives of nation', and the protagonist of these narratives is 'the individual Australian serviceman, emblematised as the Aussie digger', then the 'digger', and the force he embodies reflect back to us our most cherished ideas of who we were and what we are.[83]

As a result of this history, when the ADF headed to Afghanistan in 2001, and returned there in a larger fashion in 2006, its principal responsibility was not to re-engage with a disillusioned public, placate angry politicians or redeem its lost reputation, but to live up to and do honour by an established tradition of conduct and performance. Where the Dutch and Canadian militaries sought a clean break with the past the Australians were determined to hang onto it, to entrench their established practices and insist on the continued currency of the social and professional norms that they enshrined. If the need for rehabilitation prompted the Dutch and Canadian forces to take a leap of faith into open and cooperative relations with the media, the Australian military, its every move framed within and measured against the

80 For more on this see Marilyn Lake, 'How do schoolchildren learn about the spirit of Anzac?' *What's Wrong With Anzac?* pp.135–156; and Anna Clark, *History's Children: History Wars in the Classroom*, Sydney: University of New South Wales Press, 2008.

81 During 2012 there were a number of reviews of practices and culture within the ADF and Defence running simultaneously. These included enquiries into the Skype sex-video scandal at ADFA; the treatment of women at the academy; strategies to create career paths for women; pathways for Defence female public servants; alcohol and binge drinking in Defence; Defence's management of incidents and complaints, and a separate, major enquiry into alleged episodes of sexual abuse within the Defence Forces. Despite this, the ADF's reputation and standing remained largely undiminished.

82 Anzac Day Commemoration Committee, 'The Spirit of ANZAC', 2009, www.anzacday.org.au.

83 Ann Curthoys, 'National Narratives, War Commemoration and Racial Exclusion', *Becoming Australian: the Woodford Forum*, eds Richard Nile and Michael Peterson, St Lucia: University of Queensland Press, 1998, p.74; Catriona Elder, *Being Australian: Narratives of National Identity*, Sydney: Allen and Unwin, 2007, p.247.

Anzac tradition and its impossible legends of valour and sacrifice, stubbornly held on to the news management systems that had brought it, and its myths, safely through the Second World War, Korea and Vietnam. In this context, *why* the ADF was in Afghanistan was of far less importance than *how* it behaved there – what mattered above all else was that the men and women of the armed forces were seen to conduct themselves with a due awareness of the traditions and values they were upholding. Given the limited nature of the ADF deployment and its negligible effect on the outcomes of the broader struggle against the Taliban, for Australians, Afghanistan has been consistently regarded as less a cause than a place of performance, or more precisely, of embodied emulation. In the dusty villages of Uruzgan today's troops could be seen living up to and renewing the Anzac deeds of their grandfathers and great-grandfathers in the two world wars. Consequently, the Twenty-First century's soldiers often seemed little more than ciphers, playing their roles in a classically timeless drama. Chris Masters proposed that the ever-present shadow of Anzac hanging over 'The public accounting' of the soldiers' war in Afghanistan meant that 'Australians are more familiar with the digger drawn from history than they are with the ones doing the killing and dying in the here and now.'[84] To ensure that this was the vision of Afghanistan that came across loud and clear to the public, the ADF re-energised the practices that had shaped 'Eye-witness's dispatches in the Great War. In doing so they minimised the risk of rogue details intruding into or contradicting the established narrative of mateship, unassuming courage and steadfast professionalism. Indeed, why mention the war in Afghanistan at all when the classical myth of Australian military exceptionalism will do just as nicely?

84 Masters, *Uncommon Soldier*, p.333.

CONCLUSION

Citizens or Stakeholders?

For the greater part of Australia's engagement in the fighting in Afghanistan, political caution, cultural norms, historical precedent and the imperatives of reputation management neatly dovetailed with arguments about operational efficiency and security concerns to legitimate not greater openness from Defence and the ADF about what its forces were doing there, or a new relationship with the media founded on candour and trust, but greater caution in the minister's office about the release of information, less access for journalists to the area of operations, more control over their movements and output and a more dedicated, more coordinated effort than ever before to promote the military's version of what happened in Afghanistan, regardless of actual events on the ground.

This focus on self-promotion *über alles* is one manifestation of the increasing dominance of corporate models in the running of government departments and the seemingly irresistible rise of spin in Australian public communication. Lindsay Tanner notes that 'While the underlying elements of spin have been part of democratic politics since ancient Greece ... Spin is intensifying. Its significance is growing. Whereas once it reflected occasional embellishments and evasions, it now lies at the heart of the political process.'[1] The ADF's enthusiastic participation in this process and its absorption of its dominant ethos have led it to conceive of its relationships with its 'key stakeholders' – politicians, employers, its own personnel, their families and the public – more in terms of the strategies of brand management and client retention than the imperatives of public information provision and its requirement for full and open disclosure. This, in turn, is beginning to re-shape its relations with the fourth estate: 'Adopting the principles of strategic public affairs, militaries now seek to develop and manage relationships with media in order to achieve their organisational objectives.'[2] In the months and years after the September 11 attacks when its comparator militaries rushed to embrace the media as a force multiplier in the 'war on terror', the ADF continued to resist closer

1 Lindsay Tanner, *Sideshow: Dumbing Down Democracy*, Melbourne: Scribe, 2011, p.14.

2 Hibbert, 'Managing the "battlefield effect" of media', p.47.

relations with the fourth estate. Convinced that the media were adversarial, if not more actively ill intentioned, and that the information they might access and disseminate could do it harm, the ADF believed that it could sell its message and safeguard its organisational objectives only if it kept the media at arm's length. When it finally sanctioned an embedding program, as Jason Logue notes, the ADF found, to its pleasure, that the reporting closely mapped the key points of its official narrative of the war and thus helped project its core promotional aims. As a result, some in the ADF are slowly waking up to the fact that once a pariah and long a pest, the media are now an indispensable platform for the legitimation and broadcast of its public affairs agenda.

Yet Logue's study of the ADF's media embedding program was not only a survey of its operations and successes but also a plea for continued cooperation with the fourth estate: 'Media embedding has now become the "norm" in operations and the ADF's participation in coalitions of the future will ensure a continued requirement to support it in some form ... The ADF must stay engaged and continue to adjust its processes into the future.'[3] Logue recognises that in the context of the ADF's long-held aversion to the media, the gains made in Afghanistan are fragile and the progress they represent could easily be wiped out. The promotional imperative that has bound the armed forces and the media together could be the force that breaks them apart. In Afghanistan, embedded reporting faithfully served the ADF's public relations agenda, but what happens when the media's coverage of a given conflict contradicts or more explicitly contests the military's organisational and marketing objectives?

The military's most senior communications officers may regard their principal role as reputation management, but it is not. Likewise, though the ADF may think of itself as just another part of the government machine whose communications with its stakeholders are bound by the rules of marketing, it is not. Uniquely, its core business is the defence of the nation and its strategic interests, and in pursuit of these interests, in the people's name, it hazards the lives of its front line personnel. With these sorts of stakes at play the military have to be held to higher standards of reporting and public communication than those founded on sales and promotion. Citizens have a right to expect full and frank disclosure from Defence and the ADF and no less access to the area of operations for their media representatives than that enjoyed by reporters covering the exploits of their closest allies

3 Logue, *Herding Cats*, p.42.

and comparator militaries. After all, the wars and conflicts prosecuted by the military are fought, at the behest of their elected representatives, in the public's name, with materiel provided by the people in pursuit of broader national interests. Where the imperatives of promotion meet the demands of democracy there can be no contest of loyalties.

It may be fruitless to stand against the seemingly irresistible rise of spin and the corporate tides that power it, but it is vital to do so. Without an honest accounting from Defence and the military of how and why they acted as they did, at home and on the battlefield, contemporary debate about the aims, purposes and prosecution of a given conflict is impoverished and the historical record of the campaign will be based on little more than sunny press releases, heavily redacted reports and the self-serving recollections of the main players. The myth of Australian military exceptionalism will, doubtless, shine through any resulting account. But the determination to endlessly re-visit this paint-by-numbers celebration of moral and cultural pre-eminence, and the promotional agenda that drives it, will ensure that Defence and the ADF learn nothing from their failures in Afghanistan and the lives they cost. Primed to repeat the same mistakes wherever our military commitments take us next, it is the men and women in uniform who will suffer the consequences of their leaders' hubris.

WORKS CITED

Adams, Michael, *Sex in the Snow: Canadian Social Values at the End of the Millennium*, Toronto: Penguin Books, 1997.

Adams, Valerie, *The Media and the Falklands War*, London: Macmillan, 1986.

Anderson, Fay, 'The New and Altered Conventions of Reporting war: Censorship, Access and Representation in Afghanistan', in *What are we Doing in Afghanistan?* ed Foster, 2009, pp.119–141.

Anderson, Fay, and Richard Trembath, *Witnesses to War: The History of Australian Combat Reporting*, Melbourne: Melbourne University Press, 2011.

Anzac Day Commemoration Committee, 'The Spirit of ANZAC', 2009, www.anzacday.org.au

Arnett, Peter, *Live from the Battlefield*, London: Corgi, 1995.

Australian Associated Press, 'Afghanistan troops face long, difficult task: PM', Melbourne: AAP, 10 April 2007.

Australian Associated Press, 'Australia Committed to Afghanistan conflict: Rudd', Sydney: AAP, 15 October 2008.

Australian Associated Press, 'Australian terror threat comes from Afghanistan says Labor', Sydney: AAP, 12 July 2005.

Australian Associated Press, 'Digging in for Taliban fight', Sydney: AAP, 20 April 2006.

Australian Associated Press, 'Howard warns of dangers for diggers', Sydney: AAP, 9 July 2007.

Australian Associated Press, 'PM, Nelson announce long-awaited Afghan deployment', Sydney: AAP, 10 April 2007.

Australian Associated Press, 'SAS death won't change Govt resolve on terror, says PM', Sydney: AAP, 26 October 2007.

Australian Associated Press, 'War on Terror will not end soon, PM says', Sydney: AAP, 25 February, 2006.

Australian Bureau of Statistics, 'Graphic Designer – the most popular cultural occupation', *Employment in Culture, Australia 2011*, Media Release, 20 December 2012.

Banham, Cynthia, and Jonathan Pearlman, 'It's war: minister takes aim at defence', *Sydney Morning Herald*, Weekend Edition, 28 February – 1 March 2009.

Banham, Cynthia, and Deborah Snow, 'They don't follow orders: Nelson opens fire on top brass', *Sydney Morning Herald*, 26 February 2009.

Batty, David, 'Dutch government collapses after Labour withdrawal from coalition', *Guardian*, 20 February 2010.

Blake, Hamish, and Andy Lee, www.2dayfm.com.au/shows/hamishandandy/australian-troops/the-giggle-bunker

Bowden, Tim, *One Crowded Hour: Neil Davis Combat Cameraman, 1934–1985*, Sydney: Angus and Robertson, 1987.

Braestrup, Peter, *Battle Lines: Report of the Twentieth Century Fund Task Force on the Military and the Media*, New York: Priority Press, 1986.

Braestrup, Peter, 'Foreword', *Hotel Warriors: Covering the Gulf War*, by John J. Fialka, Washington: Woodrow Wilson Center Press, 1991.

Brown, James, 'And then there's their battle back home', *Sydney Morning Herald*, 28 July 2010.

Canadian Broadcasting Corporation, 'Afghanistan is no longer a risk: Harper', www.cbc.ca/news/politics/story/2011/05/30/pol-harper-afghanistan.html.

Canadian Broadcasting Corporation, *The Somalia Affair*, http://archives.cbc.ca/war_conflict/peacekeeping/topics/723/.

Cantwell, John, 'They Died in Vain', *The Monthly*, October 2012.

Cantwell, Major General John, with Greg Bearup, *Exit Wounds: One Australian's War on Terror*, Melbourne: Melbourne University Press, 2012.

Carruthers, Susan, *The Media at War*, Second Edition, New York: Palgrave, 2011.

Chandler, Jo, 'Women at War', *The Age: Good Weekend*, 23 January 2010, pp.12–19.

Christensen, Christian, 'Uploading dissonance: YouTube and the US occupation of Iraq', *Media, War and Conflict*, Vol. 1, No. 2, (August) 2008, pp.155–75.

Clark, Anna, *History's Children: History Wars in the Classroom*, Sydney: University of New South Wales Press, 2008.

Clark, Wesley K., *Waging Modern War: Bosnia, Kosovo, and the Future of Combat*, New York: Public Affairs, 2001.

Cloud, David S., 'As "insider attacks" grow so does U.S.-Afghanistan divide', *Los Angeles Times*, 7 November 2012, articles.latimes.com/2012/nov/07/world/la-fg-afghan-insider-attacks-20121107.

Commission of Inquiry into the Deployment of Canadian Forces to Somalia, *Dishonoured Legacy: The Lessons of the Somalia Affair*, Ottawa: Minister of Public works and Government Services, 1997, Executive Summary: www.dnd.ca/somalia/somaliae.htm.

Coorey, Philip, 'Labor faces wipeout', *Sydney Morning Herald*, 7 June 2010.

Cosgrove, General Peter, (retd), 'Inconvenient Truths: The Military and the Media', *The Information Battlefield*, ed. Foster, 2011, pp.1–5.

Crosier, Colin, 'Walls separate diggers from Afghans', *The Age*, 14 November 2012.

Cumings, Bruce, '"No More Vietnams": The Gulf war', *War and Television*, London: Verso, 1992, pp.103–128.

Curthoys, Ann, 'National Narratives, War Commemoration and Racial Exclusion', *Becoming Australian: the Woodford Forum*, eds. Richard Nile and Michael Peterson, St Lucia: University of Queensland Press, 1998, pp.173–90.

Daley, Paul, 'Defence versus Parliament: the next great debate', *The Sunday Age*, 1 March 2009.

Dalton, Trent, 'Brave Digger "Poppy" Pearce gets Afghan Memorial', *Courier-Mail*, 8 October 2008.

Danner, Mark, 'Bosnia: The Great Betrayal', *The New York Review of Books*, 26 March 1998.

Department of the Army, *Public Affairs Tactics, Techniques and Procedures*, Field Manual 3–61.1, Maryland: Department of the Army, 2000.

Department of Defence, 'Afghanistan. Fact Sheet', www.defence.gov.au/op/afghanistan/info/factsheet.htm.

Department of Defence, 'Australian Defence Force Parliamentary Program Brochure', 2012. www.defence.gov.au/adfpp/index.htm.

Department of Defence, *Defence Instructions (General) Public Comment and Dissemination of Official Information by Defence Personnel*, Canberra: Department of Defence, 2007.

Department of Defence, *Defence White Paper 2013*, Canberra: Department of Defence, 2013.

Department of Defence, *Defending Australia in the Asia Pacific Century: Force 2030*, Canberra: Department of Defence, 2009.

Department of Defense, *Doctrine for Joint Operations*, Joint Publication 3–0 Washington: Department of Defense, 2001.

Department of Defence, 'Exercise Boss Lift', www.defencereservessupport.gov.au/for-employers/get-the-reservist-experience/exercise-boss-lift.aspx.

Department of Defence, *Operationally Sensitive Information Brief*, Canberra: Department of Defence, 2009.

Department of Defence, *Statement of Understanding For Accredited Media (Ground Rules)*, Canberra: Department of Defence, 2009.

Department of Defence, 'Trooper David "Poppy" Pearce Memorial Service', www.defence.gov.au/media/download/2008/oct/20081009/index.htm.

Dodd, Mark, 'Battle for progress', *The Australian*, 9 October 2008, p.11.

Drape, Julian, 'Attacks on diggers "corrodes" trust: PM', *Sydney Morning Herald*, 9 November 2011.

Dudink, Stefan, 'The Unheroic Men of a Moral Nation: Masculinity and Nation in Modern Dutch History', *The Postwar Moment: Militaries, Masculinities and International Peacekeeping*, eds. Cynthia Cockburn and Dubravka Zarkov, London: Lawrence and Wishart, 2002, pp.146–61.

Editorial, *The Age*, 23 June 2010.

Editorial, *Courier-Mail*, 10 March 1966.

Editorial, 'Need-not-to-know doctrine', *Sydney Morning Herald*, 27 February 2009.

Elder, Catriona, *Being Australian: Narratives of National Identity*, Sydney: Allen and Unwin, 2007.

Elegant, Robert, 'How to lose a war', *Encounter*, Vol. 57, No. 2, 1981, pp.73–90.

Epstein, Rafael and Dan Oakes, 'Rats in the Ranks', *The Age* 2 June 2011.

Essential Research, *Essential Report*, 30 March 2009, Melbourne: Essential Media Communications, 2009.

Essential Research, *Essential Report*, 21 June 2010, Melbourne: Essential Media Communications, 2010.

Essential Research, *Essential Report*, 9 May 2011, Melbourne: Essential Media Communications, 2011.

Essential Research, *Essential Report*, 21 November 2011, Melbourne: Essential Media Communications, 2011.

Essential Research, *Essential Report*, 6 February 2012, Melbourne: Essential Media Communications, 2012.

Essential Research, *Essential Report*, 19 March 2012, Melbourne: Essential Media Communications, 2012.

Essential Research, *Essential Report*, 10 September 2012, Melbourne: Essential Media Communications, 2012.

Faulkner, Senator John, '2010 C.E.W. Bean Foundation Dinner Address', www.senatorjohnfaulkner.com.au/file.php?file=/news/KSBKDMDOTF/index.html.

Felbab-Brown, Vanda, www.brookings.edu/research/testimony/2012/08/02-afghanistan-security-felbabbrown.

Ferguson, Adam, 'The long and the short of covering a war', *The Walkley Magazine*, Issue 64, October–November 2010.

Fialka, John J., *Hotel Warriors: Covering the Gulf War*, Washington: Woodrow Wilson Center Press, 1991.

Filkins, Dexter, *The Forever War*, New York: Vintage, 2008.

Flitton, Daniel, 'Divided we Stand', *The Age* 23 June 2010.

Foster, Kevin, *Fighting Fictions: War, Narrative and National Identity*, London: Pluto Press, 1999.

Foster, Kevin, ed., *What are we doing in Afghanistan? The Military and the Media at War*, Melbourne: Australian Scholarly Publishing, 2009.

Foster, Kevin, ed., *The Information Battlefield: Representing Australians at War*, Melbourne: Australian Scholarly Publishing, 2011.

Foster, Kevin, and Jason Pallant, 'Familiarity breeds contempt? What the Australian Defence Force thinks of its coverage in the Australian media, and why', *Media International Australia*, No. 148 (August) 2013, pp.22–38.

Franks, Tommy, *American Soldier*, New York: Harper Collins, 2004.

Gall, Carlotta, 'Two Claim to Lead Afghan Race for President', *New York Times*, 21 August 2009. www.nytimes.com/2009/08/22/world/asia/22afghan.html.

Gerster, Robin, *Big Noting: The Heroic Theme in Australian War Writing*, Melbourne: Melbourne University Press, 1987.

Gillespie, Lieutenant General Ken, 'Introduction', *The Military, the Media and Information Warfare*, eds Peter Dennis and Jeffrey Grey, Canberra: Australian Military History Publications, 2009, pp.1–5.

Gole, Henry, 'Don't Kill the Messenger: Vietnam War Reporting in Context', *Parameters*, Winter 1996–97, pp.148–53.

Goot, Murray, and Rodney Tiffen, 'Public opinion and the politics of the polls', *Australia's Vietnam: Australia in the Second Indo-China War*, ed. Peter King, Sydney: Allen and Unwin. 1983, pp.129–64.

Grattan, Michelle, 'Poll shows most want our troops withdrawn', *The Age* 22 June 2010.

Gray, Stephen, 'A lack of cover', *Guardian*, 15 June 2009.

Grey, Jeffrey, 'In every war but one? Myth, history and Vietnam', *Zombie Myths of Australian Military History*, ed. Craig Stockings, Sydney: New South Press, 2010, pp.190–212.

Gross Stein, Janice, and Eugene Lang, *The Unexpected War: Canada in Kandahar*, Toronto: Penguin, 2007.

Haigh, Gideon, *The Deserted Newsroom*, Melbourne: Penguin, 2012.

Hallin, Daniel, *The 'Uncensored War': The Media and Vietnam*, Berkeley: University of California Press, 1989.

Ham, Paul, *Vietnam: The Australian War*, Sydney: Harper Collins, 2007.

Hammond, William, 'The Press in Vietnam as Agent of Defeat: A Critical Examination', *Reviews in American History*, Vol. 17, No. 2 (June) 1989, pp.312–23.

Hanlon, Colonel W.R, *Inquiry Officer's Report into the Death of Corporal M.R.A. Hopkins in Afghanistan on 16 March 2009*, Canberra: Department of Defence, 2009.

Hansard, www.aph.gov.au/hansard/hansreps.htm.

Hansard, www.aph.gov.au/hansard/hanssen.htm.

Hanson, Fergus, *The Lowy Institute Poll 2008: Australia and the World: Public Opinion and Foreign Policy*, Sydney: Lowy Institute for International Policy, 2008.

Hanson, Fergus, *The Lowy Institute Poll 2009: Australia and the World: Public Opinion and Foreign Policy*, Sydney: Lowy Institute for International Policy, 2009.

Hanson, Fergus, *The Lowy Institute Poll 2010: Australia and the World: Public Opinion and Foreign Policy*, Sydney: Lowy Institute for International Policy, 2010.

Hanson, Fergus, *The Lowy Institute Poll 2011: Australia and the World: Public Opinion and Foreign Policy*, Sydney: Lowy Institute for International Policy, 2011.

Hanson, Fergus, *The Lowy Institute Poll 2012: Australia and New Zealand in the World: Public Opinion and Foreign Policy*, Sydney: Lowy Institute for International Policy, 2012.

Haste, Cate, *Keep the Home Fires Burning: Propaganda in the First World War*, London: Allen Lane, 1977.

Havemann, Joel, 'Convoy Deaths May Undermine Moral Authority', *Los Angeles Times*, 15 April 1999.

Hibbert, Zöe, 'Managing the "battlefield effect" of media in Afghanistan', *What are we Doing in Afghanistan?* ed. Foster, 2009, pp.47–64.

Hillier, Rick, *A Soldier First: Bullets, Bureaucrats and the Politics of War*, Toronto: HarperCollins, 2009.

Hilvert, John, *Blue Pencil Warriors: Censorship and Propaganda in World War II*, St Lucia: University of Queensland Press, 1984.

Hobbs, Sean, 'How to build a pergola: with the ADF in Afghanistan', *What are we Doing in Afghanistan?* ed. Foster, 2009, pp.89–101.

Hobson, Sharon, *The Information Gap: Why the Canadian Public Doesn't Know More About its Military*, Calgary: Canadian Defence and Foreign Affairs Institute, 2007.

Honig, Jan Willem, and Norbert Both, *Srebrenica: Record of a War Crime*, New York: Penguin, 1997.

Hopkin, Deian, 'Domestic Censorship in the First world war', *Journal of Contemporary History*, Vol. 5, No. 4, 1970, pp.151–69.

Humphreys, Brian, 'The Australian Defence Force's Media Strategy: What it is and Why, and Why it Needs to Change', *What are we Doing in Afghanistan?* ed. Foster, 2009, pp.31–46.

Hyland, Tom, 'Death inquiry reveals Afghan troop failings', *The Sunday Age*, 26 July 2009.

Hyland, Tom, 'Funny Old war: The News from the ADF', *What are we Doing in Afghanistan?* ed. Foster, 2009, pp.102–18.

Hyland, Tom, 'Media squabbles miss the real question about war', *The Sunday Age*, 5 June 2011.

Hyland, Tom, 'Stifling soldiers of spin', *The Sunday Age*, 20 July 2008.

Hyland, Tom, 'The Media Never Lose', *The Information Battlefield*, ed. Foster, 2011, pp.41–9.

International Security Assistance Force, www.isaf.nato.int/troop-numbers-and-contributions/index.php.

Jackson, Ian, '"Duplication, Rivalry and Friction": the Australian Army, the Government and the Press during the Second World War', *The Information Battlefield*, ed. Foster, 2011, pp.74–85.

Jockel, Joseph T., 'The Dutch Army in Afghanistan', *The Dorchester Review*, 20 October 2011. *The Dorchester Review*, 20 October 2011 www.dorchesterreview.ca/2011/10/20/the-dutch-army-in-afghanistan/.

Kelly, Jeremy, 'Afghans just waiting for hell to break loose', *The Weekend Australian*, 29–30 December 2012.

Kimball, Jeffrey P., 'The Stab-in-the-Back Legend and the Vietnam War', *Armed Forces and Society* Vol. 14, No. 3, (Spring) 1988, pp.433–57.

Knightley, Philip, *The First Casualty: The War Correspondent as Hero and Myth-Maker from the Crimea to Iraq*, Third Edition, Baltimore: Johns Hopkins University Press, 2004.

Knott, Matthew, 'Foreign bureau get the chop as News, Fairfax cut costs', *Crikey*, 9 January, 2013. media.crikey.com.au/dm/newsletter/dailymail_e034edb700ec5d29edf45c4d76b17320.html article_22103.

Koch, K., 'Civilian Defence: An Alternative to Military Defence?' *The Netherlands Journal of Sociology*, Vol. 20, No. 1, 1984, pp.1–12.

Lake, Marilyn, 'How do schoolchildren learn about the spirit of Anzac?' *What's Wrong With Anzac?* 2010, pp.135–156.

Leahy, Peter, 'The Government, the Military and the Media: Hurry, Hit the Reset Button', *The Information Battlefield*, ed. Foster, 2011, pp.6–18.

Lee, Sandra, *Saving Private Sarbi: The True Story of Australia's Canine War Hero*, Sydney: Allen and Unwin, 2011.

The Liaison Office, *The Dutch Engagement in Uruzgan, 2006–2010: a TLO socio-political assessment*, Kabul: The Liaison Office, 2010. Formerly available from www.humansecuritygateway.com/documents/TLO_Dutch_Engagement_In_Uruzgan-2006-2010.pdf.

Lion, Patrick, 'Death in the night for Diggers', *Herald Sun*, 31 August 2012.

Logue, Lieutenant Colonel Jason, *Herding Cats: The Evolution of the ADF's Media Embedding Program in Operational Areas*, Canberra: Land Warfare Studies Centre (Working Paper No. 141), June 2013.

McEwen, John, 'The National Press During the First world war: Ownership and Circulation', *Journal of Contemporary History*, Vol. 17, No. 3, 1982, pp.459–86.

McGeough, Paul, 'How the ADF tried to control the real story of Oruzgan', *The Saturday Age*, 16 March 2013.

McLeish, Kathy, www.abc.net.au/news/2012-07-06/730s-kathy-mcleish-joins-qld-troops-in-afghanistan/4115848.

McKenna, Mark, 'Anzac Day: How did it become Australia's national day?' *What's Wrong With Anzac? The Militarisation of Australian History*, eds Marilyn Lake and Henry Reynolds with Mark McKenna and Joy Damousi, Sydney: New South Press, 2010, pp.110–134.

McPhedran, Ian, 'War! What War?' *What are we Doing in Afghanistan?* ed. Foster, 2009, pp.65–74.

McPhedran, Ian, '"Embedding" Trial Report', www.abc.net.au/mediawatch/transcripts/0935_report.pdf.

McPhedran, Ian, 'Defence coy on embedding media', *The Australian*, 14 September 2009.

McPhedran, Ian, 'Cook Lance Corporal Andrew Jones killed by a coward in Afghanistan', *Daily Telegraph* (Sydney), 18 June 2011.

Maiden, Samantha, 'Deaths fuel withdraw push', *Sunday Herald Sun*, 2 September 2012.

Mandelbaum, Michael, 'Vietnam: The Television War', *Daedalus,* Vol. 111, No. 4 (Fall) 1982, pp.157–169.

Mans, Ulrich, Christa Meindersma and Lars Burema, *Eyes Wide Shut? The Impact of Embedded Journalism on Dutch Newspaper Coverage of Afghanistan*, The Hague: The Hague Centre for Strategic Studies, 2008.

Marr, David, and Marian Wilkinson, *Dark Victory*, Sydney: Allen and Unwin, 2002.

Martinkus, John, 'The Road to Tarin Kowt': Australian Military-Media Relations in Afghanistan', *What are we Doing in Afghanistan?* ed. Foster, 2009, pp.75–88.

Mascall-Dare, Sharon, 'An Australian Story: Anzac Day Coverage Investigated', *The Information Battlefield*, ed. Foster, 2011, pp.162–180.

Masters, Chris, 'The Media's Left and Right of Arc', *The Information Battlefield*, ed. Foster, 2011, pp.33–40.

Masters, Chris, *Uncommon Soldier: Brave, Compassionate and Tough, the Making of Australia's Modern Diggers*, Sydney: Allen and Unwin, 2012.

Media Entertainment and Arts Alliance, www.alliance.org.au/news-limited-redundancies-should-be-the-last 2012.

Mercer, Derrik, Geoff Mungham and Kevin Williams, *The Fog of War: The Media on the Battlefield*, London: Heinemann, 1987.

Metcalf, Vice-Admiral J. III, USN (retd) 'The Press and Grenada, 1983', *Defence and the Media in Time of Limited War*, ed. Peter R. Young, London: Frank Cass, 1992, pp.168–174.

Middleton, Karen, 'Who's Telling the Story? The Military and the Media', *The Military, the Media and Information Warfare*, eds Peter Dennis and Jeffrey Grey, Canberra: Australian Military History Publications, 2009, pp.147–57.

Middleton, Karen, *An Unwinnable War: Australia in Afghanistan*, Melbourne: Melbourne University Press, 2011.

Miller, Charles A., *Endgame for the West in Afghanistan? Explaining the Decline in Support for the War in Afghanistan in the United States, Great Britain, Canada, Australia, France and Germany*, Carlisle, PA: Strategic Studies Institute, 2010.

Ministerie van Defensie, *Communicatieplan* www.communicatieplan.info/wp-content/uploads/2008/02/communicatieplan_mindef_uruzgan_2006.pdf.

Ministerie van Defensie, www.defensie.nl/english/tasks/missions/afghanistan

Moskos, Charles C., 'Armed Forces in the Warless Society', *Armed Forces After the Cold War*, eds. Jürgen Kuhlmann and C. Dandier, Munich: German Armed Forces Institute for Social Research, 1992, pp.3–10.

Moskos, Charles C., John Allen Williams and David R. Segal, eds, *The Postmodern Military: Armed Forces after the Cold War*, New York: Oxford University Press, 1999.

Mueller, John E., 'Trends in Popular Support for the Wars in Korea and Vietnam', *The American Political Science Review*, Vol. 65, No. 2 (June) 1971, pp.358–75.

Nautilus Institute, *Australia in Afghanistan Briefing Book*, www.globalcollab.org/publications/books/australian-forces-abroad/afghanistan.

Neighbour, Sally, 'Taliban conflict "cannot be won" in Afghanistan', *The Australian*, 10 July 2008.

Netherlands Institute for War Documentation, (NIOD), www.srebrenica-project.com/index.php?option=com_content&view=article&id=140:niod.

Netherlands Institute of Military History, International Security Assistance Force (ISAF), Mission Overview, The Hague: Ministry of Defence, 2009. www.defensie.nl/english/nimh/history/international_operations/mission_overview/48178809/international_security_assistance_force_(isaf).

Neuman, Johanna, *Lights, Camera, War: Is Media Technology Driving International Politics?* New York: St Martin's Press, 1996.

Nicholson, Brendan, and Jeremy Kelly, 'Slain Digger Andrew Jones "shot at random"', *The Australian*, 3 June 2011.

Nicholson, Brendan, and Amanda Hodge, 'Five fall in darkest day for army since Vietnam', *The Australian*, 31 August 2012.

Nonaka, Ikujiro, 'A Dynamic Theory of Organizational Knowledge Creation', *Organization Science*, Vol. 5, No. 1 1994, pp.14–37.

Nossal, Kim Richard, 'The Unavoidable Shadow of Past wars: Obsequies for Casualties of the Afghanistan Mission in Australia and Canada', *Australasian Canadian Studies*, Vol. 26, No. 1, 2008, pp.73–106.

Nossal, Kim Richard, 'Making Sense of Afghanistan: The Domestic Politics of International Stabilization Missions in Australia and Canada', Paper presented at the Conference of the Association for Canadian Studies in Australia and New Zealand, University of New England, Armidale, New South Wales, 5 July 2010, http://post.queensu.ca/percent7Enossalk/papers/Nossal_2010_Making_Sense.pdf.

Oakes, Dan, 'Main parties will keep Afghanistan off radar', *The Age*, 26 July 2010.

Oakes, Dan, 'Defence in "beyond tolerable state" says analyst', *The Age*, 27 June, 2011.

Oakes, Dan and Tom Hyland, 'Toll adds to exit pressure', *The Age*, 26 August 2010.

Office of the Assistant Secretary of Defense for Public Affairs, *Public Affairs Guidance (PAG) on Embedding Media During Possible Future Operations/Deployments in the U.S. Central Commands (CENTCOM) Area of Responsibility (AOR)*, Washington: Department of Defense, 2003.

Oliver, Alex, *The Lowy Institute Poll 2013: Australia and the World: Public Opinion and Foreign Policy*, Sydney: Lowy Institute for International Policy, 2013.

Olivier, Fritz, and Ger Teitler, 'Democracy and the Armed Forces: The Dutch Experiment', *Armed Forces and the Welfare Societies, Challenges in the 1980s: Britain, the Netherlands, Germany, Sweden and the United States*, ed. G. Harries-Jenkins, New York: St Martin's Press, 1983.

Olson, R. L., *Gulf War Air Power Survey, Volume Three: Logistics; Support*, Washington DC: Government Printing Office, 1993.

Parnell, Sean and Rory Callinan, 'Soldiers' despair confronts Defence', *The Weekend Australian* 10–11 July 2010.

Payne, Trish, *War and Words: The Australian Press and the Vietnam War*, Melbourne: Melbourne University Press, 2007.

Piggott, Peter, *Canada in Afghanistan: The War So Far*, Toronto: Dundurn Press, 2007.

Pinch, Franklin C., 'Canada: Managing Change with Shrinking Resources', *The Postmodern Military*, eds Moskos et al, 1999, pp.156–81.

Polling Report, www.pollingreport.com/afghan.htm.

Potter, Mitch, 'Kandahar, Inside and Out', *Toronto Star*, 10 February 2002.

Price, Dominique L., *Inside the Wire: A Study of Canadian Embedded Journalism in Afghanistan*, Unpublished MA Thesis, Ottawa: Carleton University, 2009.

Price, Steve, 'Homeward bound', *The Townsville Bulletin*, 9 October 2009. www.townsvillebulletin.com.au/article/2009/10/09/85131_rightprice.html

Probyn, Andrew, and Nick Butterly, 'Enemy toll as high as 1500', *The West Australian*, 25 May 2011, http://au.news.yahoo.com/thewest/a/-/national/9509508/enemy-toll-as-high-as-1500/.

Pugliese, David, 'Canadian Forces Pass Up Spotlight', *Ottawa Citizen*, 6 March 2002.

Reader's Digest, 'Australia's Most Trusted Professions 2011', 22 June 2011, www.readersdigest.com.au/australias-most-trusted-professions-2011.

Rid, Thomas, *War and Media Operations: The US Military and the Press from Vietnam to Iraq*, New York: Routledge, 2007.

Rid, Thomas, and Mark Hecker, *War 2.0: Irregular Warfare in the Information Age*, Westport CT: Praeger Security International, 2009.

Rohde, David, *Endgame: The Betrayal and Fall of Srebrenica. Europe's Worst Massacre Since World War 2*, New York: Farrar, Straus and Giroux, 1997.

Rural Press Club, www.ruralpressclub.com.au/item.cfm?page_id=10.

Senate Select Committee, *Report into a Certain Maritime Incident*, Canberra: Commonwealth of Australia, 2002.

Shea, Dr Jamie P., 'The Kosovo Crisis and the Media: Reflections of a NATO Spokesman', *Lessons from Kosovo: the KFOR Experience*, ed. Larry Wentz, Washington: Department of Defence Command and Control Research Program, 2002, pp.153–74.

Sheridan, Greg, 'Over-exposed, over-sacrificed … and over it', *The Australian*, 31 August 2012.

Sheridan, Greg, 'Too much for too few in the Defence con job', *The Weekend Australian*, 9–10 July 2011.

Shotwell, John M., 'The Fourth Estate as a Force Multiplier', *Marine Corps Gazette*, (July) 1991, pp.70–9.

Sion, Liora, '"Too Sweet and Innocent for War"? Dutch Peacekeepers and the Use of Violence', *Armed Forces and Society*, Vol. 23, No, 1 2005, pp. 454–74.

Smith, Phil, 'The Story of Aceh', *The Defence Reserves Yearbook 2004–2005*, ed. Bill Rowling, Melbourne: Executive Media, 2005.

Snow, Deborah, and Cynthia Banham, 'Calling Shots in Defence', *Sydney Morning Herald*, Weekend Edition, 28 February – 1 March 2009.

Southernwood, Ross, 'Review of *Uncommon Soldier: Brave, Compassionate and Tough, the Making of Australia's Modern Diggers*', by Chris Masters, in *The Sunday Age*, Melbourne Inside, 30 December 2012.

Special Inspector General for Afghanistan Reconstruction, www.sigar.mil/pdf/inspections/2013-01-29-inspection-13-05.pdf.

Starkey, Jerome, and Jon Swain, 'President Hamid Karzai takes 100 per cent of votes in opposition stronghold', *The Sunday Times*, 6 September 2009.

Tanner, Lindsay, *Sideshow: Dumbing Down Democracy*, Melbourne: Scribe, 2011.

Tanter, Richard, 'Memo to Kevin Rudd: why are we in Afghanistan?' *Arena Magazine*, No. 92 (December-January) 2007/08.

Taylor, Philip, *Munitions of the Mind: A History of Propaganda from the Ancient World to the Present Day*, Third Edition, Manchester: Manchester University Press, 2003.

Taylor, Philip, *War and the Media: Propaganda and Persuasion in the Gulf War*, Manchester: Manchester University Press, 1992.

Thomson, Mark, *Serving Australia: Control and Administration of the Department of Defence*, Canberra: Australian Strategic Policy Institute, 2011.

Tiffen, Rodney, 'News Coverage of Vietnam', *Australia's Vietnam: Australia in the second Indo-China war*, ed. Peter King, Sydney: George Allen and Unwin, 1983.

Tiffen, Rodney, 'The War the Media Lost: Australian News Coverage of Vietnam', *Vietnam Remembered*, Updated Edition, ed. Gregory Pemberton, Sydney: New Holland Publishers, 2009, pp.110–37.

Trainor, Bernard, 'The Military and the Media: A Troubled Embrace', *Parameters*, (December) 1990, pp.2–11.

Trute, Peter, 'News Limited announces redundancies', *Sydney Morning Herald*, 6 December 2012.

United States Air Force, *Information Operations*, Air Force Doctrine Document 2–5, Washington: United States Air Force, 1998.

van der Meulen, Jan S., 'The Netherlands: The Final Professionalization of the Military', *The Postmodern Military*, eds. Moskos et al, 1999, pp.101–20.

Walters, Patrick, 'Out of our depth', *The Australian*, 3 May 2008.

Welch, Dylan, 'Defiant PM vows to stay the course', *The Age*, 31 August 2012.

Welch, Dylan, and Tom Hyland, 'Defence releases over 100 documents on "hot issues"', *The Age*, 21 January 2012.

White, Hugh, 'Afghanistan mission a total failure', *The Age*, 5 February, 2013.

White, Hugh, 'The Defence Minister', *The Monthly*, November 2010.

Wieten, J., *Background and Influence of Media Reporting of the Conflict in the Former Yugoslavia During the Period 1991–1995: A Study of Views and Methods of Dutch Journalists*, Amsterdam: Netherlands Institute for War Documentation, 2002.

Williams, Glen, 'Aussie women on the front line in Afghanistan', *Woman's Day*, 19 April 2010.

Williams, John F., *ANZACS, The Media and the Great War*, Sydney: University of New South Wales Press, 1999.

Winslow, Donna, 'Canadian Society and its Army', *Canadian Military Journal*, Winter 2003–2004, pp.11–24.

Wroe, David, 'Defence in the Dark', *The Saturday Age*, 23 March 2013.

Young, Peter, and Peter Jesser, *The Media and the Military: From the Crimea to Desert Strike*, Melbourne: Macmillan, 1997.

INDEX

INDEX

INDEX

INDEX